THE DAY WILL PASS AWAY

THE DAY WILL PASS AWAY

The Diary of a Gulag Prison Guard

1935-1936

IVAN CHISTYAKOV

PEGASUS BOOKS
NEW YORK LONDON

Contents

List of Illustrations   vii

Introduction   ix

The Diary of a Gulag Prison Guard   1

Translator's Note   193

Appendix   197

    Rebels   199

    Shock Workers   212

    The Hunt   219

Memorial International Human Rights Society,
Moscow, and the Preservation of Historical
Memory   244

Illustrations

All images and captions have been provided by Memorial International Human Rights Society, Moscow.

1 Pages from Ivan Chistyakov's diary
2 Aksametova, leader of a *zek* women's phalanx
3 Cover of a magazine for BAMLag guards: *Bulletin of the Consultative Bureau of BAMLag NKVD Armed Guards*, No.1, 1935. State Archive of the Russian Federation
4 *Zeks* checking the laying of sleepers on the track
5 Backfilling the track with aggregate
6 A *zek* bugler signals a warning of explosives detonation
7 *Zek* with pickaxe
8 *Zeks* eating in the open
9 Chekists in charge of the BAM camp and construction project
10 *Zek* women's brigade loading wagons with subsoil for track subgrade
11 Pages from Ivan Chistyakov's second notebook

Introduction

Irina Shcherbakova

'My life is in this diary ...'

Ivan Chistyakov's diary is unique historical testimony. He commanded an armed guard platoon on a section of BAM, the Baikal–Amur Mainline railway, which was built using forced labour. We have few memoirs written by people on this side of the barbed wire. Chistyakov's diary, written inside the Gulag, gives a day-by-day account of life there over twelve months in 1935–6 and is probably unique. The original diary is in the safekeeping of Memorial International Human Rights Centre in Moscow which, since the late 1980s, has been collecting documents, testimony, memoirs, and letters relevant to the history of political repression in the USSR. It was given to them by people who had stumbled upon it among papers left by a distant female relative.

The diary consists of two medium-sized exercise books. One describes three days in August 1934, which Chistyakov spent hunting, before he was conscripted into the interior troops and sent to BAM. His notes, illustrated by the author, are reminiscent of Ivan Turgenev's classic *A Hunter's Sketches* and are included here as an appendix. They suggest nostalgia for the old, pre-revolutionary Russia and are in total contrast to the second notebook, written in 1935–6 when Chistyakov was working in the Gulag, and which makes up the body of this book.

We know very little about the man. Apart from his notebooks, we have only a blurred snapshot, on the back of which there is a note: 'Chistyakov, Ivan Petrovich, repressed in 1937–8. Died at the front in Tula Province in 1941'. All other biographical information has to be gleaned from the diary.

How old was its author? Evidently over thirty because he mentions that he has already lived half his life, and that he had been at the front. Even if that refers to fighting in 1920–21 towards the end of the Civil War, he would have to have been at least eighteen or nineteen years old.

Before being conscripted into the army (to his great misfortune he was drafted into the interior troops), Ivan Chistyakov lived in Moscow, not far from Sadovo-Kudrinskaya Square on the inner ring road, and probably had secondary vocational education. He took the tram to work, went to the theatre, played sport, enjoyed sketching, and in general lived much like any other relatively educated Soviet city dweller of the early 1930s. (Their way of life is characterized in the prose of such writers of the time as Yury Olesha, Mikhail Zoshchenko, and Mikhail Bulgakov.)

Ivan Petrovich Chistyakov had a thoroughly ordinary Russian name, but also had non-proletarian social antecedents, which would have counted against him at that time. He was expelled from the Communist Party during one of the extensive purges of the late 1920s and early 1930s when 'socially alien elements' were deprived of their Party card. (Chistyakov believed he was sent to BAM because the authorities already regarded him as suspect.)

What his work was before he was conscripted is not clear

from the diary. He may have taught at a technical college or been an engineer. He does not seem to have had a family; although he occasionally mentions receiving a letter or parcel, he never refers to a wife or children.

Chistyakov was drafted into the interior troops just as Stalin's vast projects, under the direction of the OGPU-NKVD* secret police, were getting under way. The Gulag,† a vast network of forced labour camps, was in the course of being created and had an acute shortage of staff. In autumn 1935 he was sent to one of its most remote and terrible locations, BAMLag: the Baikal–Amur Corrective Labour Camp.

BAMLag

In 1932, the Council of People's Commissars of the USSR gave orders for a Baikal–Amur Mainline railway to be constructed. BAM was a project of strategic importance, and was initially entrusted to the Commissariat of Transport and Communications. It was given a mere three and a half years to complete the project because of the situation in the Russian far east. Japan had occupied Manchuria in 1931–2, effectively depriving Russia of the Chinese Eastern Railway.‡ This was the main link between Vladivostok, Russia's only major port in the region and home port of the Pacific Ocean Fleet, and Siberia

* The GPU of Soviet Russia in 1923 became the OGPU; this was the United State Political Directorate of the Council of People's Commissars of the USSR; the NKVD was the People's Commissariat for Internal Affairs.

† The GULag was the State Directorate of Camps of the NKVD.

‡ The Chinese Eastern Railway (KVZhD) in north-east China passed through Manchuria, part of China, and linked Chita with Vladivostok and Port Arthur. It was built in 1897–1903 as a southern branch of the Trans-Siberian Railway, belonged to Russia, and was maintained by Russian subjects. In 1928 all the Russians servicing the railway were expelled from China, and in 1934 it was sold to the government of Manchuria. In 1945 it was returned to the USSR, and in 1952 transferred back to China.

and the central regions of Russia. The remaining Trans–Siberian Railway was single track in many places, and for more than 1,000 kilometres ran close to the Soviet border with Manchuria. The southern part of Sakhalin Island belonged to Japan, and a second, more northerly, outlet to the Pacific coast was of major strategic importance to the USSR.

Despite a propaganda campaign, it proved impossible to mobilize the huge numbers of workers needed for hard labour in the extreme conditions of what a popular song in a Soviet propaganda film called 'our near and dear Far East'. It was soon clear that the only way to complete the task set by Stalin in such a short time was to use unpaid forced labour.

Accordingly, responsibility for the project was transferred to the OGPU. Following completion of the White Sea–Baltic Canal, the first large-scale construction project of the Gulag using forced labour, thousands of people were redeployed to BAM. Vast numbers of prisoners and exiles (mainly dis-possessed, so-called 'wealthy' kulak peasants) flooded into BAMLag.

In mid–1935, shortly before Chistyakov arrived, some 170,000 prisoners were already working there, and when the camp was disbanded in May 1938 the number had risen to over 200,000. The total number of prisoners held in the Soviet Gulag at that time was over 1.8 million.

Administration

In 1935, BAMLag extended over an enormous area, from Chita to Ussuriysk (about a hundred kilometres short of Vladivoskok), a distance of more than 2,000 kilometres. It was administered from Svobodny in the Far East Region.

The first director of BAMLag was Sergey Mrachkovsky, an old Bolshevik and, in the recent past, a member of the

Trotskyite opposition. In September 1933, when the project was vastly expanded, the entire management of BAMLag, including Mrachkovsky, was arrested in connection with a criminal case against the 'Counter-Revolutionary Trotskyite Group'.

The new director of BAMLag was Naftaliy Frenkel, one of the most odious creators of the Gulag system. Prior to being put in charge of BAM, Frenkel had had an extraordinary career. In the early 1920s he was found guilty of embezzlement and smuggling and sent to the Solovki camp on islands in the White Sea. In the course of a few years, Frenkel transformed himself from a convict into the director of the camp's production section. On his release he enrolled in the service of the OGPU. From 1931–3, Frenkel was chief of works on the OGPU's White Sea–Baltic Canal project.

In his novel *Life and Fate* Vasily Grossman portrays this new world of prison camps and its organizer:

At the beginning of Lenin's New Economic Policy, Frenkel set up a motor factory in Odessa. In the mid-1920s he was arrested and exiled to Solovki. While serving his sentence, he submitted a brilliant plan to Stalin in which he proposed, with full economic and technical argumentation, that huge numbers of prisoners should be exploited to create roads, dams, power stations, and reservoirs. The Leader was greatly taken by his suggestion. The traditional pattern of forced labour, with its hallowed convict battalions and old-fashioned penal servitude, toiling with spades, axes, pickaxes, and saws, was invaded by the twentieth century.

The world of the camps began assimilating technical progress, drawing into its orbit electrically powered locomotives, excavators, bulldozers, electric saws, turbines, ore-cutting machinery, and a vast fleet of vehicles and tractors. This world mastered the use of aircraft for transportation and communications, wireless and intercom telephony, automated machinery, and ultra-modern ore enrichment technology. It planned, designed, sketched and created mines, factories, new seas and gargantuan power stations. It developed explosively, leaving the old-time forced labour looking as touching and comical as children playing with toy bricks.*

One of these ambitious new Gulag projects was BAM, a complex railway project extending over many kilometres. Like all the other camp construction projects, however, its implementation involved the murderous exploitation of manual labour, of hundreds of thousands of prisoners using spades, wheelbarrows, pickaxes and saws.

Grossman fully recognized the importance of Frenkel's role. He survived in charge of the BAMLag project for the whole of the subsequent period, and was one of the few Gulag officials not to be arrested. He managed to stay in this highly risky position, and even to advance his career.† Frenkel began his period in charge of BAMLag by radically restructuring the camp subdivisions. As a master organizer and connoisseur of camp life, he created 'phalanxes', specialist brigades of 250 to 300 men in which all the prisoners were dependent on each other to ensure they met their obligations under the Plan and competed successfully for rations. Chistyakov frequently mentions these phalanxes in the diary. The realities of the new system are accurately described by Varlam Shalamov,‡ the author of *Kolyma*

* Vasıliy Grossman, *Zhizn' i sud'ba*, Moscow, 1988, pp.790–1.

† By 1940, Frenkel was head of the Directorate of Railway Construction of the NKVD Gulag. That is, he was ın charge of all the raılway-buıldıng camps of the USSR.

‡ Varlam Shalamov (1907–82) was one of Russia's most gifted writers of the second half of the twentıeth century. He spent seventeen years ın Stalın's camps.

Tales, who in the early 1930s found himself on the wrong side of the barbed wire:

> It was only in the early 1930s that a solution was found to the crucial question of what was more effective: the stick, or the carrot of linking the level of food rations to production output. It was realized that a sliding scale of rations and/or the promise of a remission of sentence could induce even 'saboteurs' and career criminals to work hard and effectively, without pay, even when the guards were not present. They would also inform on and betray their fellows for the sake of a cigarette or an approving glance from the concentration camp bosses.*

The system proposed by such Gulag innovators as Frenkel consisted of using 'unpaid forced labour where a variable scale of food rations was combined with the hope of early release in return for accumulated labour credit points. This was worked out in immense detail, with extremely large variations in the inducements and punishments in the camps. A prisoner in the punishment cells would be allotted 100 grams of bread every second day, while one who achieved the onerous "Stakhanov norm", as it was officially called, would qualify for a whole 2 kilograms of bread daily.† That is how prisoners were incentivized to construct the White Sea–Baltic Canal and the Moscow–Volga Canal built during the First Five-Year Plan. It had a major economic impact.

'It had a no less major impact on the moral degradation of those in charge, on the prisoners, and other citizens. A person

* Varlam Shalamov, *Vishera: Antiroman*, Moscow, 1989, p.43.
† The Stakhanov norm was a heightened production quota. The term appeared in 1935 and is associated with the name of Alexey Stakhanov, a coal miner who purportedly exceeded by many times the quota for mining coal.

who is strong in spirit grows stronger in prison. The camps, however, with their tantalizing promise of early release, degraded everyone: the chief and his subordinate, the free, employed labourer and the prisoner, the platoon commander and the hired metal worker,' Shalamov writes.[*]

Every month, Frenkel received contingents of new convicts and his camp mushroomed. In early 1933 the BAMLag network consisted of only two camp divisions constructing the main branch of BAM, but later a majority of prisoners were redeployed to build a second track for the Trans-Siberian Railway. Numerous sections and independent camp centres were set up along this entire stretch of the railway. The second section of BAMLag (where Chistyakov ended up) was a vast, industrious anthill. It was engaged in constructing this second railway track, locomotive maintenance depots, railway stations and other civilian facilities. These included engineering workshops, ancillary farming projects, its own propaganda brigade, and a camp printing press. There were production phalanxes consisting of hundreds of prisoners (or 'soldiers of the track' as they were called in NKVD propaganda in the first half of the 1930s), phalanxes for miscreants and malingerers, and isolation cells for offenders.[†]

The BAMLag prisoners built the railway in unbelievably severe geographical and climatic conditions, in extremes of cold and heavy downpours of rain. They laid the rails through untamed territories of the Far East, building through mountains, rivers and swamps, overcoming cliffs, permafrost, and sodden subsoil. Under such conditions construction work would normally be considered possible for no more than a hundred days in the year, but the prisoners worked all year round,

[*] Shalamov, ibid., p.45.

[†] 'Malingerers' were prisoners who for one reason or another refused to go out to work.

whatever the weather, for sixteen to eighteen hours a day. Many contracted 'chicken blindness': when darkness fell they ceased to be able to see; malaria, colds, rheumatism and gastric ailments took their toll.

As a result of the inhuman exploitation of the labour of tens of thousands of people, by the end of 1937 the main part of BAMLag's task of laying a second track on the line from Karymskaya to Khabarovsk was completed. The prisoners were now switched to laying a second track of the Trans-Siberian Railway all the way to the Pacific Ocean, to building a number of military highways, and to embarking on construction of BAM itself, running from Taishet, north-west of Lake Baikal to Sovetskaya Gavan, a total length of 4,643 kilometres.

What Frenkel had under his command was no mere camp, but an enormous army of slaves and overseers scattered across vast expanses of territory from Lake Baikal to the Pacific Ocean. The previous management system was no longer adequate, and in May 1938 BAMLag was split into six separate camps under a special NKVD Gulag Directorate of Railway Construction in the Far East, headed by Frenkel.

With the outbreak of the Second World War in 1941, this enormous construction effort was halted; the Gulag simply had insufficient people and resources. The laying of the new section of the Baikal–Amur Railway from Taishet to Sovetskaya Gavan was resumed only in the 1970s, when thousands of youth brigades, which were designated Young Communist Shock Troops, were sent out there. The project took a further twelve years and was completed shortly before the start of perestroika. This section of the railway has since been renamed. It is no longer known as BAM.

Cogs of the system

Our picture of the world of the camps comes primarily from memoirs left by former prisoners who were victims of repression. Nowadays we can learn how the Gulag system functioned, its mechanisms and structures, from archives where thousands of documents are preserved. We also know a lot more about the organizers and those in charge of the Gulag.

We know little, however, about the 'man with a rifle' on the other side of the barbed wire. We have little understanding of the so-called cogs of that enormous machine of repression. Ex-prisoners, as we see from numerous memoirs, most often recalled their investigators, the interrogators in prison after their arrest who compiled records and indictments, to say nothing of those investigators who were unambiguously sadists and torturers and were widespread in 1937–8 during the Great Terror. It would be difficult not to remember such people. Moreover, it was the investigators who determined the fate and length of sentence in the camps of those arrested. Prisoners often saw that particular individual, rather than the repressive machinery of the state, as the source of the violence, injustice, and brutality visited on them.

Those who guarded the prisoners tend not to figure in the reminiscences of people who spent many years in the camps. Guards changed frequently, all looked much the same, and the prisoners generally only recollected a particular one if he unexpectedly acted with compassionate humanity or exceptional cruelty. The prisoners' attitude towards those guarding them is described by Alexander Solzhenitsyn in *The Gulag Archipelago*:

> It was a failing on our part: when you are in prison or a labour camp the personality of the jailers interests you only to the extent that it enables you to avoid being threatened by them

or to exploit their weaknesses. For the rest, you have no incli-
nation to take an interest in them: they are unworthy of your
attention ... but now, belatedly you realize that you failed to
take a sufficient interest in them ... Would anyone who was in
the least capable of useful activity go to work as a prison camp
guard? We need to ask the more general question of whether
a camp guard could ever be a good person. What system of
moral selection had life put them through? Any human being
with the least glimmer of spiritual maturity, with the least
stirrings of conscience, the ability to distinguish good from
evil, would instinctively struggle with all the means at his
disposal against ending up in the ranks of that dismal legion.
But suppose he didn't succeed? A secondary selection follows
during training and the initial period of service, when the
administration itself looks closely and winnows out all those
who manifest, not a strong will and firmness (brutality and
heartlessness), but weakness (kindness). After that comes a
third phase of selection over a period of many years: those who
did not realize where they were headed, and what was being
proposed to them, now understand and are horrified. To be
continually the tool of violence, a constant participant in evil,
is not something everybody is immediately capable of. You
are trampling other people's destinies underfoot. Inside you
something is resisting, and breaks, and you simply can't go on
living that way! Very belatedly, people did start struggling to
get out, claiming to be ill, obtaining certificates, taking a cut
in salary, stripping off their epaulettes – anything just to get
away from it all! Were the rest, then, sucked in? The others
got used to it and their fate struck them as normal. Of course
it was 'useful', even honourable. And some had no need to be
sucked in, because they were already there.[*]

* Alexander Solzhenıtsyn, *Arkhipelag GULAG*, vol. 2, Moscow, 1988, p.494.

Solzhenitsyn's words about those who failed in their struggle to avoid working in the camps, who felt they couldn't go on living that way, who just wanted to get away from it all, are wholly applicable to Ivan Chistyakov. The diary he left gives us a unique insight into the thoughts and feelings of someone who found himself in that role.

'They just called me in and sent me off . . .'

It was through no choice of his that Chistyakov was sent to the ends of the earth to command a unit of VOKhR* marksmen, whose job was to guard the prisoners on their way to work, to patrol the camp perimeter, to accompany echelons, and to catch anyone who tried to escape.

From that moment, every day he spent at BAM was filled with just one wish: to get himself out of that nightmare world by whatever means he could. He describes it endlessly: the severe climate, the disgusting accommodation in which your hair would freeze to your forehead at night; the lack of a bathhouse, of decent food, the constant colds he suffered, the stomach pains:

> It would be bearable if we could at least relax in a warm building, but we don't have even that. The stove heats you on one side of your body while the other freezes. You become lackadaisical: why care about anything? Yet every day that passes is part of my life, a day I could have lived instead of wasted.

Chistyakov was in command of a platoon of guards. He was the very lowest link in the chain of command and was under

---

* The Armed Guards Unit, *Voenizirovannaya okhrana*.

pressure from two directions. On the one hand there were the coarse, illiterate, drunken guards, many of whom were themselves prisoners serving short sentences, or had been prisoners in the past. He writes: 'There is no one to talk to here. I can't talk to the *zeks*,[*] obviously, and if I talked to the guards they'd become overfamiliar and I'd lose my authority. We are just a prop for the system, and when the project is finished we will leave the stage unnoticed.'

On the other hand, he was also being pressured by his more bloody-minded Chekist superiors in the secret police, who had been transferred to BAM from the dreaded Solovki complex where they had been trained in the ways of Solovki power, which had replaced Soviet power.[†] It was a school whose approach was now extended to the entire Gulag system. The brutal methods used against the prisoners (which Chistyakov was to encounter at BAM) are described by Varlam Shalamov on the basis of his own experience of the camp in the early 1930s:

> Somebody must have shot those three escapees. It was during the winter, and their frozen corpses were stood by the guardhouse for a full three days to demonstrate to the camp inmates the futility of attempting to escape. Somebody must have given the order to parade those corpses to teach us a lesson. There in the North, which I knew like the back of my hand, someone must have issued instructions for convicts to be given 'the mosquito treatment', to be tied naked to a stake for refusing to work or failing to achieve the output quotas.[‡]

* '*Zek*', abbreviation from 'zaklyuchenny', a prisoner.
† A pun in which 'Sovetskaya vlast', Soviet power, is replaced by the brutal 'Solovetskaya vlast', Solovki power. The Solovki special-purpose forced labour camp was set up in 1923 and closed in 1933.
‡ Varlam Shalamov, p.43.

It is obvious from this kind of testimony that Chistyakov's role in BAMLag must have been deeply repugnant to him, and indeed he writes about that quite openly in his diary:

Nightfall brings disturbances, escapes, killings. For once, though, may the gentle autumn night extend its protective mantle over the captive. Two runaways this time. There are interrogations, pursuits, memoranda, reports to HQ. The Third Section* takes an interest, and in place of rest night brings unrest and nightmares.

This man is no Chekist. He is an outsider, here under duress, and from time to time he is given to reflection. He remembers 'for some reason, the number of people I have burdened with a longer sentence. I try to stay calm but sometimes lose my temper. Some I send to the punishment cells.'† He was stunned by the appalling conditions in which prisoners, engaged in the heavy labour of building a railway, were kept.

We check out the huts ... bare bunks, gaps everywhere in the walls, snow on the sleeping prisoners, no firewood. A mass of shivering people, intelligent, educated people. Dressed in rags filthy from the trackbed ballast ... They can't sleep at night, then they spend the day labouring, often in worn-out shoes or woven sandals, without mitts, eating their cold meals at the quarry. In the evening their barracks are cold again and people rave through the night. How can they not recall

* Third Section – the Third Cheka Operational Unit was a section in the camp administration representing the NKVD or interior ministry. Its task was to monitor the mood and behaviour of the prisoners. It had powers to bring criminal charges, carry out arrests, and conduct preliminary investigations.

† All penalties imposed on prisoners were likely also to deprive them of the right to early release.

their warm homes? How can they not blame everyone and everything, and probably rightly so?

In his jottings shortly after arriving at BAM, we still find clear expressions of sympathy for those he is obliged to guard. He understands why people refuse to go out to work, and why, given the least chance, they try to escape.

We have been sent juveniles: louse-ridden, dirty, without warm clothing. There is no bathhouse because we cannot go sixty rubles over budget, which would work out at one kopek a head. There is talk of the need to prevent escapes. They look for causes, use guns, but fail to see that they themselves are the cause, that escapes are a result of their slothfulness, or their red tape, or just plain sabotage. People are barefoot and inadequately dressed even though there is enough of everything in the stores.

Chistyakov is incensed by the methods in use on this project, a combination of muddle-headedness and profound indifference and heartlessness towards people deprived of the barest necessities. His diary is one of the few reliable sources exposing the perversity of Stalin's forced labour system. Its uniqueness lies in the fact that the author is describing what happened day after day from inside the system.

At every step he encounters evidence of the inanity and inefficiency of organizing labour in this manner. For example, the administration fails to provide firewood for a contingent of new prisoners, and at −50°C people simply must find a way to keep warm. As Chistyakov admits, they have no option but to steal and burn precious railway sleepers intended for the project.

The *zeks* are burning railway sleepers by the cartload. They poach a few from here, a few from there, and in total they destroy thousands. So many that it's terrifying to think about. The top brass either can't or won't recognize that it is because these people must be given firewood, and that their burning of sleepers is the expensive alternative ... The brass, the Party members, the old Chekists, all work in a slapdash way, not giving a damn about anything ... Discipline is maintained solely by fear of the Revtribunal.*

On almost every page of the diary Chistyakov expresses irritation and dissatisfaction with the Chekist leaders, who are constantly in hysterics, 'the company commander kicks me out of his office, shrieking', because their superiors are demanding that they should at all costs fulfil the Plan and complete the project in an absurdly short time. He also expresses his lack of faith in their coercive work methods, although it would have been dangerous for him to say anything about that openly: 'If you try talking out loud about the real state of affairs you'll be in big trouble.'

From what Chistyakov describes, he appears to have behaved in substantially the same way as the prisoners. In other words, he tried his best to avoid carrying out inane orders. He understands something the camp bosses do not, when:

they imagine that a subordinate who has been given an order is duty bound and willing to carry it out promptly and punctiliously. In actual fact not all are slaves. A whole category of sloggers among the prisoners strain every fibre not to carry out any order they are given. This is the natural

* Chistyakov often uses the outdated term 'revolutionary tribunal', an institution created in 1917 which existed only until 1922. As an army officer he was in fact answerable to a military tribunal.

reaction of a slave, but the camp bosses in Moscow and those below them for some reason suppose that every order they give will be carried out. In fact, however, every order from above offends against a prisoner's dignity, irrespective of whether the instruction itself is constructive or destructive. The prisoner's brain has been deadened by every conceivable order, and his free will is impugned.*

The real tragedy of Chistyakov's situation is that, whether he likes it or not, and as he himself occasionally realizes to his horror, he is growing into BAM. Gradually the sympathy he felt towards the prisoners atrophies until it all but disappears. Fights and murders among the criminals, endless escape attempts for which he is answerable, blunt his empathy. This is more pronounced in BAMLag because few of the prisoners are educated. That time, of educated prisoners, had not yet come; the mass terror of 1937 was still ahead.† The main contingent were criminals, jailed for ordinary crimes, dispossessed 'wealthy' peasants, and street children who had been rounded up. These were prisoners who were particularly likely to attempt escape, and circumstances were in their favour: the constant moving of the phalanxes as the railway track advanced and the lack of a fixed camp infrastructure. Chistyakov writes that every day he covers many kilometres on foot or horseback. These conditions made it almost impossible to prevent escapes.

For the women prisoners (mainly criminals or prostitutes) he felt horror and revulsion, mixed, at times, with pity:

* Varlam Shalamov, p.25.

† Of course, there already were some educated prisoners in BAMLag. Until 1934 the renowned scholar and philosopher Pavel Florensky was there serving a ten-year term. Chistyakov's diary contains no mention of anybody sentenced for political crimes, however.

... there is a fight in the phalanx, a fight between women. They are beating the former top shock worker to death and we are powerless to intervene. We are not allowed to use firearms inside the phalanx. We do not have the right even to carry a weapon. They are all 35-ers,* but you feel sorry for the woman all the same. If we wade in there will be a riot; if they later recognize we were right, they will regret what they have done. You just get these riots. The devil knows but the Third Section doesn't. They'll come down on us and bang us up whether or not the use of firearms was justified. Meanwhile, the *zeks* get away with murder.

The sound of trams

Did echoes of events in the rest of Russia in 1935–6 reach the Far East? In his diary Chistyakov several times mentions Communist Party officials like Klim Voroshilov and Lazar Kaganovich, and current political events. This is mainly in connection with his obligation to conduct political indoctrination sessions, based on the newspapers, with his guards. He reads them Mikhail Kalinin's† speech about the draft of a new Soviet constitution.‡ He tells them about the building of the Moscow Metro and the world situation, mentioning Hitler. He does not, however, give the impression of having thought overmuch about the significance of these events, or even about how hollow the word 'constitution' sounds in the context of the situation he himself describes in BAMLag. Chistyakov

* Article 35 of the Criminal Code provided for up to five years' imprisonment for violating the passport laws or for those categorized as 'socially harmful elements'. These included tramps, prostitutes and petty criminals.

† Mikhail Kalinin was a Soviet party and government official, at that time chairman of the All-Russian Central Executive Committee of the USSR.

‡ A new Soviet constitution was adopted on 5 December 1936.

writes derisively about a meeting which took place in the canteen in support of the trial, which was just beginning, of the 'Trotskyite-Zinovievite bloc'.* What he mocks, however, is not the show trial of the political opposition as such, but the absurd and illiterate speeches by Chekists, none of whom 'can carry the masses with them, inspire them, know how to guide the listener's mind'.

Neither, however, does Chistyakov have any fanatical belief in communism, or any particular enthusiasm for the 'great construction projects'. He knows that he and others like him are mere rubble for Stalin's 'foundation pit': 'The Armed Guards Unit is part of a great construction project. We're devoting our lives to building a socialist society, and what recognition do we get? None. Unless we get hauled before the Revtribunal.'

Chistyakov is a fairly typical bit player of the early Soviet era. He only wants to be a loyal citizen. His aspirations are modest. He wants to live a life full of ordinary human joys:

> I want to play sport, to learn about radio, I want to work at my real profession, study, keep up with metals technology and try it out in practice. Live among educated people, go to the theatre and cinema, to lectures and museums and exhibitions. I want to sketch. Ride a motorbike, and then perhaps sell it and buy one of those catapult-launched gliders and fly . . .

---

* The 'United Anti-Soviet Trotskyite-Zinovievite Centre' was a criminal case fabricated in the mid-1930s, in which a number of individuals were accused of conducting anti-Soviet activity, espionage, sabotage, terrorism and complicity in the murder of Sergey Kirov, and preparing terrorist acts against leaders of the Communist Party and Soviet government. There were sixteen accused, including Grigoriy Zinoviev who had already been imprisoned in connection with a 'Moscow Centre' criminal case, and Lev Kamenev, who had been imprisoned in connection with a 'Kremlin' criminal case. The trial was held in Moscow on 19–24 August 1936, and all the accused were sentenced to death by firing squad.

He was to enjoy none of these things. It was the way of the times he lived in. Soviet power was to give him no opportunity of acquiring even a minimum of personal freedom, and the hopelessness of his situation is something he felt from his very first day at BAM. He sensed that even the modest life he had lived as a Muscovite was over. In the first half of the 1930s Moscow was a grey city, with communal flats, crowded trams, queues, food ration cards and badly dressed people, but now it seemed to Chistyakov the most beautiful place on earth. He outdoes even Chekhov's three sisters in his yearning to return there: 'I pictured Karetno-Sadovaya Square, the noise of the trams, the streets, the pedestrians, the thawing snow, and the yard sweepers clearing the pavements with their scrapers. I thought about it till my head ached ... and even some remembered ramshackle fence in the Moscow suburbs seems near and dear to me.'

From today's viewpoint, this sense of nostalgia and fatalism seems strange, almost neurotic. Chistyakov had probably been conscripted for only one year, and soon that ill-starred year would end and he should return home. He knew only too well, however, the country he was living in. He knew he was powerless when faced with the authorities, who could deal with him as they pleased. Most importantly, he was aware of the fragility of the partition that separated him from those he was compelled to guard. A recurring motif in the diary is the constant expectation of his own arrest. He is undoubtedly aware that the whole tenor of his life at BAM is going to lead inevitably to his exchanging the status of commander of an armed guard platoon for that of a prisoner.

The threat of arrest dogs him. He is in genuine danger of facing the tribunal his superiors keep threatening him with, either for failing to prevent escapes, or for any of the other actions and inactions which could provide grounds for accusing him of negligence. He might be consigned to the Gulag for many years. In the climate of denunciation which reigned among the Chekists in BAMLag, with everybody spying on everybody else, Chistyakov was vulnerable from virtually every angle. He was an outsider in terms of social class, he had been purged from the Party, he criticized his bosses, and he didn't take orders seriously. The fact that he kept his distance from the others, didn't get drunk along with everybody else, and was constantly writing and drawing alerted the Chekists and made them suspicious of him.

Chistyakov gradually grew reconciled to the idea of his impending arrest. He told himself he might only get a short sentence and, having served his time, at last be able to return to his old life.

> I really will have no option but to earn myself a prison sentence and get out. It won't be that bad. I certainly won't be the only person in the USSR with a criminal record. People just get on with it now, and will in the future. That's how BAM has re-educated me, how it has refined my thinking. By making me a criminal. In theory I already am. I'm quietly sitting here among the 'soldiers of the track', preparing and resigning myself to that future. Or perhaps I will top myself.

'I am going out of my mind . . . '

It may be that the nostalgia and despair Chistyakov increasingly felt during his year at BAM were intensified by a sense that any other way of life was now a mirage. The whole world seemed to be one big BAMLag.

'There was something else I realized: the camps were not a hell in comparison with a paradise elsewhere but a mask copied from that other life,' Varlam Shalamov was to write, formulating what Chistyakov, the armed guard platoon commander, is attempting to say in his diary. Shalamov goes on:

Why is the camp's mask copied from the outside world? The camp mirrors that world. There is nothing in the camp that you would not find in the world beyond the barbed wire, in terms of the social and moral arrangements. The ideas in the camp only replicate ideas from outside, transmitted downwards in the form of orders from superiors. Any social movement, campaign, twist or turn in the world outside is promptly reflected in the camp. It reflects not only the struggle of political cliques succeeding each other in power, but the culture of these people, their secret urges, tastes, customs, their suppressed desires. The camp is a mask of society also because everything there is the same as in the world outside. Blood is just as bloody, and the secret policemen and stool pigeons are working flat out, initiating new cases, compiling profiles, conducting interrogations, carrying out arrests, releasing some and arresting others. It is even easier to control other people's destinies in the camp than outside. Everybody works every day, just as in the outside world, and working outstandingly well is supposedly the only way to be released. Just as in the outside world, however, these promises prove false and do not lead to release. The motto on the gates of the camp is constantly repeated: 'Labour is a matter of honour, glory, valour, and heroism'. Lectures are given about current affairs, national loans are signed up for, meetings attended. People succumb to the same diseases as in the world outside, are hospitalized, get better or die. Nowhere are blood and death illusory. It is the blood that makes this mask a reality.*

* Varlam Shalamov, p.46.

Gradually, indeed, the sense of isolation, doom and fear take hold of Chistyakov so powerfully that the possibility of death nearly becomes a reality. He contemplates suicide ever more frequently. After the terrible cataclysms of the Revolution and Civil War, suicide became almost a fad. That choice struck many of Chistyakov's contemporaries as virtually the easy way out. Reporting a suicide in the camp, he writes about it as a possible escape for him too.

> One of the *zek* armed guards has shot himself.* The report claims he was afraid of being sentenced to a new term, but the reality is probably different. They write these reports to keep up morale. What will they write if I top myself? I am going out of my mind. Life is so precious, and wasted here so cheaply, so uselessly, so worthlessly.

As time goes by the idea of killing himself becomes increasingly real, and seems simple, almost commonplace:

> I took out my pistol and put it against my throat. It would be so easy to press the trigger and then . . . feel nothing. How easily it could be done, as if you were only joking. It's nothing to be scared of, nothing supernatural. Just like supping a spoonful of soup. I don't know what held me back. It was all so real, so natural, my hand didn't even tremble.

When Chistyakov writes about suicide he quite deliberately lowers the pathos and tragic nature of such a decision. Several times he chooses a slang term for it that was common during the Civil War: to 'top yourself'.

* The reference is to an armed guard who was also a prisoner or former prisoner.

XXXI

For all that, although in places this seems almost the diary of a suicide, he did not kill himself. In a world which for Chistyakov had been reduced to the confines of the camp, he nevertheless still had supports which held him back. He drew strength from the countryside, the *taiga* forest, the hills he described, the landscapes he drew. These are the things that he had to set against the horror of life at BAMLag.

The main thing that held him back, however, which gave him strength and enabled him to survive in BAM, was his diary. Writing it was risky. He paints an unflinching picture. It is full of such despair and such descriptions of what was really going on there that almost every line could be said to reveal anti-Soviet attitudes and hence used as grounds for imprisoning him. He sometimes speaks openly about this: 'What if the Third Section read these lines, or the Political Department? They will interpret them their way.'

But he cannot stop making the entries: '. . . my life is in this diary.'

Ivan Chistyakov was a minor figure, as he himself often says, but this awareness brings him to a point where he begins not only to complain in the pages of the diary, but to rebel against the system which was trying to swallow him alive. In this awareness he occasionally rises to tragic heights. He writes, 'Alas, the days here are filled with longing and anger, sorrow and shame.'

He comes to an almost Kafkaesque understanding of his powerlessness in the face of an inhumane state machine which erases the boundary between freedom and unfreedom. He rises to tragic irony when he writes about the 'historical inevitability' of the camps:

A path of defeats, misery and rage. A path that makes you even more contemptible, a path humiliating to the humanity in you. Sometimes, though, you try cold-blooded analysis and much of that peters out for lack of fuel. There have been prisons throughout history so why, ha ha ha, shouldn't I be in one rather than only other people? This labour camp existence is necessary in particular historical circumstances, hence necessary also for me.

This is only a diary, but Chistyakov, a guard at BAM who, against his wishes, became a cog in an enormous machine of repression, defends in it his right to at least jot down these entries.

In 1935, when Chistyakov was sent to BAM, Stalin famously announced, 'Life has become better, life has become merrier!' In his diary this minor figure, astonishing as it may seem, himself unaware of the fact, flatly gainsays the all-powerful Leader. If only in a whisper, if only in secret, Chistyakov announces something both terrible and crucial for Russia: 'In the state system a human being's individuality doesn't matter.'

The destiny of the diary's author was played out as he had foretold. In 1937 Chistyakov was arrested, but was probably not sentenced to a particularly long term, since otherwise he could not have been on the front line in 1941. He was killed 300 kilometres from his beloved Moscow, which he probably never saw again.

We do not know where Ivan Chistyakov was in 1939 when, along the railway built by the labour of prisoners he had guarded in 1935–6, long echelons of wagons passed bearing new prisoners to BAM. Among them was one of Russia's greatest twentieth-century poets, Nikolai Zabolotsky. Years later he was to describe BAM as, in all probability, Ivan Chistyakov might have wished to:

Our train of sorrows trundled along the Siberian Railway for two months and more. Two small, iced-up windows near the roof timidly illuminated our goods wagon for a short while during the day. The rest of the time the stump of a candle burned in a lantern, and if no candles were issued, the wagon was immersed in impenetrable darkness. Huddled close to each other, we lay in this primal darkness, listening to the thudding of the wheels and abandoning ourselves to cheerless thoughts about our lot. In the mornings we were able barely to glimpse through the tiny window the boundless expanses of the fields of Siberia, the infinite snowbound *taiga*, the shadows of towns and villages canopied by plumes of vertical smoke, the fantastic sheer cliffs of Lake Baikal. We were transported on and on, to the Far East, to the world's end. In early February we arrived at Khabarovsk. We stood there for a long time. Then suddenly we were pulled backwards, travelled to Volochaevka and turned off the main line to the north along a new branch line. To either side of the track we passed columns of camps with their watchtowers, and settlements with new gingerbread houses built to a standard design. The Kingdom of BAM welcomed us, its new settlers. The train stopped, the bolts clattered, and we emerged from our refuge into this new world, bright with sun and fettered by 50 degrees of frost, and surrounded by slender, spectral Far East birch trees which rose to the very sky.*

It is a miracle that Chistyakov's diary, whose entries break off, probably, with his arrest, somehow survived, that it did not fall into the hands of NKVD officials, that it was not discarded and destroyed, and that somebody managed to send it to Moscow.

Thanks to this miracle, one more voice of a lonely man who lived in a fearful era has come down to us.

* From *'Strange' Poetry and 'Strange' Prose: a philological Festshrift in honour of the centenary of N. A. Zabolotsky*, eds., E. A. Yablokov (Moscow) and I. E. Loshchilov (Novosibirsk), Moscow: 'Pyataya strana', 2003, p.13.

9 October 1935

A new stage in my life.

10 p.m. It's dark and damp in Svobodny. Mud and more mud. The luggage store is cramped and smoke-filled. A prop holds up the sagging ceiling, people sprawl on the floor. There is a jumble of torn quilted jackets with mismatched patches. It's difficult to find two people who look different, as they all have the same strange expression stamped on their faces, the same suspicious, furtive look. Unshaven faces, shaven heads. Knapsacks and trunks. Dejection, boredom. Siberia!

The town hardly lives up to its name.* Fences and more fences, or empty land. Here a house, there a house, but with all the windows shuttered from the outside. Unwelcoming, spooky, depressing, cheerless. My first encounter: not a smart, upright soldier of the Red Army but some sort of scruffy partisan in a shabby greatcoat, no tabs on his collar, scuffed boots, cap plonked on his head, rifle over his shoulder. The local community hotel is a village house partitioned into cramped rooms. Overheated. Incessant snoring.

10 October 1935

Morning. I walk down Soviet Street. Unmetalled, no pavement. More fences, pigs, puddles, dung, geese. I could be in Gogol's *Mirgorod*, but this is Baikal–Amur Mainline Railway Central.

* The town of Svobodny (which means 'Free') was the headquarters of BAMLag, the Baikal–Amur Corrective Labour Camp administration, part of the Gulag system. [Tr.]

HQ is a two-storey brick building, with flowerbeds and a modern electric clock. Road signs: two reflective triangles and a 30 km speed limit. Same mud. Hostel. More mud.

First night in my life feeding bedbugs. Cold. No discipline here either. Incessant swearing.

'Panteleyev, don't give me that crap. Malingering, that's what it is. You know what we call that?'

We call it a crime.

Swearing to the rooftops, incessant, so dense you could lodge an axe in it.

VOKhR, the Armed Guards Unit. Bunks, coloured blankets, illiterate slogans. Some men in summer-weight tunics, some in winter tunics, jackets quilted and not, leather or canvas or string belts. They lie on their beds, smoking. Two are grappling, rolling around locked together, one with his legs in the air, laughing, squealing. Another laments his lot with a wheezing accordion, bawling, 'We are not afraid of work, we just ain't gonna do it.' Men cleaning rifles, shaving, playing draughts, one even managing to read.

'Who's on duty here?' I ask. 'Me,' another partisan replies, getting up from poking embers in the stove. He's wearing padded winter trousers, a summer tunic, winter felt boots, and a convict's hat back to front on his head with a tuft of ginger hair sticking out. There's a canvas cartridge pouch on his belt.* He starts trying to tidy himself up, shifting from foot to foot, uncertain how to behave. I find out later this sentinel has never been in the army and only had a few

---

* The uniform for staff in the GPU (later NKVD) prison camp system, as specified by GPU Order 207 of 21 May 1923, was: greatcoat with red collar tabs and red piping; jacket and jodhpurs, dark blue with red piping; cap with dark blue band and red piping. Not everyone in the security services was an established NKVD staff member; some were prisoners, so they could be dressed variously. It is also possible there was simply a shortage of regulation items in the store at the time.

months' training on the job. What a hero! Few of them are any better.

What am I doing here? I ask myself. I feel ashamed of the little square lieutenant's insignia on my collar tab, and of being a commander, and living in 1935 across the road from the nationally celebrated Second Track of the Trans-Siberian Railway, shamed by a brilliant, soaring concrete bridge.

21 October 1935
Arkhara is a hill surrounded by a hole, a village at the foot of a three-humped mound, with 200 rickety all-but-windowless hovels.* At the foot of the hill trucks trundle from the sand quarry down a dirt track to the station. What a desolate, lonesome place.

22 October 1935
I spent the night in a barracks hut. Cold. Killed a louse. Met the platoon commander.† He seems pretty thick etc. Walked back along the railway track.

My thoughts are all over the place, like pages torn out of a book, shuffled, stacked, crumpled, curling like paper on a fire. I'm disorientated. Lonely. Sad.

Twenty days ago I was in Moscow, alive, living my life, but

---

* Arkhara is in the south-east of Amur Province, and was close to the border with Japanese-occupied Manchuria. It is the fifth stop on the Trans-Siberian Railway from Vladivostok.

† Chistyakov probably had the status of a junior officer drafted for twelve months. A law 'On Compulsory Military Service' was adopted by the Central Executive Committee and Council of People's Commissars of the USSR on 13 August 1930. Section 10 sets out the regulations and length of service for graduates of technical colleges and institutes. While writing his diary, Chistyakov had no rank and the 'little square insignia' on his collar tab indicated only his function as a platoon or section commander. On [p.35] of the diary he says he is not a 'Chekist' (secret policeman); in other words, he is a soldier of the Workers' and Peasants' Red Army, seconded to the NKVD to serve on the BAM construction project.

now? There's no life here. There's no telling how high the clouds are, and it's impossible to take in the endlessness of the hills and the emptiness of the landscape. One hill, then another, then another, then another, on and on for thousands of kilometres. It's bewildering. Life starts to feel insignificant and futile. It gives me the creeps.

Moscow! Moscow! So far away, so out of reach!

Freezing temperatures. I hope they finish the earthworks on the bridge soon and I'm moved somewhere else. A comforting thought, providing I ignore the possibility it might be somewhere even worse.

23 October 1935
I slept all night in the warm. The joy of sleeping without needing a pile of bedclothes.

The day greets me with a stiff breeze as I walk along the track. *Zeks* grafting, inching towards freedom with every cubic metre of earth they shift and every metre of rail they lay, but what do I have to do to get demobbed? I didn't wash today: no water. Tomorrow? Probably still none. I can only dream of steaming in a bathhouse. Bathhouses make you happy. Bathhouses are heaven.

24 October 1935
I met our company commander this morning. He looks like a moustachioed Ukrainian anarchist from the Civil War, like most (all) of the rest of them. Quite some creek I'm up!

Could I ever have imagined I would one day stomp the hills of Arkhara? I never even knew they existed.

Unencompassable vastness, bleak and wild. How small and insignificant a thing is man, how frail his grasp of time. We think two or three months ahead but beyond that is bafflement. It all just telescopes into an unfathomable future.

Autumn is all around. There are haystacks, and the first ice on the River Arkhara appears. Autumn is brown. The haze above the distant hills merges with the horizon and you can't make out the sky, what are hilltops, what are rainclouds. A steady wind blows constantly and the oak leaves rustle in lifeless synchrony. The sun does shine, but it's pale and cold, a nickel-plated disc you can stare at. Was I really born to be a platoon commander at the Baikal–Amur Mainline forced labour camp? How smoothly it happened. They just called me in and sent me off. Party members have the Party Committee, the factory management, and the trade union to intercede, so Bazarov gets to stay in Moscow. For the rest of us, nobody puts in a word.

25 October 1935
Life is like riding a bicycle: you pedal along and try to steer, but first there is mud, then a pothole, then you have to swerve to avoid a sharp stone. But if you stop pedalling, you'll fall off.

Incessant swearing in the barracks, by grunts and commanders alike.

26 October 1935
A raging wind drives the thunderclouds low. Autumn! The russet incline of the hill is hacked into a cliff face day by day, exposing layers of geology. Trucks drive up, and moments later drive away, shuttling without respite between hill and railway station. The people, like ants, are patiently, persistently destroying the hill, transforming its hump into a square in front of the future station. The gash widens: fifteen hundred workers are a mere sprinkling in the maw of the hill, but their crowbars and shovels are having an impact. They count the cubic metres, fighting for the right to live outside, to be free. They rush through everything, whatever the weather. There is a hunger to work and work and work.

There are only statistics, statistics, statistics.

Days, cubic metres, kilometres.

If their strength did not give out, these people would work here night and day.

They work a ten-day week.

The USSR is impatient for the Second Track. The Soviet Far East is impatient for goods.

The Second Track will open up this region, speed its development. And so on.

27–28 October 1935
I count the phalanxes of prisoners in.*

The prisoner-run administration seems to have better living conditions than the guards.

I can just hop on a moving goods train and hop off again. Life goes bowling along, except when you have a 30 km footslog.

29 October 1935
Rain and slush. The clay has been churned into sludge, which makes walking tough. Today is a footslog day. Twenty km to Phalanx 13.

We've been invited to dinner by the section commander.

We walk into the village and enter a huge Ukrainian-style house that has been plastered from the inside with clay then whitewashed. Icons are draped with embroidered linen. The bedstead is a trestle bed with a lacy coverlet and the pillows are in grey chintz pillowslips. Everything is incongruous: the rags stuffed in windows where the glass is missing, the Russian stove, the icons, the bed. Dinner is different too. We have borsch with meat from a goat slaughtered yesterday, then noodles in milk with white gingerbread, home-made with butter. The

* On the vast BAM labour camp complex, the basic administrative unit was the 'section' (*otdelenie*), subdivided into what, for a time at BAM, were known as 'phalanxes', consisting of about 300 prisoners.

6

Ukrainians are in their third year here and have a smallholding with a cow, three pigs, ten chickens. Sometimes they even have honey. Life could be worse for them.

The guards are permanently in a foul mood because their food is so bad.

'They're stashing food away for Revolution Day, so we get no fats.'

The camp administration have everything: meat, butter, everything.

In the evening we get an escape alert and everyone fans out. I walk along the track towards Ussuriysk. It's very still. The sun hovers over a hilltop, its last rays playing over the russet brown leaves of the trees, creating fantastic colours that contrast with equally fantastic shadows. It's exotic scenery for a European: a dwarf oak forest, the hills receding, one higher than the other far into the distance, their summits fanciful, humped animals. The haystacks look like the helmets of giants half rooted in the soil.

Construction of the Second Track is nearing completion. Only yesterday this was a graceless, jagged precipice with gnarled shrubs jutting out of it, but today? Today a women prisoners' brigade appeared and now for 150 metres there is an even, two-storey high embankment with regular lines and a smooth surface that is a sight for sore eyes.

Hills are sliced through, marshes drained, embankments embanked, bridges straddle streams coaxed into drainage conduits. It's the result of concrete, iron, human labour. Stubborn, persistent, focused labour.

And all around, the *taiga*, the dense forests of Siberia. As Pushkin never said, how much that word contains! How much that is untouched, unknown, unknowable! How many human tragedies, how many lives the *taiga* has swallowed up. I shudder when I think about the trek to Siberia, to exile, to prison. And now here is Petropavlovka, a village whose buildings bear the mark of a past of direst penury, but where a collective farm now thrives.

30 October 1935

To the bathhouse, the miraculous bathhouse! It's just a wooden shed, its inside walls pointed with cement, although you could stop up scores of cracks and still be left with as many again. There's a layer of slime on the floor, a cauldron plastered in place on top of the stove. The bathhouse is warm now, but how will it be in winter? The roof leaks – but still, I have a good scrub. It feels so good after twenty days!

I couldn't help getting nostalgic over the bathhouse in Moscow. It would be so nice to have a proper night's sleep too, but we are here to work. Nightfall brings disturbances, escapes, killings. For once, though, may the gentle autumn night extend its protective mantle over the captive. Two runaways this time. There are interrogations, pursuits, memoranda, reports to HQ. The Third Section takes an interest, and in place of rest night brings unrest and nightmares.

31 October 1935

I didn't write a diary entry yesterday, and now I remember nothing. The days hurtle by, faster and faster, a spiral narrowing towards the end of a life, except that here at BAM the spiral is rusty and distorted and may snap at any moment.

1 November 1935

Then there are prisoners who refuse to go out to work. They're just the same as all the others, no less human. They get just as upset at losing that roving red banner as anyone else.* They cry just as bitterly. They have the same psychology as anyone serving

* A mark of distinction awarded temporarily to the winning team in a 'socialist competition' contest

a sentence, the same oppressive thoughts about backbreaking toil, bad conditions, hopes for the future. The same faith that some day they will be free, the same disappointed hopes, despair, and mental trauma. You need to work on their psychology, be subtle, be kind. For them kindness is like a second sun in the sky. The competitiveness here is cut-throat. A foul-up in recording their work credits can drive them to attempt escape, commit murder, and so on. No amount of 'administrative measures' help, and nor does a pistol. A bullet can only end a life, which is no solution, and a dead prisoner can cause a lot of grief. A wounded *zek* is a wild beast.

4–5 November 1935

(On 3 November), the duty officer bangs at the door. What's up?

Urgent telephone message!

I read, 'Your responsibility to unload fifty wagons of railway sleepers.' Head of Security, signature.

'What's the time?'

'03.00 hrs, Comrade Commander!'

We must commence unloading at dawn, so I have to get up, walk 1.5 km to the siding, rouse the brigade, brief them, deploy them and so on.

It's a spring-like day. I wear lighter clothing. After lunch the wind picks up from the west. Winter is on its way. The sleeper layers work fast, followed by those laying the rails. And-one, and-two, and move it through! Eastward! Eastward! Come on, come on! They waddle rhythmically along, followed by the spikers:

Aaargh-clunk, aaargh-clunk.

It turns cold and starts snowing. Minus 16 Celsius. I hop on a passing train, travel 25 km out to the phalanx and walk back on foot. I feel fine, the hike doesn't leave me too tired.

Five hours' sleep in the past forty-eight. It snowed during the night, icy cold. At five in the morning there's a noise, a knock. I hear the duty guard reporting to the deputy head of GHQ that it's not easing off. It's as cold in the room as outside in the snow.

We check out the huts. Oh, life! How can you do this to people? There are bare bunks, gaps everywhere in the walls, snow on the sleeping prisoners, no firewood. A mass of shivering people, intelligent, educated people. Dressed in rags filthy from the trackbed ballast. Fate toys with us all.* To fate, none of us matter in the slightest.

They can't sleep at night, then they spend the day labouring, often in worn-out shoes or woven sandals, without mitts, eating their cold meals at the quarry. In the evening their barracks are cold again and people rave through the night. How can they not recall their warm homes? How can they not blame everyone and everything, and probably rightly so? The camp administration don't give a damn about the prisoners and as a result they refuse to go out to work. They think we are all bastards and they are right. What they are asking for is the absolute minimum, the very least we are obliged to give them. We have funds that are allocated for it, but our hoping for the best, our haphazardness, our reluctance, or the devil only knows what, means we deprive them of the very minimum they need to work.†

---

* A reference to N. Kozlov's popular song of 1859, 'The Fire of Moscow Roared and Blazed' ('*Shumel, gorel pozhar moskovskiy*'), in which Napoleon looks down ruefully from the Kremlin walls.

† After the diary entries in his notebook, Chistyakov has a draft or re-working which appears to relate to this entry. It reads:

> Oh, life, why do you so mock people? The hut at Phalanx 7. There are gaps everywhere in the walls, snow on the sleeping prisoners. No firewood, and perhaps in this sieve firewood would be of little help. A swarm of living creatures, not human beings. Why is it like this? Rags! Dirt! They sleep wearing jackets, felt boots and fur hats. If you look in, you wouldn't guess straight away what you are looking at. A store for old surplus uniforms, or a rubbish tip? There are groans, shouts, whistling snores, curses from sleepers. It's a madhouse
>
> One man is sprawled out, his arms hanging lifelessly down, his legs splayed. He looks as if he's been murdered. On his face there is a plea combined with horror.

6 November 1935

The frost is really setting in. Minus 18. I've put on my felt boots, a very good invention. We go through another one of our farces, searching the *zeks* for knives etc. They are so indignant. People need to be able to slice bread, peel potatoes, chop firewood, don't they? If they had any serious weapons, they certainly wouldn't store them in the huts. Budnikova (Article 35)* rightly protests, and very forcefully. I would have done the same.

I give them a talk in the evening. They listen silently, mistrustful of every word. There is tension whenever we are present. I decide to leave. Budnikova has a way of petulantly kicking off her shoes. They dream of having boots, glance at my leather coat and say, 'Nice boots that would make up into.'†

'I'll nick silk stockings just for you, but only tell me yes or no,' a baby-faced *zek* serenades me sarcastically.

7 November 1935

Revolution Day. We're run off our feet. The prisoners are supposed to be behind the barbed wire but one has gone off looking for milk, another to see the management, a third here, a fourth

White grinning teeth, his mouth twisted in soundless laughter. His eyes flicker open for a moment, then close again.

There is not a single joyous expression. Where are all the smiles and happy dreams? Even in sleep they're still living in a labour camp. Sleep brings not peace and rest, but nightmares and delirium.

A day at work. Rain, snow, mud At night, more raving. Conditions like these inevitably make you think everyone is guilty. The camp administration does not take care of its prisoners. It wastes and embezzles the rations they are entitled to. The railway labourers can't see that Soviet power has anything to give them.

What they get they drink or gamble away and, of course, they never get anything above the official allocation.

* Sentenced under Article 35 of the Penal Code as an 'element harmful to society'.

† A fantasy at the end of the book may be wish fulfilment, a rewriting of how Chistyakov would have preferred this evening to have gone. See 'Rebels' in the Appendix [p.199].

11

there. They all have some reason, some human reason, some trivial reason they think is tremendously important.

'They deprive us of even the little things, like milk for today's holiday, the bastards.'

23.00. A delivery of ballast needs to be unloaded, so out we go. A delay here, a cock-up there, and we end up freezing in the cold. And there is always a mischief-maker not far away.

8 November 1935

Fight.

The *zeks* are fighting. The women beat up the carpenter and threw logs at him. I talked them out of it, it's possible to do that. It's in the tone of voice, stern and masterful at the right moment, or gentle and coaxing. Women are all primarily women.[*]

9 November 1935

I walked 50 km down the track. Wandering along the Ussuriysk line, right in the middle of nowhere.

10 November 1935

This life is nomadic, cold, transient, disordered. We are getting used to just hoping for the best. That wheezing accordion underscores the general emptiness. The cold click of a rifle bolt. Wind outside the window. Dreams and drifting snow. Accordion wailing, feet beating time. There's heat from the stove, but as soon as it warms up one side, the other gets cold. A fleeting thought: am I really going to have to put up with this for long? Is life just one perpetual shambles? Why? I want to let

---

[*] There is a related variant after the end of the diary which reads:

FIGHT

There's a commotion in the phalanx. I need to go. The noise is coming from the club. No human voices. A thump, a crack, the sound of broken windows. The ringing of an overturned iron stove. Then a moment before – more noise.

everything go hang and just float downstream, but I'd probably get banged up myself. Come on, head, think of something and I'll buy you a cap!

Alas, the days here are filled with longing and anger, sorrow and shame. Your work is slapdash and you just hope for good luck. It's degrading. Nobody thinks of us as people; they think of us as platoon commanders and that's it. Periodically someone calls you a representative of the USSR government. I 'sadly look back at the life I have lived',* and kick myself yet again. I have to get out of this place! Think of something, wise up!

11 November 1935

Commanders' training day. I spend it instructing squad commanders 'at home', in the warm (while the heating is on). It goes all right. The lads sing, 'How many thoughts those bells recall.'† They surely do. I look back from the railway bridge at my ark and smile wryly. Here we are, stuck in the middle of the *taiga*, living our lives, laying a railway, worrying about things, doing our geometry. There is life everywhere (only, what sort of life?).

12 November 1935

An influx of juvenile delinquents: the *zeks* call them 'sparkies'. We count them: five short. Count them again: still five short. We check them again: ten short, so another five have got away. We bring out extra security. Thirty sparkies are working; there is no way any of them can escape. We count again: twenty-nine. They cover themselves with sand or snow and, when everyone else has left, come out and leg it. Three more escaped during the night.

I talk to their top dog.

'Can you find them?'

* A line from 'Sleigh Bells', a popular ballad by the Imaginist poet Alexander Kusikov.
† A line from 'Vesper Bells' ('*Vecherniy zvon*', 1827), a ballad by Ivan Kozlov.

13

'Sure!'

He did. They won't do it again. It turns out he sent them off himself and they got drunk but they're back now. Others will do the same tomorrow. I let a man out for a pee and he just disappeared. I saw a woman standing there. She pulled out a skirt she'd tucked into her trousers, put a shawl over her head, and before I knew it she'd vanished.

One of the sparkies says: 'There's this woman selling ox meat, so I sit there watching how much she's making, beg some money off her, then nick her bag and scarper. I fill another bag with stuff, old rubbish, find someone to buy the meat, take their money while holding the bag between my legs, another kid swaps the bags round and the deed is done.'

13 November 1935

I walked to Arkhara this morning. Twenty km hardly counts here. We talked shop: someone got killed, someone else got killed. In 3 Platoon a bear ripped the scalp off a hunter and smashed up his rifle. They bayoneted it.

I bought frozen apples. They were a delight to eat. I spent the day hanging around at the station, which is regarded as normal. What can you do if there are no trains? Hang around.

14 November 1935

I went to check the rails and sleepers and so on with the political instructor. We are building BAM, but whether that is our job or not we haven't been told. It's difficult to know who's supposed to be doing what. We met a commissioner who cheered us up by asking, 'Have they been stealing sleepers from the Ussuriysk track? Been using them as firewood, have they?'

As if we are going to tell him. Here's the thing: if there's no firewood, cold, hungry people refuse to go out to work and I'm to blame. If there is firewood and those people get fed and keep warm, I'm still to blame. I decide to be to blame for one thing. One of life's lessons: learn to steal but don't get caught.

15 November 1935

The day fades slowly here. It seems endless. I'm up at five in the morning and go to bed at eleven at night. The west wind is blowing in cirrus thunderclouds through which the last rays of the setting sun stream, creating a fabulous picture in the sky. The background is grey, the horizon amazingly distant. The firmament is suffused with pale yellow; pink clouds edged with crimson look like poppies. The horizon, a red line, burns ever brighter until it overflows and spills out, flooding the sky and turning everything purple. As a blindingly red sun begins to sink below the horizon, purple yields to hues of yellow tinged with green, and these in turn give way to violet and deepest blue. The base of the hills becomes shrouded in mist and the reddish-brown grass on their summits is streaked with gold before slipping slowly into blackness. The darkness deepens upwards and downwards. A last red line limning the horizon narrows and then, lingering a moment in your imagination, dies. A tardy ray flashes out, as if hastening after the sun and, as it vanishes, bestows a smile, like a girl who has said goodbye and, walking away, looks back from a distance.

Night. It's dark outside. I can only sense the thirty-metre high embankment, just fifty metres away, because I know it's there. With a clattering and scattering of sheaves of sparks, a freight train steams across the bridge. Smoke comes from the little chimney of a wagon heated by a stove. Conscripts. Perhaps they look at us and think, even out here, there are people living. Yes, even out here there is some godforsaken gypsy encampment.

These years of impressions are going to leave their mark on me.

16 November 1935

It's 26 degrees below zero and a gale-force wind is blowing. Cold. Cold outside, cold indoors. Our building seems to have more holes than wall. The building's superintendent comes in and cheers us up:

'Don't worry, lads, it's going to get twice as cold as this.'

How wasteful human mismanagement is. Nobody thought to lay the sub-grade before the frost came and now the labourers are forced to dig a trench, 30 cm deep, into frozen clay as viscous as tin.

The days roll by. What lies ahead? I have no desire to serve in the army, let alone at BAM, but what else can I do? It would be bearable if we could at least relax in a warm building, but we don't have even that. The stove heats you on one side of your body* while the other freezes. You become lackadaisical: why care about anything? Yet every day that passes is part of my life, a day I could have lived instead of wasted. There is no one to talk to here. I can't talk to the *zeks*, obviously, and if I talked to the guards they'd become overfamiliar and I'd lose my authority. We are just a prop for the system, and when the project is finished we will leave the stage unnoticed. The whole, or a large part, of the burden of this project is borne by us, the guards and platoon commanders.

17 November 1935

Midnight. The duty officer calls the guards out to supervise the unloading of ballast. I get to join them. It's a shambles. The shuttle truck hasn't arrived and probably won't, so people are freezing in the minus 35 degrees cold. This isn't how I would do it. I would lay a secondary track and run the ballast and backfill along that.

Do you know what it feels like to be out in the *taiga* at night?

* The stove, a wood-burning iron 'burzhuika', was suitable for heating only a small room.

Let me tell you. There are oak trees, perhaps three hundred years old, their branches bare, like giants' arms, like tentacles, paws, beaks of prehistoric monsters, and they seem to reach out to seize and crush anyone they can catch.

You sit round a campfire and the flickering shadows make all these limbs look like they're moving, breathing, animated, alive. The quiet rustling of the remaining leaves and the branches tapping other branches make you think even more of the Cyclops or other monsters. You are overhearing a conversation you can't understand. There are questions being asked and answers given.

You hear melodies and rhythms. The flames of the fire pierce the darkness for five metres or so, and sparks fly like long glow-worms in the air, swirling, colliding and overtaking each other. The face of your comrade opposite, vividly lit by the flames against the backdrop of the night, with shadows darting from his nose and the peak of his Red Army helmet, looks theatrically grotesque. You don't want to talk loudly. It would be out of place. You want to sit and doze and listen to the whispering of the trees.

18 November 1935
I ride out in the morning to Phalanx 13.

We have been sent juveniles: louse-ridden, dirty, without warm clothing. There is no bathhouse because we cannot go sixty rubles over budget, which would work out at one kopek a head. There is talk of the need to prevent escapes. They look for causes, use guns, but fail to see that they themselves are the cause, that escapes are a result of their slothfulness, or their red tape, or just plain sabotage. People are barefoot and inadequately dressed even though there is enough of everything in the stores. They don't issue supplies even to those who are able and willing to work, claiming it would just be wasted. So the prisoners don't waste it, don't work, and run away.

19 November 1935

An empty sort of day. Apathy, indifference. In the political study class I ask, 'Who is Vasiliy Blyukher?' He's only the military commander of this entire Far East Region. The best guess I get is, 'Ex-commissar of the Second Track?'

20 November 1935

An escape. A 58.8-er.* Silly bugger. In frost like this, with no money, he doesn't stand a chance. What was he thinking of? The professional criminals are a different matter. They could bring it off.

Emptiness. Perhaps it is always going to feel like this now. I'll get used to it and think it nothing out of the ordinary, normal.

We're going hunting tomorrow. What will that be like?

The political instructor says he will find goats. We'll see.

21 November 1935

At 5.15 a.m. I hear a train crossing the bridge with what sounds like a loose brake shoe knocking. I'm just dozing off again when the duty officer reports:

'Crash at Kilometre 752!'

'What kind of train?'

'Don't know.'

I leap out of bed.

'Platoon Commander! Send four men to the accident and the rest to breakfast. After breakfast, send a relief shift.'

'At once, Comrade Commander!'

---

* Article 58.8 of the 1926 RSFSR Penal Code covers 'organization for counter-revolutionary purposes of terrorist acts against representatives of Soviet power or officials of revolutionary organizations of the workers and peasants, as well as participation in performance of such acts, even if the individual participating in such an act does not belong to a counter-revolutionary organization'.

The rear wheels of a flat wagon loaded with timber derailed on the bridge and the wagon broke all the railings. How the whole thing didn't derail I can't imagine. Having trailed along for over a kilometre, the part of the train with the broken wagon decoupled and blocked the track. The driver continued almost half a kilometre to the station and received the baton to proceed, but was stopped at the signal just out of the station. We dumped the timber, lifted one end of the wagon on to a trolley and shunted it into the siding.

It messed up our hunting, but the superintendent and I went anyway. Looking at a hill, you don't see the snow because the grass is higher than a man. A swamp, full of goat tracks. It looked to be no distance but was 5 km. Walking through an oak forest in winter gives you the willies. It feels strange for someone from Russia. I didn't even notice the two goats skipping past. The superintendent did but couldn't shoot for fear of killing me.

I want to get to bed.

22 November 1935

Life just bowls along. We had to travel to Arkhara, although 'travel' is putting it too grandly. First we had to plod 5 km to the rise where the train slows down and you can jump aboard. We sped through the last 12 km on an express carrying firewood and timber. The political instructor was reminiscing about the Far North camp at Solovki, where the Solovki officials, not the Soviets, are in charge. Not Soviet but Solovki power there! The appropriateness of their methods for educating and rehabilitating the prisoners can be judged by the sentence passed on F.* and some others.

You can find yourself in a stupid situation and the regulations are no help at all. I arrived wearing an Abyssinian-style cowl, and must have looked a right prick because the chief said, 'What's this in aid of?' The political adviser, adjutant and entire

---

* It is not known who 'F.' is. [Tr.]

HQ staff came out to take a look, even the political adviser to the head of the entire Armed Guards Unit. What could I say? They took the HQ clerk's snazzy Red Army helmet from him and put it on me. I could see that cap meant a lot to the boy and made his life a bit more bearable. How easily his pride and joy was taken off him. The position I was in, as a commander. I would not have done that.

23 November 1935

One more day crossed out of my life in the service of pointless military discipline. What if the Third Section read these lines, or the Political Department? They will interpret them their way.

I walk through a part of the site where women are working and hear long torrents of virtuoso abuse, with Siberian trimmings. To think that women can sink this low. They imagine gutter language is chic and raffish. They disgust me. This lot really do deserve the rough end of Solovki power.

And yet the countryside is enchanting in its wild beauty. The slope of a hill stretches further than imaginable and dissolves in the distant purple haze. Your body trembles as you take in the immensity, this sparsely populated landscape untouched by man. Beyond the nearest hill are others, and beyond them yet more, and more, and more, as many as you can picture, all the way to the Arctic Ocean. You feel as if you own all this space and that, if you wanted, you could come and live here, and sow, and plough, and reap to your heart's content, with no boundaries, unfettered.

24 November 1935

Have you seen the sun rise in these hills?

Something unexpected is the way the darkness disappears instantly. You look one way and it is dark, then you turn, close your eyes for a moment, and it is day. It's as if the light had been stalking you, waiting for you to open the door so that it could slip in, as iridescent as mother-of-pearl. The sun has not appeared yet but the sky is already ablaze, not only on the horizon but everywhere. It is aflame, changing like a theatre set under the skilled hand of a lighting technician; as the action unfolds, it is painted every colour. Rockets explode, firing rays of light from behind the hilltop. There is a stillness, a solemn silence, as if a sacrament is to be administered that cannot be celebrated without it. The silence intensifies and the sky reaches the peak of its brilliance, its apogee. The light grows no brighter but, in an instant, from behind the hill, the fireball of the sun emerges, warm, radiant, and greeted by an outburst of song from the dawn chorus.

Morning has broken. The day begins, and with it all the vileness. Here is one instance: there is a fight in the phalanx, a fight between women. They are beating the former top shock worker to death and we are powerless to intervene. We are not allowed to use firearms inside the phalanx. We do not have the right even to carry a weapon. They are all 35-ers,* but you feel sorry for the woman all the same. If we wade in there will be a riot; if they later recognize we were right, they will regret what they have done. You just get these riots. The devil knows but the Third Section doesn't. They'll come down on us and bang us up whether or not the use of firearms was justified. Meanwhile, the *zeks* get away with murder. Well, what the hell. Let the prisoners get on with beating each other up. Why should we get their blood on our hands?

25 November 1935

After work I went walking in the hills. There were lots of tracks but not a goat to be seen. The company commander arrived. He seemed to find everything in order with the platoon but couldn't bring himself to say so.

* Article 35 of the Criminal Code provided for up to five years' imprisonment for violating the passport laws or for those categorized as 'socially harmful elements'. These included tramps, prostitutes and petty criminals.

26 November 1935

For a second day I feel fagged out. Today, we went hunting in the hills.

We walk for ages but see only tracks. We head up the path on the hill. I hear a rustle of dry leaves, look round, see two goats leaping. 'Over there!' I say to the hunter standing behind me. The goats hear and scarper. I take a potshot, miss. Miss a second time. He misses too. It's the first time I've ever seen, and shot at, goats in the wild.

Back at the hostel they are winding up Armed Guard Sigitov:

'They escaped only to die in Arkhara. What a place to choose! You should've ordered them to lie down first and then shot them!'

27 November 1935

This is how we live: in a cramped room furnished with a trestle bed and straw mattress, a regulation issue blanket, a table with only three out of four legs and a creaky stool with nails you have to hammer back in every day with a brick. A paraffin lamp with a broken glass chimney and lampshade made of newspaper. A shelf made from a plank covered with newspaper. Walls partly bare, partly papered with cement sacks. Sand trickles down from the ceiling and there are chinks in the window frames, door, and gaps in the walls. There's a wood-burning stove, which, while lit, keeps one side of you warm. The side facing towards the stove is like the South Pole, the side facing away from it is like the North Pole. The amount of wood we burn would make a normal room as warm as a bathhouse, but ours is colder than a changing room.

Will they find me incompetent, not up to the job, and kick me out? Why should I be sacrificed like so many others? You become stultified, primitive, you turn into a bully and so on.

You don't feel you're developing, either as a commander or a human being. You just get on with it.

28 November 1935

It's cold outside, it's cold inside, and it's cold and cheerless inside me. How can you do a job properly if you have no interest in it and no wish to do it? And why is that? Because you don't have the bare necessities of life and culture. The top brass don't even talk about these things. Today we are faced with the fact that there is no firewood. I have to order people about. I don't need all this. Why does it always turn out this way?

My hands are stiff with cold. Why is no one looking after us commanders? What do all the brave words amount to? If we had even a hundredth of what Voroshilov promised here, on the railway, we would at least have a little hope. All the talk is of The Second Five-Year Plan, Maxim Gorky, Klim Voroshilov. The USSR has unparalleled aeroplanes, but here we don't have even the bare minimum. Oh, hell! The only consolation is that it was even worse at the front. Some comfort! I sleep under two blankets, a leather coat and a sheepskin jacket.

I just can't find my place here in the Baikal–Amur Mainline system, probably because it doesn't exist. It's different for peasants. They get something out of it, learn new tricks, find out things they didn't know. All I'm going to learn here is how to be a slob, not give a damn, and not get caught.

29 November 1935

More emptiness. Nothing worth noting down. Even my mood is empty. I don't care about anything. If there is an escape I won't go out. To hell with it all! I'm not bothered that the women's team has made good progress on the ballast. I'm not moved to see a train speeding round the bends with steam billowing behind it. Even sighting a fox can't rouse my hunting instinct. I no longer wince at the duff notes played on the balalaika. Who cares?

30 November 1935

A south wind brings warmth and now it's only 16 degrees below. Clouds in the sky. I go hunting with the political instructor. The nearest hill seems no distance away, but it's 5 km and that's far enough to warm us up.

That's how we spent the day, moving from one hill to the next, one ravine to the next. It's highly addictive. Spiralling goat tracks make patterns in the snow, loops, zigzags, triangles, all interlocking, mixed up together, sometimes forming a kind of oriental ornamentation, or something like the inscription on the tomb of an Ethiopian emperor. We must have walked for three hours, climbing hills, pushing through undergrowth, going down into ravines. Sometimes we came upon melted snow where a goat had been lying, but not the goats themselves. One might at least have skipped teasingly by.

Suddenly, just behind a projection, we saw a dugout and behind it a ramshackle cabin. There must have been a hundred beehives. We moved closer. Not only was there no lock on the door, but it wasn't even tied shut. There were some bits and pieces under a shelter – carpenter's tools, hive tops, cans, pottery and so on. It was warm in the hut and there were perhaps fifty cans of honey, scales, utensils, food. We could just go in and help ourselves. Here were the old Siberian customs and decency. And all around the forest were oaks broken by the storms, felled, collapsed from age, half-rotten, re-rooting in the ground. Freedom, space. We stalked for another four hours, to no avail.

We were both dog-tired. The political instructor barely made it back. Dinner, then relaxation.

The superintendent came in with good news: 'The bathhouse is working.' Cause for celebration.

31 November 1935

My day off. Went hunting again, and again bagged nothing. I didn't even see anything to shoot at. Cold. Minus 29, with the wind searing my face and hands. The trees are beautiful, covered in hoar frost. Telegraph wires iced up and looking like threads of fire in the sun. No thoughts in my head. Well, perhaps just the one: some day I will make it back to Moscow.

   I still have that hope. Hurray!

1, 2 and 3 December 1935

Wrote nothing in the diary: no time. Two days travelling round the sections. Escapes, and worse: in one phalanx someone caused an explosion.

4 December 1935

Before I am even out of bed, another escape. I'll have to go looking for him tomorrow. We should just shoot three in each phalanx to put them off the idea. Escapes disrupt everything. What a dog's life, sniffing around like a bloodhound, browbeating everyone all the time. Banged one *zek* up for twenty-four hours.

5 and 6 December 1935

On the 5th I was going round inspecting. If I keep this up who knows what'll happen. Getting put away might get me kicked out sooner.

> *Morn catches fire above the hill*
> *And fills with light the darkest creeks.*
> *Blue the sky as lovers' eyes,*
> *Dawn the blush on lovers' cheeks.*

Only I've been sent an official report. Oh, *hell*!

★

14. 6–1 29. 6–2 . . . Seriously!*
Anger jeopardizes joy
Bile will flood, afflict the soul.

7 December 1935

I have to admit, I am growing into BAM. Imperceptibly the environment, the way of doing things, the life are sucking me in. Perhaps inevitably.

Tried studying Leninism but it only made me feel worse by rubbing in the kind of life we are living. What positive thing can I occupy myself with? Nothing. Knowledge which hasn't been refracted through life's practicalities is fairly useless. There's no one here to talk to, joke or argue with. Feeling superior among inferiors is cold comfort. I need to feel I'm the best among equals. I need to be challenged, to have something to rise to. I need people to test me, goad me, and be able to hold my own. A year from now people will probably look down on me the way I look at this lot now. Awful, but a fact. Where's my alternative?

8 December 1935

Thirty-three degrees below. Wind and snow. Our burzhuika stove is our salvation, our South Pole. How strange that in the era of the Second Five-Year Plan we should be using a word like that, and indeed using the mechanism itself in our everyday life. When it goes out, the heat is immediately gone too. Quite odd. You sit with a fur jacket over the arm towards the door, while your other side is blazing hot and sweating. When I am back home I may find it interesting to remember that, but right now it's just really annoying.

Above the hills there are whirlwinds and snowstorms.

---

* A cryptic entry but which probably means 'Phalanx 14, 6 escapes, 1 caught; Phalanx 29, 6 escapes, 2 caught.'

26

Everything is milky white. The silhouettes of trees make it look as if they are walking towards us as, now here, now there, the blizzard relents. But then there's another flurry, and tongues of dry, prickly snow inflict thousands, millions of venomous snakebites. Branches as thick as your arm, thicker even, snap off readily in the icy cold.

I sleep soundly and wake up refreshed. The air is clean and frosty and sometimes there is even a dusting of snow. My lecture programme flaps on the wall. By lunchtime the temperature is down to minus 40 and the cold attacks every exposed part of my body. I stare longingly at a log of firewood, imagining the energy, the warmth within it. It's so cold in the room that a wet hand freezes to the door handle. Soap doesn't lather until the heat of my hand has melted it. Smoke from a steam engine doesn't disperse but hangs in the air like tufts of cotton wool. It mixes with steam to form snowflakes, an impenetrable haze obscuring a window like nets.

The lads have formed a jazz band with penny whistles and pipes, balalaikas and rattles. Music can also be warming, literally.

Meanwhile, *zeks* are on the run. Freedom. Freedom, even with hunger and cold, is still precious and irreplaceable. They may get away for only a day, but at least they get out of the camp. I wouldn't mind a day away from this job myself.

9 December 1935

Minus 42 degrees during the night and very, very quiet. The air chimes like crystal. The dry crack of a gunshot. It feels as if the air could break like glass and splinter. In places the ground has fissures as wide as my hand. It's so cold that even the rails can snap, with a sound unlike anything I've ever heard.

A message over the intercom to the railway station duty officer:

'Comrade Duty Officer, a rail has broken at Kilometre 755. Hold the trains!'

They work quickly and efficiently. It's just another job for the accident brigade. Silently and confidently, everyone does his bit and the passengers in the trains have no idea that their lives have been saved in this quiet, straightforward, businesslike, understated way. It's a simple truth that, in many ways, people going about their daily work without a fuss are the real heroes.

I had to go all the way to Zhuravli. Murderously freezing. My fur jacket rigid in the cold, my felt boots like blocks of wood. Didn't see a single bird.

10 December 1935

The water in our building has frozen so we can't wash. When I splash water in one eye out of a mug, the other eye opens by reflex. Minus 45 degrees. The trains run slowly. Only the moon, with a superior air, glides serenely through the sky . . .

> The moon looks down above the hills, two-horned and bleak and pale,
> Reminding us it's cold enough to make us quake and quail.
> Centuries-old oak trees sway, their branches snap and break
> And forest creatures shun the chill until it's time to wake.

I stay indoors all day, wearing outdoor clothing. The stoves can't compete with the cold. My ink has frozen. I sleep in breeches and sports training top, my hair freezing to the cold sweat on my forehead.

What fun. That's it! I've had enough.

11 December 1935

Today it's minus 47. One cheek has puffed up and I have swelling on my forehead, near my eye. This kind of cold makes you swell up. The prisoners are working, hacking at part of the embankment. Still, knowing the right people is a good thing. How can we combat nepotism, and do we need to? Without it I might have caught pneumonia or worse, but pulling strings was my salvation: I got my felt boots re-stitched. Good, fast work. That's all very well, but there's no escaping the fact we now have three and a half months of frost ahead. We've got no lining for insulating the walls and no prospect of getting any. No caulking either.

I got a letter from the railway office. Civilians don't know how lucky they are. When you are warm at your workplace and at home and have enough to eat, you take everything for granted. Everything is under control, so why bust a gut? Then you get bored. Things are different if you are constantly wondering when this is going to end, when you will get time to rest, when you will have the bare essentials, when you will even get a little time to plan your day, when you will no longer have the sword of the Revtribunal hanging over your head.* I will hold life so dear when I can go out and buy whatever I want at any time I please. White bread, for instance. Right now I feel every passing day is another one I haven't lived.

12 December 1935
Last night I was warm, but only because I kept my all my clothes on. You feel tied and tethered and weighed down. I spent the

---

* Chistyakov's constant fear of punishment derives from Article 193.17 of the RSFSR Penal Code. Paragraph a) provides for punishment for 'exceeding authority, failing to exercise authority, or neglect of duty by a person in a position of command within the Workers' and Peasants' Red Army' by imprisonment for not less than six months. Paragraph b) provides for punishment of the same offences where there are serious aggravating circumstances by penalties up to and including capital punishment.

Article 193 was usually invoked to punish service personnel, including NKVD officers, for serious neglect of duty, such as allowing escapes, riots or causing delays through inaction.

day trudging 45 km. After that, the boots mended two days ago were falling apart again. I got to bed at four in the morning.

13 December 1935

Out on the tracks again. I ride to Domikan on horseback. Look like I'm going to the wars. The phalanx leader there, a *zek*, wants to lord it over us. Surprising. Perhaps he would like to try lording it over the prosecutor. An armed guard sings the ballad of faithless Murka. Pleasant baritone. Very moving.

A sleepless night makes itself felt; my eyelids droop and I'm barely able to keep my eyes open. Then it is one thing after another. I have to imprison one woman, there's some muddle about an escape, a conflict with the phalanx leader, a knife fight. Someone's injected something and is dying. To hell with the lot of them! Life doesn't wait, it passes. I'll never get today back again. What has it given me? Nothing. The question is more, how much have I lost? For many there's nothing corrective about these labour camps. The phalanx bookkeeper has five years to serve and he's still cooking the books. What is he hoping for? What is he expecting? He'll get it sooner than he thinks.

14 December 1935

A bright, joyful, sunny day. A mere minus 34. Soon the Green Attorney will be releasing *zeks* in large numbers.* There is talk about it already. We'd be in big trouble without the sloggers, the ordinary prisoners, to rely on.

15 December 1935

A long drawn-out hoot from an engine on the Baikal-Amur Mainline. It's the stop signal. An odd-looking train stops. The

---

* The coming of the Green Attorney was prison camp slang for escaping in the spring.

30

freight wagons have a second cladding of planks, there's *glass* in the hatches, and a chimney on the roof puffing away as blithely as the engine. The brakes platforms are festooned with all sorts of things: the wheels of a field kitchen, urns for boiling water, bales of straw, tarpaulins, buckets and cauldrons. From the wagons come human voices, neighing of horses, grunting of pigs and mooing of cows. The passengers wear warm tunics and sheepskin jackets, felt boots and Abyssinian-style rag boots. We can see all the men but we also hear a lot of women's voices. What's going on?

What's going on is that all the women are dressed like men. The first things they unpack are kettles and cooking pots. Y-shaped sticks, kindling, fires, and tea is served. There's a clattering of pans and bowls, spoons, mugs and buckets. How ridiculous and wonderful that these people have just turned up, found themselves out in the open here, and made themselves at home. Someone strikes up a bawdy song. From the far end of the train comes the clanging of shovels, crowbars and pickaxes. A blacksmith is already working the bellows on a mobile forge.

There's a cook with a sack of potatoes on his back, a laundress with washing, and several grooms with hay and buckets. They hack at nearby trees to chop down firewood. Wash themselves, shake out clothing and straw mattresses. One is looking over the terrain, another selects a small, wizened tree for firewood, another may be thinking about home and the familiar places he has left behind, and some may be dreaming of escape. Different people, different perspectives.

The group stands around smoking. The group argues. One man is working hard to persuade them of something, gesticulating wildly, constantly straightening his hat before it falls off. Some spit with gusto to one side, coughing and clearing their throats. Three walk down the line, inspecting something, stamping on the ground, pointing at the embankment and rails of the old section. One waves a rod at the far distance and round about. The others follow the movements of his hand, turn, consider something, note something down.

A new phalanx is born.

In a day's time there will be tents, huts, dugouts, a whole movable town just a few metres from the railway. It will come to life in the mornings, get quieter during the day, come back to life in the evening. They don't consider or comment on whether this place is better or worse than the last. Everywhere is much the same to them. They will live here for the next three to five months and then move on. If they get through the winter, every bush will provide shelter in the summer.

'Momma! Momma!' I hear someone shouting, but it's not someone's son or daughter. This is how the 35-ers address their brigade leader. You don't find that kind of team spirit among the men, they don't band together the same way. The women are different, but only the 35-ers. They form gangs with thieves' rules and customs. For them the brigade leader is their *ataman*, their boss, their godmother. Momma rules everything and everyone. Momma beats or pardons, decides who gets work, feeds them or leaves them to go hungry. Momma is in charge. Men keep themselves to themselves or, occasionally, pair up. When they're playing cards, whether they're winning or losing, their sense of what belongs to them counts for more than friendship. They can make a pack of cards in ten minutes, so it's a waste of time confiscating them. They gamble away anything and everything. They gamble the stores, which means we can expect robberies. They lose and their forfeit is to say something filthy to the guards. They lose parts of their body: fingers and toes, hands. The person who has lost hacks off a finger or a hand in front of everyone and throws it on the table saying, 'Drink my blood, you parasites!'

32

Aksametova, leader of a *zek* women's phalanx.
BAM – the Second Track

16 December 1935
Motorized Unit 10 are leaving. The company commander
orders me to supervise the departure. I trudge 13 km there,
another 13 back.

Chernigovka village. A grey winter's day. Low sky. Here and
there smoke rises from people's chimneys. The smoke is very
still, like a pillar to the sky, merging with the background. Not
a soul in the streets. Silence. The shadoof stretches its neck high
above the huts, trying to look out beyond the village and warning
people not to make a noise. There's a particular smell of smoke, of
ordinary hot cabbage soup and the warmth of a hut. An unhur-
ried conversation with its hospitable owner puts my soul at rest.
But then I have to march back along the sleepers. How easily I've
been deprived of even this small happiness in life.

33

That is how modest our desires and aspirations are now. It is perfectly true that, for the present, we are a republic on wheels, the front line; for the present we have no rights and cannot yet enjoy the achievements of the First and Third Five-Year Plans, free trade and so on. How many more construction projects will there be? How many more criminals? Siberia is boundless. There's no shortage of work.

Many company commanders hit the bottle in the hope of being fired. I have every sympathy for them. I'll come up with something after I've been here a year.

17 December 1935
There are talk and rumours that we'll be going east, or maybe to the Volga–Don Canal project, or to the goldmines in Aldan in Yakutia. Nothing to report today. Emptiness and more emptiness, which is not the same as tranquillity.

18 December 1935
Commanders' training day. Called in by the Third Section, then by company HQ. Change my horse. I'm told it's a Mongolian Blaze. Looks ungainly but moves all right. I'll give the nag a go. You're running around, surrounded by other people, making yourself useful and barely aware of the time. Or standing by the intercom in the phalanx office, a place stained by paraffin fumes and tobacco smoke and which smells of sweat. Some indolent carpenters are reluctantly repairing a partition. If you don't pay people then that's the work you get.

19 December 1935
The nag is a star. It did 36 km at a trot through a cold night. We went riding along, skirting a hill in the dark. Silhouettes of bushes, telegraph poles, a train coming towards us. Frost. My knees are chilled. The collar of my fur jacket frosts over and

my eyelids freeze up. There's hoar frost everywhere. The horse throws back its head, snorts, waggles its ears. Frost creeps into my sleeves. My gloves are covered in hoar frost from the heat of my hands. You don't want to turn your body or move your arms. Any movement loses body heat.

Got 'home' at 1.30 a.m. I had a mug of tea with pancakes, yes, pancakes, and then went to bed. Sleep is the best. It lets you forget everything and everyone. It's too cold to undress, it's cold getting into bed. I'm often cold in the night but I can warm myself by keeping the stove going. That's nice.

20 December 1935
Gap in my memory.

21 December 1935
I waste an hour knocking frozen dung off the horse's hooves. He's not having it. Keeps butting me with his back and front, the Mongolian devil. I get in the saddle and we're off. We ride to Zhuravli and back, at a trot and galloping. I tried to catch up with the deputy head of the Education and Culture Unit but no luck. Couldn't match his fiery steed.

I spent the afternoon going round the squads. In Moscow Centre the NKVD are celebrating the anniversary of the Cheka with feasting, and here at the railway we are celebrating it in our own way. We have to complete the Second Track at top speed, so there's no time for holidays, not even a day off. I'm no Chekist and don't even want a rank, but I would like civilized living conditions. I confiscated a pack of cards and a whole printing works and trekked 20 km on foot. That was how I celebrated Secret Policeman's Day.

Like yesterday, I spent a sloppy day at 'home'. A brigade leader got hit by a train, which cut off his ear and flesh from his thigh. Meanwhile the track is being completed and soon we'll be off somewhere else. It would be good if we were sent to Russia.* I've had enough of interesting places, enough of the Far East. I want no more of it.

23 December 1935

Spent the whole day making a billiard table. There was an escape in Phalanx 29 but I'm not going out there. Sod it! I've been given a deputy. I expect he . . . Let's wait and see.†

24 December 1935

My deputy arrived. He seems all right. I'll check him out and help him where I can. I'll be glad if he learns well, it'll make things easier for me. He might even be my replacement. We went to Phalanx 13, then to Uletui. An unprepossessing *zek* comes up to us:

'Let me visit Arkhara.'

I don't. She drops the angelic tone. Now she's an animal.

'You won't let me? I'll cut someone's head off and bring it to you. Shoot me if you like.'

No problem. If need be, we will.

25 December 1935

An escape and a half! Group of seven. To hell with them. The top brass care more about the 'soldiers of the track' than us. Do they think I'm a ready-made expert who doesn't need support and guidance? Well, perhaps we can get by without support, but someone needs to take a minimum of interest in the commanders. They're surprised some get drunk on their day off. Well, what

---

* Chistyakov was serving in Amur Province in the Far East Region of the Russian Socialist Federative Soviet Republic, which is included in the broader definition of Siberia. Strictly speaking he was already in 'Russia', but would just like to be somewhere nearer Moscow, and with a less severe climate.

† He evidently suspects his deputy has been appointed to spy on him.

else is there to do? There's no recreational centre, not even a doss-house like the one I stayed in for those few days in Svobodny. We have nowhere to meet up with friends. I need to let off steam. I need to joke, have a laugh, play the fool, tell tall tales. Where can I do that? Where is the club to meet up with the other commanders? You can't let your hair down with the squaddies, because commanders and guards look at things differently.

Here's an order from Company Commander Gridin, complaining about negligence and so on. Does he think I'm trying for a criminal charge? Does he think I'm my own enemy? That I don't want to see everything in good order?

Supposing there is negligence – why could that be? Perhaps because there's no sense of commitment from anybody else, because there is no incentive, because the whole armed guard organization is . . . whatever the hell it is. You don't know what you're supposed to do, how you're supposed to do it or why. Sometimes, you find you've apparently done the right thing, but then the next time you do exactly the same and you're told it's completely wrong. You'd like to be doing a good job, but at the same time you think that if you do they might keep you at BAM for the rest of your life. Sod that!

The newspapers are enough to drive you crazy. They write about what's being done here, what's being done there, but they never write about us. All they report are escapes, more escapes, guards arrested and the Revtribunal. Makes me feel really great.

26 December 1935
Got back last night at 2 a.m. Freezing cold, with the wind blowing outside and through the building too. It's best not to talk about it. In the morning I finish off the billiard table, and then from lunchtime I'm at Phalanx 13 in Zhuravli. I have to motivate them, push them. What a lot of tosh I've started talking. Wonderful.

You are on horseback and the 'soldiers of the track' are on

foot. Hundreds of them on foot to one supervisor on horseback. Suppose ten or twenty decide to take off, what can you do? I feel such despair, such frustration and hopelessness. It would be so much better, almost beyond my wildest dreams, just to be any-where else, even if it wasn't Moscow, even if I was somewhere way out in the sticks.

Just to be shot of all those Article 59.3-ers, 58.7-ers, 35-ers and so on.*

27 December 1935

Commissioner Morozov from the Third Section: what can he actually do, what guidance is he supposed to offer, when he doesn't have a clue about the situation or the measures we have already taken, when he doesn't know that we have already tried everything, we're not our own enemies, and we're not trying to get ourselves awarded fatigue details or arrested. All they do is swear at us, punish us: the commissioner, the political adviser, the company commander, the head of the Third Section. That's all any of them do. Who is there to advise, support and explain? Nobody. Just get on with your job!

That's what the Cheka call leadership. I spent from lunch-time to 1 a.m. trudging 26 km to Phalanx 14. Warm breeze and flurries of wet snow. 'Warm' for us is minus 27. If you take your hand out of your glove, it'll go numb. We picked up a stray artist along the way. He was bare-headed and drunk, asked us to take him back to Phalanx 7. With pleasure. We'll take you there and put you in the cells.

---

* 59.3 was an article of the Penal Code from 1926 until 1959 that covered criminal activity and exceptionally grave crimes against governance, not undertaken for counter-revolutionary purposes.

58.7 covered 'sabotage', defined as 'counteracting the normal functioning of state institutions and enterprises or related exploitation of the same to destroy and subvert state industry, trade and transport in order to commit acts covered by Article 58.1 (economic counter-revolution).'

28 December 1935

I wait all morning for the squad commanders to turn up for lectures. They appear in time for lunch. I give them two hours on tactics and geometry.

Shouting and fighting in the phalanx. I go to see what's going on, truss up two and put them in the sin bin. Osipov got punched in the eye, hard. Pity it wasn't me. I'd have shot one of them and the rest would soon have calmed down. I bet Company Commander Gridin doesn't see this side of things. If he actually came and worked here, he'd soon find out what it's like. Anyone can order people about, for better or worse. Anyone can do it. Anyone can issue demands.

How can I just get away from BAM? If you can think that one out, head, I'll buy you a new cap. I don't have time to think, but I will all the same. I have to get out of this place. I can't just hit the bottle because I'd only end up in 1 Squad. Can I get myself sacked for incompetence? No platoon commander ever has been, but if anyone thinks up a way to alter that I'll be next in line. I'll work something out.

29 December 1935

In anything you do, opportunity plays a big part, and your attitude is crucial to success or failure. I don't see any opportunities yet. Perhaps it's too soon, but getting a chance is a matter of chance.

If one turns up, too soon or not, I'll be waiting for it.

The phalanxes are gradually reducing. The prisoners are going home. I can only imagine how they feel. What a completely barbaric nightmare the camp must seem to them now, as it does to me. I still can't believe I am actually working in a forced labour camp. There's no need to be educated or intelligent here, you just have to stop people escaping. I went to Arkhara. What a dump! You arrive and there's nowhere you can spend an hour or two relaxing. And it's minus 37.

30 December 1935

It's cold during the night and I don't want to get up. The latrine is outside and it's freezing cold, minus 45. I try to warm up with tea, but it doesn't help much. My hands are so numb I can barely write. I'd forgotten tomorrow is New Year's Eve. That's something that happens for people who live in cities. In two days' time they'll be wishing each other success and happiness and so on. No one is going to wish us anything other than ten days in a cell or the Revtribunal. The prisoners don't respond to kindness. Well, too bad! Let's at least get warm as soon as possible and that will be one thing dealt with. I need to get through the next sixty days. By hook or by crook I shall, but my health is fading, and so is my life, pointlessly.

I sat chatting with the political instructor. There's bedlam even among the top brass. Everything is turning against us. I think about the Maikher case: that could happen to me. Best not to cheek the bosses. I'll wait to see what they have to say to me. I took on a squad who were slobs in terms of their combat and political training and raised their morale. I'm on the road to demob. Maikher actually wants to work here, because in civilian life he'd be a complete loser.

31 December 1935

Nothing to note other than that it's minus 42. A shuttle crashed and a wagon and flat truck derailed.

Maybe it happened by accident, but maybe it didn't; maybe someone shoved a trolley under it. Their efforts to lift the wagons were frankly criminal. Faffing about, wasting time, cursing and swearing, but all for show, senseless and disorganized.

I got stuck in and within an hour the wagons were back in place. A commanding tone of voice is all it takes to get people working effectively. Without authority nothing gets done. They fuss over trivial details and hold everything up. It's just as well they didn't block the Ussuriysk track; slacking would not have been tolerated over that.

I got a poor night's sleep because of the cold. It was cold even under two blankets, a leather coat and a fur jacket. My rheumatism is back and I have aching calf muscles and a cramp in my legs.

1 January 1936
New Year's Day. Day off. I go hunting with my deputy and miss a goat. I'm dog tired. I'm thinking over a lot of things, but all my thoughts centre on getting demobbed, getting rid of those tabs on my collar and of BAM. Even moving into the personnel section is an impossible dream. The Armed Guards Unit is part of a great construction project. We're devoting our lives to building a socialist society, and what recognition do we get? None. Unless we get hauled before the Revtribunal.

I haven't been to the bathhouse for the past fifteen days and see no prospect of it. Smashing!

2 January 1936
Minus 40 and chilled through. The *zeks* are breaking the camp up. They need fuel too, to keep warm, to cook. There's been so much big talk in the past, and big talk now, with more to come, and yet we never see a stick of firewood delivered. The era of War Communism is over and the Cheka should have changed. Stalin has said 'A greater concern for people should be shown in full measure.' But here? Here I'd be reluctant to even imagine Stalin's words might be applied. Everyone should apply them for themselves. That's the Party line. They say it's your own fault if something hasn't been done. BAM is a complete shambles. The camp guards force the *zeks* to lie down in the snow. Sigitov's approach is:

'If you want to stand, you can stand out here for four hours, or sit for two hours, or lie in the snow for one. The choice is yours.'

Fedosov was fondling Kalugina. 'It was a bullet that tore my socks and trousers but it missed me. Broke into pieces, nearly hit me. I'll get them mended at the end of the week.' What a load of nonsense.

3 January 1936

And now it's 52 below freezing. I'm gasping for air like a fish out of water. The wind is searing. I'm on my way to Arkhara, summoned by the company commander. Well, you see, the problem is this, as it were . . .

I went into a shop. Sod all. It didn't even have sugar, let alone butter. I've had nothing to eat since morning and there's nowhere to get a meal. The buffet at the station is closed until 8 p.m. There's no train and nobody knows when the next one will come. I hung around till the buffet opened. Dinner was 5 rubles 40. Soup was probably yesterday's leftovers, and it was a good four days since the carp was fried.

At 10 p.m., I got an express freight train. At last. Hardly able to breathe.

At 11 p.m., I was back in my room. Need to sleep now.

4 January 1936

To Phalanx 13. The head of the section invites me out hunting. We go: me, the section head and the stationmaster. We don't spot anything. I hand back the rifle and on the way home, to rub it in, see two goats. Could've had meat for dinner tonight.

How beautiful is nature here
Where all around is wild and sere.
A desolate, silent, hungry place,
Nor bird nor beast nor human face
Nor sound, nor aught to fear.

5 January 1936

Still cold. *Zeks* not working so we get to take it easy. I give the lads a talk about astronomy. They're really interested. We go to the bathhouse in the evening. Some bathhouse! Five degrees of frost with ice on the floor, walls and ceiling. The water is barely warm. Once you get your kit off you can't stop your teeth chattering. The political instructor says he's been poisoned by carbon monoxide from the stove. I tell him he looks a healthy pink. We wash our legs and bodies but can't wet our heads or our hair would freeze. Even so, we get scales of ice on our bodies. It must be good for us.

6 January 1936

Do the rounds of the phalanxes, 35-ers. Pretty weak after riding 40 km.

I'm in an odd mood, don't care about anything. I feel jaded, empty.

7 January 1936

Go hunting with my deputy and Romanenko. There are plenty of tracks, just no goats. Hunting them is a matter of chance. If you see one in the right position you're in luck and should be able to kill it. If you don't, you won't.

An agent turns up with information. Hell, what a trickster. They checked a suspect, searched him and packed him off to the Third Section. At the siding he tried to escape, immediately swapped clothes with another *zek* and denied who he was.

'I'm a passenger. I've just got off the train and have no idea what you are talking about.'

We'll have to wait and see what happens. They've caught Vasiliev. He'd been living at Phalanx 7 for fifteen days, wearing a skirt and a towel round his chest to pad himself out. They arrested him anyway.

I've got a pain in my left temple from the cold. I just hope it isn't meningitis. My feet are freezing at night, and my shoulders. I can't step on the floor, it's colder than ice. Undressing and dressing would be suicide. I go to bed at night and worry myself sick over whether tonight's the night the bridge gets blown up or burned down.

8 January 1936

It all took off in the night. Batonogov turned up to report that some arrested prisoners were not on the train. I spent a restless night wondering whether they would bring them in or not. They didn't arrive in the morning either. One had escaped by knocking out a window. He disappeared, jumping in different directions in the snow. The devil only knows why. Perhaps it's a trick to put pursuers off his track, or perhaps he's one of several. Two others arrested, both of whom gave the same surname. Sent them to the Third Section to sort out.

Commanders' training day. One commander is missing, with a woman in the stables. Another is missing because he's too busy commanding a division. A five-storey building is going up at HQ. 'I expect that's for us!' More likely we'll get a dugout, and get to dig it out ourselves.

No class timetables, no syllabus, no textbooks. It's stupid and pointless to complain about lack of support. Who could provide it? Rank doesn't confer knowledge and there's no instruction manual. Rank teaches some of them how to strike a pose, which they think proves what a lot they must know. In fact, it just makes them look stupid and ignorant.

They've started burning coal in the stove. It does seem to make the place warmer, or perhaps it's just because it's got warmer outside. You can get frozen apples for 4 rubles 50, which is good news. Fruit, fruit! I manage to get butter too, an achievement here. We get what we think might eventually come in handy. We're not yet at the level where we can just go and buy what we need. That's sometime in the future.

9 January 1936

As we're using coal for heating, a thick layer of dust settles on everything. It seems a bit warmer and you get used to it. We still have a North and South Pole in the room. We're still burning railway sleepers. There's no other solution, and both the Third Section and the phalanx leader look the other way. For the first time in two years they are training the middle ranks. It'll be interesting to see how the company commander measures up.

We're handing over the Zhuravli–Uletui stretch of the track tomorrow. You keep your spirits up with talk and speculation. It helps. I've been issued a greatcoat from the clothing section. I'm accumulating military bits and pieces now, but I have no interest in life – meaning life out here, of course. I've learnt a lot: don't worry too much about orders, escapes, or training the armed guards and junior commanders. You teach them in order not to fall behind yourself, to retain at least something in your memory. My manner and attitude probably seem odd. I'm beginning to have that mark on my face, the stamp of stupidity, narrowness, a kind of moronic expression.

I remembered my white collar. Useless luxury here, of course. I haven't been in the bathhouse for a month, but my collars used to be dazzling. I can't get my hands clean. Everything I handle is covered in dirt, dust, and soot.

10 January 1936

Feeling foul. I'm waiting for something bad and unpleasant to happen. What could be worse than BAM? If they demote me, it's probably for the best and means I'll be out sooner. I feel rotten about angling for that. The guards are all talking about who will go home and when. I reckon right now they're luckier than us.

11 January 1936

It's only three months since I arrived here from Moscow but it feels like a year. Leshchuk, the platoon clerk, is going home and doesn't want to. Incredible. I would cheerfully live in even worse conditions if it meant leaving BAM. He says he's got nowhere else to go. Odd. A state farm is being organized on land allocated to my platoon and with people from my subdivision. Life might be easier there, although it would increase the likelihood of staying here permanently, which is definitely not what I want. I pictured Karetno-Sadovaya Square, the noise of the trams, the streets, the pedestrians, the thawing snow, and the yard sweepers clearing the pavements with their scrapers. I thought about it till my head ached. I have less than half my lifetime left now, and BAM is eating into even that. Nobody cares about my life. How do I gain the right to control my own time and my own life?

12 January 1936

I ride out to Phalanx 13 and round all the territories: Krasnaya Gorka, Antonovka, Klyuchi, Nizmennoye. Thought I might happen upon some game. Nothing. I see a local hunter on the trail of a wolf. He's wearing a goatskin jacket and matching goatskin boots and cap, and is carrying a five-chambered Berdan rifle.

Sivukha tells me the story of how he tested the guards:

I came to Klyuchi in the night. The armed guards were all asleep, the sentry out somewhere in the phalanx. I lifted out a pane of glass, flicked the catch, and took all the rifles and ammunition. They were fast asleep. I took up position round the corner. Bang! They were still sleeping. Bang again! I hear 'To arms!'

'Lads, there are no rifles! We've been disarmed!'

Bang, bang!!! Bullets! Where? Over there! Get under the bed! Bang, bang! Up runs the sentry. ' "To arms!" What do you mean, "To arms!?" There are no rifles. Get under the bed, there are no rifles.' I show myself. Sufmis is on his knees, his hands crossed like Jesus on his chest. Speechless. Out of his mind. A lesson he'll never forget.

A Chinese gang could have disarmed and shot the lot of them.

13 January 1936

I got a letter from Laudenbakh. Letters are a cause for celebration. I spent all day writing a reply. Yesterday they filled up the gaps in the walls with clay and now it's warmer. Last night, though, my sides still got cold. I felt as if I'd been used to pull a plough, and stayed home all day.

A delivery of sleepers. Yes, I know they need heat but this is not a bloody holiday resort. We keep being ordered to work with the masses, to take them under our wing, but they just spit in our faces. Bloodsuckers! That and more. You want me to try to teach that lot? First let's see all those superiors of ours have a go. They just want someone else to pull their chestnuts out of the fire. Well, sorry! Mikhailov fixed himself up nicely and has managed to leave. Norokhodov lived with a *zek* and what happened? They suspended him and will probably transfer him. The top brass can do whatever they please and get away with it. Party members just say, 'Oops, sorry. Won't do it again.' But non-Party members? The flotsam and jetsam of society? Where do we go, who do we ask for protection and help? Anyway, what does 'non-Party member' mean? We're just dross. The quartermaster and phalanx boss get drunk, and where does that money come from? They're selling the railway workers' food. The 'soldiers of the track', poor sods, eat badly but still stand up for them. The Third Section chooses to be broad-minded. Well, to hell with them. A pity, though, to watch state property being embezzled.

14 January 1936

This place is so empty it makes the Torricelli vacuum look bustling. Admittedly, there's plenty of work of one sort or another: prisoners being redeployed, replacements arriving, the Third Section, the lecturing, inspections. We are gradually moving eastwards. Money makes the world go round. Money is what lured the hired armed guards here. When they've lived at BAM for a while, they'll see what they've landed in. There is disorder everywhere and no firewood anywhere, people refuse to go out to work, and quartermasters sell the food in the stores and spend the money on drink. The camp administration is down on us, the railway workers are down on us. That's a real classless society.

But the fact remains that we've built a railway!

With each passing day my stomach problems get worse.

15 January 1936

Every day is as like every other day as two drops of water. There was another flurry of escapes. I need to go and lay down the law, and I will. The top brass are all over the supposedly record-breaking Stakhanov 'shock workers' and reward them with this and that, whereupon they escape.* If I don't describe

---

* The Stakhanov movement took its name from Alexey Stakhanov, a worker who allegedly mined fourteen times his quota of coal on 31 August 1935. The Soviet authorities claimed the movement increased labour productivity by 82 per cent during the Second Five-Year Plan of 1933–7.

the weather, I have nothing to write about. Insufferable. I'm so disgusted with this whole foul place. Sometimes I don't feel like writing, it's all filth and savagery. But my life is in this diary. Administrators deal with lofty matters, plans for the future. They are enthusiastic, excited, but what about us?

The sword of the Revtribunal is always hanging over us. We don't want all those awards and other perks they have at our local HQ. Just give us our rations, our firewood, and potatoes that are not frozen and rotten. I took a trip to the bathhouse at Uletui and felt reborn. I hadn't washed properly for a month, and suddenly I was in a warm place that even had steam. The floor may have been cold, but it was still luxury. An hour of bliss. Deserting your post can get you solitary.

16 January 1936

I went to Kulustai, travelling on the shuttle as far as Domikan and trudging the rest. The wind was as sharp as a razor. I enjoyed sitting with the lads, told them about things they'd never heard of. They found it interesting. It was an occasion for them and they enjoyed it.

I walk back. Milky fog. The outlines of the bushes are blurred and obscure. You can't see ten metres in front of you. All kinds of thoughts crowd in while you're walking 42 km, you can turn everything over in your mind. A train flies by, clacking on the joints of the rails. Light shines from the windows, curtains sway. Those people are thinking too. It would be good if their ideas could be written down as well. So many tragedies and joys, so much despair and hope. How many lives destroyed! How many emotions and aspirations, how much apathy endured! For now I have to turn away from the world and all its pleasures. I have to be only part human because so much is out of reach. But still, no frontal attack. I need to scheme and wriggle and connive. The straight road invariably leads to disaster. I suppose that's how diplomacy works, who can outsmart whom. Let's see how good I am at it. Let's tr-y-y!

17 January 1936

I go to Phalanx 13 with a squad commander. There's a shop wagon. What to buy? There is nothing. I just wish I could escape from all this, if only for a day. But where to and how? When it's warm again I'll be able to go and lie on a hill and clear my head, but right now? I know I make the guards uneasy. Wouldn't want them to see and hear too much.

18 January 1936

I went hunting with the squad commander. Shot at a goat on the run but missed. Reluctant to go back to my room, where there's no space. I can only sit on a stool or stand immobile. The guards are going away on leave and I'm actually pleased for them. I'll do the same sometime, and not come back. A crow flew by and my thoughts followed it. 'Free as a bird.' Human beings, the most intelligent of creatures, hem themselves in with the most complicated laws, restrict themselves with rights and customs and all the rest. Form, style.

19 January 1936

They say Stakhanov methods are a grand thing, and I agree, but what does over-fulfilling the Plan's quotas actually achieve? I am a pragmatist. I play a small role in something major, but I do it in such a way that I can say, 'I've done that in an exemplary manner.'

20 January 1936

Got a dressing down over the intercom from the company commander over Squad Commander Krivosheyev. Cursing and swearing as usual! Went to Arkhara.

21 January 1936

Scandal! That son of a bitch Osipov has hit the bottle. There's going to be thunder and lightning from the company commander, ranting and raving, but what good will that do? None, other than fuelling resentment. I went to Zhuravli with the political instructor. We talked as we walked, about the company commander, the way BAM is run, and times past.

The company commander kicks me out of his office, shrieking. He offers no constructive suggestions or advice, probably because he has none to give. Fat chance of the Party organization taking him in hand. It stands up for Party members, not for the rest of us. Look at how they handled the case of Political Adviser Molchanov against Platoon Commander Maikher. Everything gets turned against the lower orders. The company commander needs sorting out, although how much good would that actually do? Not a lot.

That sky! All the beauty and magnificence, all your finest feelings get trampled in the mud of BAM. Delighting in the sunrise, though, you can forget the lot of it. What a life!!!!! What if . . . ' But no, that's not an option. We just have to carry on. Am I really worse than other people? I'm used to moving up every couple of months, but here I'm probably better off without promotion, because otherwise I may never get away. I have been issued a passport which gives my permanent place of residence as Arkhara. Isn't that something?

It's only January, but already you can feel the sun. It just might be getting warmer. The birch trees seem like a brown backdrop, misty and spring-like, against the white of the snow.

Nature will come back to life, wake up, and people will follow. They will meet her with joy and happy smiles. But here? When I think about it I feel sick at heart. Some prisoners are such vipers you can't scare them with the threat of solitary or a longer sentence. They don't care. They're not fools by any means; intelligent, creative people, but they behave disgustingly and cheat themselves out of so much. Osipov has drunk himself stupid. Fine, join the ranks of the labourers. Hack at the ground and freeze. Drink their gruel and feed the lice until you've atoned and get remission.

People don't think. They throw away the few blessings we have: warmth, food, work that is light in comparison with what most people have here. Human beings always just hope for the best, which is destructive and pointless and against their own interests. Live for ages, learn for ages, and you'll probably still end up dying a fool.

The company commander has nevertheless had a treat in store for me, may he be struck by a thunderbolt! I am on the career ladder. He is giving me a bonus, so now, like a serf, I'll be in the military for decades. How do I get out of this one?

What can I think up? I've been here just three months, two of them completely on my own. A new man in an unfamiliar job. They took me on when the political instructor was away. I had to work at it, invent, slog and wriggle my way out of trouble, with no real support (or unreal support, come to that).

What a job! Still, Lawrence of Arabia didn't start out legendary. I'll get stuck in. The political adviser came in the evening. Gave me a pep talk — keep up the good work. He played billiards with me until four in the morning then left. It was entertainment of a sort, or at least the nearest we come to it. Should I make a go of it at BAM? That would be stupid, the easy way out. When spring comes it will be even harder. For me, freedom is over 80 per cent of what life is about. Minus 38, wind. You can turn one side then the other to the stove, but at the moment we have the right to turn only one side of us towards life.

22 January 1936

Looked out the window and pondered. I'm not in prison but what's the difference? Emptiness all around. It's cold and windy. I don't feel like walking, and anyway there's nowhere to go. Today is my day off but I feel ill at ease, so what sort of break is that? The Plan has us spending the winter here.

23 January 1936

I go wading through knee-high snow in the forest to Territory 14 and all I can think about is how to get fired. Even the incident with the sparkies didn't make much of an impression on me. They're madcaps who don't want to go to the phalanx and that's all there is to it. They stripped naked in 40 degrees of frost and ran all the way from the station to the phalanx. The little devils didn't freeze to death but it beats me why they did it.

There's no way you can get women to go into the guardhouse cells, so they've worked out a ploy. They put a newly arrived armed guard on duty with a pencil and paper. The women are called out, questioned, and then told to wait inside while he clarifies something, then they repeat it with the next ones.

I brought back ten kilos of soused apples. How great it is to eat something tart. Underneath my bunk is like an icebox and the apples freeze. This is the life! I walked to Uletui wearing a greatcoat this evening. The cold got to me. The oil lamp is flickering and smoking. I imagine after BAM I will find electric light amazing. January is passing, but then there will be February, then March. Spring and summer will fly by. Why are we always in such a hurry? Where do we think we are going? Damned if I know. You rush ahead expecting things to get better, but after all that waiting we look and find life has flown by. I am pleased about that bonus, but I also really don't want promotion. It looks like a future of serfdom beckons.

24 January 1936

Wish it would warm up. Firewood is an issue, so is life, and so is the end of the project. Increasingly, the guards' relationship with the prisoners is becoming an issue. The *zeks* are burning railway sleepers by the cartload. They poach a few from here, a few from there, and in total they destroy thousands. So many that it's terrifying to think about. The top brass either can't or won't recognize that it is because these people must be given firewood, and that their burning of sleepers is the expensive alternative right now and in the future. In all probability, just like me, nobody actually wants to be working here at BAM, and that's why they don't pay attention to anything. The brass, the Party members, the old Chekists, all work in a slapdash way, not giving a damn about anything. What, I wonder, should I be doing? I've got no chance of demob for now so I'll need to accept my commendation, but stay alert. Then there are the soldiers, blast them. They're just figureheads. The prisoners only want to get to the end of their sentence. Voluntary paid labourers come to BAM only if absolutely nowhere else will have them. People like Sinilov and Zuinin are just tailor's dummies, dead wood. It might be something if they could behave professionally, but they don't even do that. Discipline is maintained solely by fear of the Revtribunal.

You have to be an actor. Do I need promotion? Would I be better off as a company commander?

25 January 1936

You work better and more enthusiastically if you are getting support, advice, instructions from your superiors. Many trials are easier to bear. The constant tension, the hierarchy of rank, the endless rushing around, that's the army way of doing things.

I got really chilled last night. I sneeze, and snot flies out like a blowout from a borehole. The days are getting longer and sunnier but no more cheerful. Our joy will be pure and unalloyed only when BAM releases us.

I spent the whole day writing the wall newspaper for the guards to read.

What does a person actually need? Three sets of underwear and bed linen, three pairs of leg wrappings and socks, felt boots, ordinary boots, three handkerchiefs, a uniform, a blanket, a pillow, and that's it. Just add a little money and I'd need no more. We live in penury at BAM.

27 January 1936
On the march to Bureya. That is, 9 km to Phalanx 29 and 28 km back home. We are not allowed on to the bridge. What sort of NKVD commander am I? Our own units want nothing to do with us. I'm tired of writing about how disorganized everything is. A couple of goats ran to within 300 m of the phalanx. While we were running about looking for a rifle they flashed their tails and were gone. One even had the cheek to run under the bridge. I got back at five in the morning. Too cold to sleep, of course. I piled whatever I could find on top of myself. It was heavy and I was still cold. I had a fit of not wanting to do anything, and thinking there's nothing agreeable to look forward to. Morozov, the Third Section's commissioner, is equally discouraging about the prospects of discharge. Time will tell. There must be some means of escape.

28 January 1936
How unhelpful regulations always are, and here in particular. We are trying to send off a contingent of prisoners. Some were accepted and checked in, some were not but went anyway. The commissioner was cursing, we were protesting. He was right and so were we. If anything goes wrong it will be our fault. If we had not sent them on it would have been our fault too.

Either way. On top of everything else there's the Plan, may the devil drag it down to hell. BAM is exile for all of us, prisoners and 'free' alike.

Yesterday's exhaustion is making itself felt today too. If I had a separate room I could leave the lads and go to bed at seven in the evening, but as things are that would be embarrassing.

Whatever next? One of the women sewed a skirt out of a mattress cover. How are we supposed to find out where she put it or who she's sold it to? I ought to write home but what is there to tell? I just want to sleep.

29 January 1936

My neck has frozen up and I can't bend or turn it. I have a headache and a runny nose. Went out to Territories 13 and 14. Squad Commander Sivukha goads his grey along at a gallop but my devil of a horse, snorting and twitching its ears and straining at the reins, doesn't let me take the lead.

My heart is so desolate, it alarms me.

I feel as if I'm not living in the real world but in some weird, unearthly world in which I can live and think but can't speak my thoughts. I can move, but everything is constrained. The sword of the Revtribunal hangs over everything I do. I feel constantly held back: you mustn't do this, you mustn't do that. Although I feel solidarity with society, I feel cut off from it by an insurmountable, if fragile, partition. I'm aware of my own strength, yet at the same time feel weak and powerless, a nonentity. I feel hopelessness and apathy, almost despair, that so much cannot be achieved. I stumble blindly along the paths of this world, unable to work out what is allowed and what is not. The thought that drills into my brain is, 'How long will this go on for?' A lifetime? I have at least ten years of life ahead of me and I'm not being allowed to live them like a normal human being. Must I despair? We have to fight for every stupid little thing:

a visit to the bathhouse, sugar, matches, clean linen, and more besides. As for heat, firewood, we almost risk our lives for that. We, the armed guards, are powerless.

30 January 1936
A purge of the guards. They retain the best.

I ought to learn from that. I am tired of writing about all the wrongdoing and bad things. But what good things can I find to write about? Perhaps the white bread roll the political instructor brought? I write a monthly report for BAM that isn't without an element of fiction. There really doesn't seem to be that much to do here, and yet I'm busy all day. Later in the day I feel shivery. I sit in my greatcoat close to the stove and my head feels leaden. There is no doctor or medicine here if you fall ill. So far, so good.

31 January 1936
January is over, joyless and bitter. February and March will come to an end in just the same way, and so will life at BAM. Today the sun cheered us with some heat. It warms you a little, and for that I'm grateful. I have a cough and a headache but will try to ignore them. I ought to go out hunting, but am I up to it? The *zeks* pilfered a load from a food truck. Nobody will do anything about it. They'll trade a sack of sugar or cereal or whatever for vodka.

Thanks for that, at least, they'll say. Soviet power is looking after us, even out here.

1 February 1936
It's relatively warm. The result of the general review shows we are one person short. Where he went and when, nobody knows.

I'm wakened at one in the morning to go and see the head of the Third Section. I go with a guard to Uletui. A train passes quietly, almost soundlessly. I sit about all day reading news-papers, which proclaim that life has become better, life has become merrier! 'Where would that be?' I ask myself. 'Do you mean here at BAM?' Here we are just running out of the last of our dried potato. So far, the life we live is purely theoretical. It is whatever they say it is in the newspapers. If you try talking out loud about the real state of affairs you'll be in big trouble. I wish we could hand over this section of the track as soon as possible. It really is best not to read the newspapers or you might go out of your mind. But still, why? Why was I selected for BAM? Why Doronin?

The day is noticeably longer. Now for some warmth, please! I'll start sketching. Perhaps I can lose myself in that.

2 February 1936

We spend the morning waiting for the BAM hikers to arrive. They are walking from Svobodny to Vladivostok wearing gas masks and with a dog called Jim. They are walking in felt boots. The world of sport long ago recognized the unsuitability of felt boots as sportswear. I am really not very interested in this event, as my personal life bears a closer resemblance to a battered tin can than to a life.

We give them a few tips and accompany them as far as Zhuravli, yet I still envy them a bit because for many days they will not be under the threat of raids and the BAM rules and regulations. Lucky them!

3 February 1936

Two guards have hit the bottle. Well, perhaps that's only to be expected. Let's face it, none of us has much to be happy about. There simply is nothing. Groats and meat. Some people pass the time by going to the theatre, but we don't have one. Some find other ways. Some turn to drink, and luckily we

Cover of a magazine for BAMLag guards: Bulletin of the
Consultative Bureau of BAMLag NKVD Armed Guards, No.1, 1935.
State Archive of the Russian Federation.

can buy as much alcohol as we want here. This place drives you to drink.

Perhaps I'm only imagining it, but I think it is getting warmer and the sun is getting brighter. I go with the political instructor to Zhuravli and he complains about life quite openly. I completely understand and sympathize. Why try to hide it? Things are bad. Quite apart from the money, we are likely to be serving here for three years. If you can save a bit of money then go home and get married after the army, buy some things for yourself . . . But for us? We earn just enough to stay alive. For now I have only one idea for getting out: write a complaint detailing all the charms of this place.

But who knows? Perhaps some opportunity will come along, they always do, everywhere, for everyone. The days are becoming noticeably longer.

4 February 1936

A dog starts barking furiously in the night. I send out a sentry and hear: 'Who goes there? Halt!'

He rushes in.

'Comrade Platoon Commander, someone is asking to see you. They know your name.'

I have to get up. They are skiers, wearing helmets and carrying pistols. They come in and sit themselves around the stove to warm up. They seem safe, but how can I be sure? We need to disarm them.

I seize my pistol and the sentry has his truncheon at the ready.

'Put down your weapons!'

'What's the problem, comrade? Why?'

'Hand over your weapons!'

I take them.

'ID!'

They hand it over. It's all in order. The duty officer of the Third Section is by the intercom.

60

'How's the file? Any information?'

'No.'

'Should we let them proceed?'

They warm themselves up. I give them each an apple, return their pistols, and they set off again (on foot through the snow, Russian-style). I go with them to Zhuravli and we pick up another skier there. He is quite awkward, but that's just how young people are. They head on to Arkhara. Nobody has organized any food or a place for them to stay. That's the way our sports organizations work. That's what enthusiasm comes up against. You can only conclude that we still have a lot of work to do, a lot of inertia and bureaucracy to break down.

5 February 1936

The sun warms us more kindly, and is even quite hot. During the day it gets as warm as 15–18 degrees. Not long now until summer and more escape attempts. The shortages of food, shoes and underwear are so tiresome. We are promised everything, and in the Centre they clearly think we are living in a paradise. In reality, we are living in theories. We have theoretical semolina, butter and new uniforms. Theoretically the Centre is thinking about us. That's supposed to be encouraging. For some reason I simply do not believe it. Perhaps I'm the wrong sort of person. I would like to be provided, simply and without rhetoric, with the basic necessities. Today we had dumplings and home-made noodles etc. Tomorrow, it will be home-made noodles and dumplings, and that has been going on for the past month.

We have 40 km to cover. I've tried to avoid this so many times, but it has to be done. At least there was no walking. I got as far as the bridge but was not allowed through. The guards are within their rights, but our superiors ... Whether they don't want to, or can't be bothered, or are mesmerized by their own red tape, or most probably are just incompetent, you can sum it all up in one word: BAM. Got to Phalanx 29 at 5 p.m., covered in mud. It's a wonder the guards can still stand. For some of them it's at least better than forced labour, others need to earn extra money, and some are under the sword of the Revtribunal. So life continues. That's the level we're on. Everyone gets issued one sheet and one towel. Find a solution to that! You have to wash every day and sleep on that sheet. The guards who came here for the pay have already seen the error of their ways and repent bitterly and loudly. Some of them amaze me. They have worked at the White Sea Canal, the Turkestan–Siberia Railway, and now are working at BAM. What kind of people are they? Fools, idiots, or people incapable of finding better work and unable to fit into normal life?

Shatakhin wants to resign and go to Rostov. Rostov may be okay. The things you grew up with, or memories of the happiest days of your life, make you want to go back to a place. I would much prefer to live in any run-down corner of Moscow than in the centre of Leningrad. Party members are made to stay on by a system of coercion known as Party discipline, while non-Party members are kept here on the basis of some government decree or order which no one has ever actually read, or even seen.

6 February 1936

At Phalanx 14 my Mongolian demon steed digs his heels in and will not move. I whip him and drag him by the reins, to no avail. Then we cover 8 km at a gallop. On the way back I come across Osmachko, the *zek* leader of Phalanx 13. A pair of fine horses are smoothly speeding his sledge along, while my demon gallops the whole way back, covered in foam, tossing his head, snorting. A real demon.

You can sense that the thaw will start tomorrow. I spend the night in the warm. What a joy! What pleasure!

7 February 1936

I've started getting everyone out for gymnastics in the morning. They are not as dozy as they were. It's warm and overcast, the air humid and misty. Your feet are not cold in leather boots. If I'm honest with myself, we live the life of convicts. A guard is on duty at the work site from 7 a.m. till six in the evening. He has to keep an eye on those sluts, and there are 300 of them. He comes back and needs to rest, but instead there are classes. His eyes are closing but he has sentry duties. So who has more freedom, the *zeks* or us?

Warm again! I was even quite hot last night. We're slowly getting started on a bridge, but there is talk that we will soon be heading east. There's noticeably more daylight.

And it's quite warm. I go out in a greatcoat and leather boots, but somehow my heart is uneasy. You know that for escapes you will only get ten days in the cooler, but still, why the hell should I have to put up with that? Morozov, the Third Section's commissioner, has been specially trained for this job. Not surprising: most people go to normal Soviet schools.

I, forgive the immodesty, find it difficult to be that stupid. I am a Muscovite, and even some remembered ramshackle fence in the Moscow suburbs seems near and dear to me. But no one is going to understand or be interested in my moods. You sit all evening in your allocated three square metres and slowly go round the bend. You could turn into a complete idiot. You have to learn to resist it.

The camp is just 100 m away. There is no sentry post here. You can go out as often as you like and wherever you like, but you are answerable for escapes. How the hell do you deal with this situation? It really would be better to have a place of my own, apart from the team. I could go there and do as I pleased. There's nothing and nowhere to help you relax. In the summer we'll be able to go up into the hills, but that's a long time from now.

9 February 1936

The thaw is continuing. That's good.

I saddle up the demon and can't get him to budge, then suddenly he takes off at a gallop and there's no holding him. I ride to Phalanx 13 and back in a complete lather. I tried riding without stirrups, which helped, but I have to cling on on the turns if I don't want to be sent flying.

Sun, sun! What joy you bring us! How life-giving are your rays! We can sometimes even forget our misfortunes. How much lovelier you would be in freedom, or have people there forgotten you? I have always thought of you as a god. You give life to the natural world, reconcile people and make them kinder and happier. You inspire and bring us joy. You are the wellspring of life and my only happiness. Many of my closest friends have stopped writing to me. They have forgotten me, but you do not. Every morning and evening you sustain my soul with beauty. During the day, when your radiant disc is high in the sky, I am in love with you. Your warm, caressing rays play on my cheek and gladden me and I am alive again and filled with energy.

Phalanx 14 are leaving, which is fine, only I am supposed to go and see that they're sent on their way. I send my deputy. He needs practice.

One thought gives me no peace of mind. I used to know things, have aspirations, be useful. I was a teacher, a textbook for other people. Now, though, the pages of that book have been scribbled over. What am I? Why do I exist? I have no idea. Not even the Red Army riflemen guarding the bridge respect me. They are right, of course, you can't go over without a pass, but they could at least treat me like an officer.

I live, lost out here in the Far East, and feel like a white crow. I worry that if I go back to civilian life I will be seen as primitive and backward and will have to face up to the full extent of my own nonentity.

You could, of course, though I do not intend to, work in the Armed Guards Unit if there were enough guards, if they had rights, if they were respected, and provided with at least the necessities. But I would prefer to endure privation than serve at BAM. What quality of service can you expect when the political instructor doesn't want to be here either, and he may not be alone. And to cap it all, you have to defer to a prisoner who is the leader of a phalanx. That's just great, really delightful.

Evening. The moon rises, a blood-red disc. The smoke between me and the moon turns crimson. Trains thunder past. People travel freely. When will we be able to travel like that?

I give the lads a pep talk. What's next? There's dinner, but after that? After that you just sit there going out of your mind. Nothing to read, nowhere to go, no one to talk to or joke with. You have to keep yourself to yourself, because the guards are there with you.

10 February 1936

What a day! It began last night. No sooner was I in bed than I was called to the intercom. At 1 a.m., again. At 3 a.m., I had to go to the station. At 6 a.m., I had to go back again. Completely knackered. Thank you, Commissar Kaganovich. One man can cause so many people so much trouble. It's good that it's getting warmer. It's hard to write anything, my head is so muddled. I yawn till my cheekbones ache. It's dire when the top brass try to be clever, innovate, have bright ideas, and leave us to carry the can. There are major redeployments in the pipeline. I'll get sent off somewhere. It's far cosier in the army, they have facilities, culture, they care about people and make sure they develop. Progress. The New Soviet Man. But here? Everybody knows we are stuck in the back of beyond and that everything is worse than backward. I would so like an answer to a question I know is ridiculous: why is everything here such a shambles?! Why are

65

we here at all and what, in the end, is the point of this? Why are we not being looked after properly? Why does everyone look down on us? And how am I different, for better or worse, from the masses (i.e., everybody else)?

11 February 1936

Making a little joke out of it, just barely hinting, the political adviser mentions mentoring. Incentivization. If a phalanx fulfils more of the Plan, the platoon commander gets paid more. I'm not swallowing that bait. How could I be a Stakhanovite when I have no wish to work at BAM for more than a year? If you stand out then you will never get away. In any well-ordered project you find some disorder, but we have more disorder than order. They put pressure on the guards and hint at incentivization, but make no attempt to address the real problem. There are all these miscellaneous 'educators' in the Education and Culture Unit slobbing about, getting drunk and generally behaving scandalously, and the guards are expected to cover for the job they are not doing.

The phalanx leaders have it in for the guards. Our superiors are supposedly rehabilitating *zeks* and we're supposed to just put up with it. Why doesn't someone put those people in their place and stop them undermining our authority! If you dismissed me now without a month's notice I'd agree to it in a flash. In fact, I'd agree to donate a month's pay on top. What sort of work can you do in that kind of mood? All the same, I wonder what they do with the educated people who would be capable of managing a phalanx, teaching them and so on.

12 February 1936

The sun is coming into its own. In the afternoon the ice on the roof starts melting and dripping. Your spirits rise, but the joy only serves to emphasize the blackness. I still haven't found the way to get myself dismissed. Through the window I can see them marking out, preparing to dismantle something and build the bridge. Axes thud, bringing so many memories of freedom to mind.

Today is a holiday in Moscow. I would be riding the tram home, planning my evening.

I went out to Territory 14 yesterday, to lecture the lads on the origins of the world and of man. Some bits of it they understood, some bits they didn't. They are so poorly educated. It was 20 km on foot but no one seems to think there is anything wrong with that. I was really angry with the Third Section, because of the way they let the phalanx leader take charge. If he feels like it, he may do something for the guards: if he doesn't, he won't. Starikova refuses to fit out a wagon for the Armed Guards Unit and that's the end of the discussion. She rants and raves. When the political instructor comes back we'll find out what's been going on and lodge a complaint.

13 February 1936

The hills, the *taiga*, my thoughts, all exist in a kind of vacuum. Not only that, but a vacuum with constraints. There is another world abroad. I know it exists, but I can't get there.

14 February 1936

A reshuffle, but not without something in it for me. I take charge of 5 Platoon. That's another 10 km for me to walk.

What a shambles! There's no discipline whatsoever. On the way back I drop in on Bureya Bridge Special Camp. They live like human beings. Their office is warm, clean, bright and spacious. They have electricity and radio. It's as spacious as an apartment and, pinned up on the wall, an official chart introducing the head of the guards, the political adviser, and the filing clerk. Compare my conditions. It's best not to dwell on it and upset myself.

A right mess at Kulustai. An engine driver went through a stop signal and our own driver then crashed into a shunting engine. That's two locomotives for the scrapyard, one shunting engine and three wagons. Those complete bastards! They already have a conviction for transport sabotage and still they got drunk, the wretches, while in charge of a locomotive. They're in for a rude awakening.

Morozov, Morozov! He's a proper commissioner, and humane with it. They're going to go after Starikova.

Got a message there was a parcel for me. I wondered for a long time who could have sent it and what could be in it. I also have another pleasant enough surprise: a telegram asking me to come and collect a bonus. What for? I don't know and it seems odd, but I must be doing something right and am climbing the ladder. It's exactly what I don't want, but what can you do?

None of the old platoon commanders or political instructors are getting a bonus, but I've been singled out. Odd. And little consolation. We are short of guards. What can I do about that? Lilin is freezing me out.

15 February 1936

Not even the devil knows what is going on now.

The top brass have gone off to swear in a new company. The phalanxes are leaving, taking guards with them. It's pandemonium, to put it mildly. I go to HQ to collect my bonus. 250 rubles. I don't know what it's for but think I can guess. I am an improvement on many of the platoon commanders and they may have me in their sights for promotion. If they knew what I think I'm sure they would be really delighted. I collected my parcel at the same time. Held off opening it for ages, trying to guess what was inside and, when I did open it . . . apples and tangerines! What a hoot. Who would have guessed?

16 February 1936

Light snow. A grey day. To get through it I go out to Phalanx 13. Out of sight, out of mind. Savchuk, the clerk from HQ, walks by my side. He reminisces about Leningrad, the White Sea Canal, cooking the books. He tells me if it hadn't been for cooking the books and ammonal explosive there would be no White Sea Canal.

We have no vehicles and the *zeks* are not allowed to give political lectures. There are knowledgeable lads among them who would be more effective than the paid help, but what can you do? It isn't allowed.

I really do need to move to a place of my own. At least I might get a proper night's sleep, and might be able to get my thoughts together.

17 February 1936

Again the sun, but still the east wind cold.
And from my thoughts there is no rest.
It seems they can't be silenced or suppressed.
Oh, thinking, thinking. Something
That I cannot stop, cannot control.
Moscow, the factory, the sound of hammers and the screech of
*   saws,*
Machinery clattering, the workshop full of dust.
A ray of sunshine makes it through the double glazing,
Plays lovingly upon the wall.
And people come to me. I go to them.
Here work is in full swing, progressing in the sweat.
And when the closing door shuts me off from the workshop,
I breathe so deep a sigh, a sigh so free . . .
And see a face before me.
The clatter of trams, the noise of cars.

Horns, sirens, signals showing red,
Feet tramping pavements,
People hastening about their business.
They all have cares, they all have lives.
One to the theatre, others to a meeting,
And I, among them, hurrying to the stadium.
How many me's? Perhaps a million?
The city's life, so various,
So tedious, so gregarious.
You sometimes wish the ground would swallow you.
You sometimes feel in Moscow like merging with this bustling
    crowd,
Joining the roundelay, plunging in head first.
But here? In Siberia? In the taiga?
Such stillness all around, such peace and all of that.
The only sound the tapping of a woodpecker, the chattering of
    crows.
I am alone and friendless, a troubled soul.
Wandering, like Berendey, a spirit of the forest, paths
    untrodden.
Bridges, depots, second tracks, a railway.
Words and rhetoric.
All needed, like the pathos.
No fraudulence, no ammonal
Would mean no grand White Sea Canal,
That's what they say.
Without the fraud and ammonal
And all that we poor suckers lack
You could forget your Second Track.

Bitter cold, the hills, the criminal underworld,
Shovels and picks and ammonal,
Orders, escape reports, and everywhere a shambles,

70

All mixed up. Confusion, endless tangles,
Till no one has a clue what's going on.
You cannot tell when you are right or if you're wrong,
Or sometimes even what you ought to do.
Comrades, you should not just forget about the people, about
  commanders.
You say we are the ones in charge,
Are representing Soviet power,
But that is not where happiness lies.
We are small fry, nothing special.
Just give us what we really need, some warmth, a clean shirt,
A private space, away from all the calves and pigs.
It's all we ask.
We claim no right to butter and white bread.
We claim no right to films and theatres.
The only thing we really want is the right to a good night's
  sleep,
And perhaps a day off to call our own.
Although actually what we really want
Is to shuck off BAM and get back home.

18 February 1936

Commanders' training day. Taking charge of a platoon requires many qualities, of which the most essential is to be as thick as two short planks. It's also useful to be able to turn up at a station at 5 a.m. and wait for the express to come through, which it will, but without stopping, so what you actually need to do is go a kilometre down the track from the signal and sit out in the open at the bottom of a hill. The more straightforward alternative is to trudge 40 km on foot.

We give the commanders a pep talk. They listen, but do they believe what they are being told? Will they take it on board?

The devil only knows. The human soul is a dark forest. You are instructing away and suddenly ask yourself: if all the commanders are here, what will happen if there's an incident in their squad? Still, the physical exercise has an effect. I go to bed and wonder whether I'll be called to the intercom or something else. It's impossible to get a good night's sleep with all that going on in my head. I wish the redeployment of phalanxes was over and everything would settle down! Snow gradually building up. The weather and my mood, as overcast as each other.

19 February 1936

I would like to write a lot, put all my thoughts into this pen, but nothing comes out. Decide to clear my mind by riding out to Phalanx 10. My amazing steed gallops the whole way. The squad commander's grey can't keep up. The lads sing well in the evening. I want to join them but don't like to muscle in on it. The anxiety over escapes is getting to me. Any time now the *zeks* will start running away.

On top of everything else, we have 250 kilos of high explosive ammonal stored in the corridor. What if it explodes? We should move it somewhere safe and post a sentry but don't have the manpower. The store at Phalanx 30 was robbed. Thieving is the only thing they know how to do.

20 February 1936

Day off. Cold. Rest.

21 February 1936

Empty. I edit the wall newspaper. Romanenko, a platoon commander, is just plain illiterate. That's the kind of person they need for BAM, someone who would be useless anywhere else. In civilian life I would be ashamed to admit that this was a platoon commander, ashamed not for him, but for myself.

I've caught a chill somewhere and have a sore back. The notes of the accordion tug at my heartstrings. It's nauseating. I could look at the map of the Far East Region, go to Bureya and say, 'Send me there,' but it's not that easy to survive even a single winter here.

In the state system a human being's individuality doesn't matter. To them you are just 'a specialist' and they don't give a damn about your aspirations.

22 February 1936

Went off into the forest this morning to forget it all, at least for a time. Trekked along the Great Siberian Highway and came upon a couple of grouse but didn't have time to shoot.

I didn't want to go back. Luckily there were no escapes. I really need to get somewhere separate from the guards. To be able to relax in the evenings at least. Our bridge is at a standstill. Of 220 *zeks* only 80 came out to work, the rest just stayed in their huts. They get the same meal rations as those who work, so, you might well ask, why would they bother to work? The company commander knows but does nothing about it. Does it trouble me more than everyone else?

I'm sure people will say, 'Why are you always writing about yourself? You should write about the life of the prisoners.' I will write about the *zeks*, of course, but only when I've got my own life sorted and can think straight. When I've at least got the bare essentials. Then I can start taking an interest in the lives of others, even marvel at the project and the building work as I might survey it from a train, especially a train taking me back home. When I'm no longer a worker at BAM.

The political instructor likes riding to visit the squads. He gets round them in two or three days. I have no idea what's in it for him.

Order received at 10 p.m.: hand over the platoon and leave.

Something is brewing. We'll get through it somehow. At BAM you aren't allowed to, but can, do anything.

23 February 1936
Red Army Day. I hand over 5 Platoon and prepare 4 for hand-over. Something is in the air. I'll be somewhere, somehow. I don't like moving, carting my belongings around, settling in. I'll even miss 4 Platoon a bit. They weren't such a bad lot.

24 February 1936
Went to Arkhara to hand over the platoon.

25 and 26 February 1936
In Zavitaya. Spent a sleepless night in a truck. I feel doped all day. The boss calls me in and appoints me commander of a division. I've drawn the short straw, I'll have to serve in this army for decades now, like a serf. I sit with Savchuk and listen to the gramophone. It's emotionally unsettling.

I receive my letter of appointment. I have to start forming a divisional HQ. I have a meeting with the men from Moscow. Someone has a keen ear and long tongue. The company commander alludes to my demob yearnings. It feels strange, after the *taiga*, to be in an actual town. I'll have to get used to it. I'm not feeling quite right in the head. Must be the sleepless nights.

Also the jubilation, the wild, throbbing jubilation, has thrown me off balance. I receive a greetings telegram to mark Workers' and Peasants' Red Army Day. I'll enter . . . [sentence left incomplete]. The violin reduces me to a quivering wreck. There's nobody to exchange so much as a word with. There's no one to answer my questions.

I can't do this. I can't.

My pen is blunt.

Just breaking off in mid-sentence.

74

27 and 28 February 1936

February has passed, just like January did. They're moving me up, if only temporarily, from platoon commander. But if they move me any further, I'll be having words. I'm taking it easy. I might be starting from 1 March, but it's unlikely. Empty, empty. Another telegram.

1 March 1936

Relaxing. The boss is away. When he does turn up, there will probably be a kerfuffle. I haven't settled in yet. I play chess with the political adviser then go for lunch. An interesting development. Canteen manager asks: 'Are you getting a rank? If so, what ration category?'

I tell him I don't yet know, but not above 8.

Political Adviser Khrenkov winces, probably thinking, 'He's got big ideas about himself.' My thoughts and diary entry interrupted.

2 March 1936

I'm running around like a scalded cat, could easily go crazy. There are problems and the boss is ranting and raving. No time to write a letter. Living conditions still not sorted. Pleasant outside during the day, warm and encouraging.

3 March 1936

Three escapes. Here we go. I run around doing what I can, trying to be unobtrusive. I'm summoned by Company Commander Gridin. Another dressing down. Things need to be sorted out. I spoke well at a meeting of trainees yesterday. For some reason I have authority; they listen attentively, keeping their eyes fixed on me. Past few days spent in a whirl of activity. Many people think that the higher your position the easier your life, but the opposite is true. I have no personal life at all.

4 March 1936

It's calming down a bit. I still have nowhere to live and no fuel. Can't get firewood or coal for love or money.

We put the finishing touches to track sections, at the price of rheumatism, flu and other ailments. I have a cramp in my legs. My room has been without heating for eight days. Commander of 3 Platoon is ill. He's unmarried and has no one to look after him. I go and pester the accommodation manager for firewood. The sunny days are good news, at least. I bully and get bullied, can't concentrate, can't even get into BAM routine. No repairs. Either they can't or won't get the materials legally. I need to turn the chaos to advantage. Haven't yet had time to look around, but will as soon as I can.

5 and 6 March 1936

A conference has been running for two days. We talk a lot, but BAM-style. People recall my Abyssinian cowl and laugh about it. Political Instructor Golodnyak was fiercely criticized. He jumps up, says he can't take any more and will shoot himself. He goes for his pistol but is disarmed. I need to think and draw conclusions. What caused that? Perhaps it can be traced back to the Maikher saga and the relations between the company commander and the political people? People envy me my position. Karmanchuk advises acting BAM-fashion under all circumstances. I certainly will. The gift of the gab is a big advantage. They listen to my speech attentively. I'm afraid BAM may suck me in. Need to keep an eye on that.

7, 8 and 9 March 1936

Just can't get my living conditions sorted, typical BAM. Pleasing weather. I like the puddles and life-giving sun.

No events, no incidents, I'm just really tired. The division is not yet sorted. I need to teach classes in the training platoon.

Gridin wants to know why I'm not riding out to inspect the periphery, with his usual delicacy:

'How many times do I have to tell you? Bloody get out there!'

'I can't just abandon the training platoon.'

That was that. Everything is unclear and unfamiliar, but the training course keeps me from feeling the empty loneliness so keenly, or the laxity and disorderliness here. Every time I get a letter it just unsettles me. Moscow is so far away, but feels much closer than Zavitaya, where I am living.

10 March 1936

There's poor political morale among the trainees, who are complaining about shortages. They are right. Who wants to eat their meals standing up? Not me. I'm told they don't usually second educated people to the guards. Great.

I remember, for some reason, the number of people I have burdened with a longer sentence. I try to stay calm but sometimes lose my temper. Some I send to the punishment cells. The political adviser tells me I should rent a place privately. Fine, if I can find a comfortable one. He might drop in for a chat if I do. I'd like to be in a training platoon. Our big problem, escapes, would just fall away.

How limited the outlook of Zavitaya's townspeople is. My digs does have separate rooms, but they're not up to much. The partitions seem to have been made, not to give the tenants a bit of privacy, but because they happened to have some spare planks to use up. The result is more peephole than partition. They're pretty rustic round here. Their narrow horizons don't extend beyond Zavitaya, and educationally they're no higher than second grade at school. They have no concern, no interest in anything. They're born, marry, have children, grow old and die. Outside that cycle, what is there worth noting in their lives?

Nothing. Our life is like the smoke from a chimney. At first it's only a wisp, then it's thick and heavy, then diffuses, dissipates and disappears. No one needs or notices it. The wind blows it back and forth and it's gone.

I sit with the political instructor at the political adviser's place and we drink together, but there's no escaping the consciousness of rank.

11 March 1936

It's my day off. A bit cooler. There's wind from the east and a pale sun. I go with the head of ammunition supplies to the range to put in some small-bore shooting practice. Don't want to miss the opportunity. Need to relax. I feel awkward lying around in the barracks. For some reason I was really tired yesterday. Just feel generally fatigued.

I fire small-bore with the political instructor and head of ammo and manage to keep up, although I struggle more with revolver practice. I hit the seven, but not consistently. The political adviser invites me back to play chess.

I need to get a decent place to live. We could play billiards there, get everyone together. It would give me something to do, and the rest of them too. We could gossip and spend time with each other. I wouldn't find myself wandering aimlessly down the track, as I did today. How likely is it?

12 March 1936

The puddles are impressive.

Interruption. The divisional commander thing isn't going to happen, meaning I'll be shot of responsibility for escapes if I can just stay with the training platoon. There's still no decent accommodation for me, now or in the foreseeable future. The top brass, needless to say, have washed their hands of us.

13 March 1936

Overcast and windy. Don't know what to do with myself. I don't feel like going back, can't work, can't relax. It's too cold and the guards are in the way. Nichepurenko seems to have been sent to keep an eye on me and check out my political and moral credentials before processing me to join the Party. We'll see who sniffs out whom! I'll hold out somehow until it's warm, work through the summer, and then see. The shambles at BAM is ubiquitous, even in positions that are officially filled. The platoon's political instructor is a Young Communist League member. How can they allow that sort of nonsense? You hardly see a regular commander, they're all 'acting' this and that.

Even squad commanders are in charge of platoons. Everywhere you look, the Party and YCL members are given priority, irrespective of whether they're competent or idiots or totally useless. It doesn't seem to matter.

Luxuriated in a bathhouse yesterday, a real one, where no one complains you're using too much water. It was warm, relaxing, clean and there was nobody rushing me. I look at the commanders and think about how they live and what they do. They've got nowhere to go, nothing to entertain them. They just drudge away at home and go to seed. The squad commanders are yokels, and the top brass are so full of their rank that they can't just strike up a friendship with anyone. They ossify.

14 March 1936

Murderously cold. The wind chills you to the marrow of your bones. There's nothing to write about because life is empty.

15 March 1936

It might be a bit warmer today. I'm teaching the squad commanders. What commanders they are! They graduated from regimental school and know sod all. They say I'm a white crow. Probably right. I feel freakish among commanders like this lot, uncouth, ignorant, barely literate and so on. But rank seems to be what matters. For some reason I just can't get my room repaired. I could try making a fuss, but something tells me that wouldn't be wise.

So it goes on. The deputy divisional commander arrived. If I'm a greenhorn in the camps, he seems like a fledgling. He's finding it hard, and bizarre. I encourage him. Resign yourself to it, young friend, remember the Party discipline. You'll get used to it. Nichepurenko is definitely an informer for the political adviser. He keeps sounding me out on my politics and morale. Let them dig.

I sit in the HQ not wanting to go home, and waste my time and my life. Pakhomov is counting the days. Are we allowed to do that? We probably are, because they are setting up a trade union of some description. If that's for real, then excuse me. I'll do a year's stint here and then I'm off.

16 March 1936

My memory seems to be playing tricks on me, or it's something else, but I simply don't remember what happened yesterday. In the evening, at 11.30, I was playing chess with the political adviser at HQ. There still hasn't been any progress with my room. The top brass can get building materials and workers but we can't, we are just small fry. Anyway, how could they spare people for this, it's a crime, the track needs to be completed. It's not a crime if a commander doesn't have a proper roof over his head. Not being helpful, not bothering about us is not a crime. The head of the Third Section had his office varnished. Who needs that? The high command, of course. All I need is a plain, warm room. That's all.

17 March 1936

Even Party members are lax on discipline.

They aren't scared of being expelled from the All-Union

Communist Party (Bolsheviks). If they need an apartment they'll take it up with the Party bureau, but who can the non-Party members take it up with? Novikov is making a fuss about having been moved without being allocated accommodation. I've had nothing since I got here and still haven't. Ordering fifty boards to mend the roof and for insulation is a crime, forbidden, but the head of the section is free to burn them if he feels like it. Who is really wasting their lives at BAM? Is it us, living in squalor in the cold, or the top brass, who seem to have it all?

I'm surprised, and can't work out why Company Commander Gridin so goes out of his way to 'help' me.

18, 19 and 20 March 1936

No personal life, no experiences. I will remember these days as a time of emptiness and failure. Life is hard here and cheerless. I no longer even hope my accommodation will be any better next month, that I'll have somewhere to live. It's as if they're determined not to extend the partition by one metre and hang a door.

21 March 1936

It's my day off. Spring is here! Puddles and streamlets. Spring and the beauty of nature. Emotions. But BAM defiles everything. I play chess with Gridin and learn an important lesson. If you lose, the company commander is pleased and happy. But if you win, watch your back! I win two out of three and the boss starts cheating. He takes a chesspiece as if to make a move, puts it on a square, then takes it off again, saying, 'It was there,' moving it to where he can take something. Which he then does. Pathetic.

The political adviser invites me over but I wriggle out of it. Ranks and people are different things. I'm not going to feel under duress. I'm not willing to pretend I'm stupider than they are. The apartment makes the man, and a life of filth, transfers and transience break a person down. No, thank you. Sometimes I don't even have a chance to wash and clothe myself hygienically.

Oh, boy, this diary is going to provide a lot of evidence.

There's no roof on the hut. Sawdust and rubbish blow around inside it. It's a stable, not a room. I give orders, I carry a fire-arm, I get held responsible, so I know I'm alive, but what kind of life is it that comes to nothing more than this? All anyone ever talks about is getting away from here. Party members are prepared to give up their Party membership to get discharged. There is a directive about a trade union, under which we are all to be categorized as paid volunteers. The implications are clear. Political Adviser Khrenkov alters the directive and keeps it quiet, muttering: 'If people find out, you can imagine what it will be like here!'

We can.

22 March 1936

It's an abomination, not weather. Hurricane-force wind, snow and slush.

The wind blows through my room. I sit in a greatcoat. This is the front line. There's nowhere to just sit, relax and forget everything. Mind you, it's good that I don't have to worry about escapes. Still, rank isn't a reward for intelligence. It's fine to be a pawn. Stay close to the king and your problems are over.

Ogurtsov is talking about getting discharged again. It's a sore point for everyone. Gridin is off on vacation soon, and hinting I can move into his quarters. Well, why not enjoy life? For a time, at least. I have a problem with beating him at chess. I need to lose more often to keep him happy. Stay smart, be diplomatic.

I have to put up with freezing tonight. But why, for heaven's sake? Because of fine words, 'Chekists Are Engineers of the Soul'! No thanks, I've lived too long to be taken in by words. I don't want to put up with it even for a stonking 400 rubles. For that money I could live in Moscow in comfort, warm, in a cultured environment and, last but not least, untroubled and free.

The guards are dunces, blockheads. They amaze and infuriate me. They match commanders to the men and vice versa. The political adviser of 1 Division was a squad commander in the army. He probably can't believe he now has those four lozenges on his collar tab. Our rank is determined by what we were earning before being drafted to BAM. I discover that Gridin was in the cavalry.

There are drifts of snow spiralling. I feel sick at heart but I'm not giving in. I will find a way out of this.

23 March 1936
Snowdrifts. Slush. The top brass are the same everywhere in BAM: barely literate, uncouth. But what managers! What disciplinarians! Bosses who periodically squawk like ventriloquists' dummies: 'Reprimand! Under arrest!! Punishment cell!!!' How can I take orders from people like that? They think they know all about politics. I don't make a thing of it, but, actually, so do I. If I decide to study seriously, watch out!

The divisional commander came in this evening, sharing his impressions, asking questions about the things that trouble him, as if looking for sympathy and advice. I am diplomatically evasive. The training courses will end soon, then where will they send me? Hurry up, summer, you'll make being moved about much less awful.

I was debating with Savchuk on the subject of propaedeutic philosophy and logic. The divisional commander was standing beside us slack-jawed, clueless and unlikely ever to catch up. The guards are beginning to disgust me. They're certainly sentient. Animals with a brain. Well, animals anyway. But they have no interest in anything, they're idiots. Blockheads. They're stoned out of their minds at night, five nights a week, for months, years. They have no desire to learn or progress.

24 March 1936
The winter's back. Heavy snow and frost.

I still have no room. Typical. One became available; they wanted to put the political instructor in it but the divisional commander is having it for himself. The company commander is getting his done up at our expense, supposedly for the sake of the guards.

25 and 26 March 1936
I went to see a room. It's a good place, clean, warm, with a rug on the wall. It felt decidedly odd. Can you really live like that? I'd be embarrassed to even occupy the room. Decent living conditions scare me. That's what it's come to.

I read a memo from the political instructor. He's illiterate, just the kind of worker BAM needs. I luxuriated in the bathhouse but then had a cold night. My rheumatism is making itself felt.

The snow is thawing. There's mud to your ears, a mush of snow and clay. Whenever commanders meet, whatever they start talking about, they invariably end up discussing how to get discharged, non-Party members and Party members alike.

The training courses for junior commanders are coming to an end. I'm going to get sent off somewhere. There's a flood in my room. Where do I sleep?

Periodically the top brass say, 'We'll knock that Moscow cockiness out of you.' Let them try. I'll take countermeasures.

27 March 1936
Soaked through from going outside. The Third Section checks our correspondence. They open the letters and stamp them 'Checked'.

Political Instructor Novikov doesn't get on with Company Commander Gridin.

There's no need for us to judge priests, that's what devils are for. Leave it to them to decide. Strange weather, a thaw during the day but the cold wind is a killer. My knees hurt, aching with no respite. There's nowhere to get dry. My memory keeps playing tricks. My head is bursting from too much thinking and the chaos.

28 March 1936

Day greets me with a ray of sunlight on the wall, shining through a crack. I experience a moment of sheer joy, like that sunbeam, then BAM immediately crushes it and our life here falls into even starker contrast. A life of never knowing and ... can't come up with a name for it because everything here is just dreadful.

1 Squad have lost it, which is no surprise. They're stuck out in the forest with none of the amenities human beings need to live, e.g., food for the soul or the mind. They're out of touch with civilization and have food only for their stomachs, so they end up behaving like animals. Even wolves gather and play together. But us? It is forbidden for two commanders of the same educational level to serve together. What sort of policy is that? They shift you from one place to another saying you were getting too close. We have screwball superiors who couldn't understand human psychology even if they were allowed to and just demoralize you. I'll stick it out till autumn, and at the end of September, that's it! Freedom or jail! I now have one idea for getting discharged – a report or speech at a meeting. I have seven months to think something up. I do want to see the Far East Region in the summer, then I'll have savoured all the seasons.

Bystrykin, a platoon commander, has TB but doesn't want to leave. Why? Because for him this life is perfect and he gets fed. For me, it would be hip, hip, hurray!

Golodnyak has arrived. Why have the top brass moved him

here? Is it clemency or does he scare them? I got talking to a doctor in the canteen and learned an interesting fact. One of our doctors qualified as a bookkeeper but is said to 'know about diseases'. How amusing.

29 March 1936

For a long time, they haven't been able to get this man they pulled off an engine to talk. He had hidden on a frame under the boiler where he'd be impossible to spot. Another got hold of a form, a train driver's travel permit, went to the station duty officer and, as soon as the man went out, stamped and signed it etc. himself. He took the place of a train driver who was late. He was brought back to the phalanx.

'Ah, welcome back!'

'I have no idea who you are.'

'Stop wasting our time!'

'Judas!'

Nichepurenko comes snooping every day, asking why I don't want to serve at BAM.

I find out I'm being appointed to the commandant platoon to strengthen discipline. It looks like they're planning to switch me from one platoon to another. As soon as the trouble-shooting at one is done, they'll move me to the next. Great.

This is the second day I've been able to rest my mind. I've been hanging around at HQ, reminiscing about phalanxes, what the *zeks* get up to – some who siphoned off porridge through a pipe, some who tunnelled out of the compound and so on. Warm sun, cold wind.

Playing chess with Savchuk.

30 March 1936

Golodnyak tells me about the virtuosity of Divisional Commander Azarov. He ought to be prosecuted but at BAM these things are shrugged off. Azarov got food off the platoon quartermaster and exchanged it for gold. He helped himself to half the guards' vegetable plot and, when he left, swapped it for a couple of piglets. Nothing out of the ordinary, then. According to the clerks, the new divisional commander (Afanasiev) gets drunk with them. They're careerists, but they're Party members who can supposedly be trusted. Although they can also be called to account.

Golodnyak wants to get out too. That is the ideological and moral state of our political guardians. He submitted an application, got called in by the boss and political adviser, was given a dressing down and threatened. Now, with no room for manoeuvre, the lad's staying. Everyone here thinks only about how to get away – perhaps the boss and political adviser too? But possibly not. They may find BAM is somewhere they can exercise power.

31 March 1936

There's an in-service review in progress, but it tests neither your politics nor anything else. The section commander in charge of staffing hasn't a clue. What a lot of cobblers! The general knowledge of the divisional commander, according to Golodnyak, was no more than passable. I'm conscious that I'm well ahead in all disciplines.

Company Commander Gridin declined to sit the exam in order not to undermine his authority (by displaying his ignorance). Khrenkov claims to have conducted school-leavers' exams but has no pedagogical theory or practical skills. He's a Party member, so perhaps he did just sit there applauding or asking preposterous questions and being given preposterous answers. It was all over by 2 p.m. and the afternoon was warm and wonderful. Rapid thaw, mud.

1 April

They give the order and now, so easily and straightforwardly, Savchuk is stuck in 1 Squad.

The sun is really hot. Bloody hell! I play chess with the company commander. I probe him. S's prediction was right. The commander is not a chess player but a big baby. He calls me a cheat. Your heart and soul are petty, sir, base and spiteful.

The mud is completely impassable. One person is out in felt boots, another squelching through in woven shoes, and nobody turns a hair. I wander down the track. Thoughts, thoughts.

At the end of the squad commanders' training course, the head of section delivers a 'speech'! It's a mishmash of vacuous platitudes, often beside the point. Commanders, commanders!

I've still got nowhere to live but I need to hold out in Zavitaya till the autumn. I can't hunt game in summer anyway. Come the autumn I'm going to be in Moscow! The guards are drinking themselves into a stupor. The Third Section staff are on the bottle too.

I have an inexplicable sense of anticipation. It's warmer with every passing day. My mind is muddled, my thoughts don't make any sense. People are really living in Moscow, although in Moscow, it so happens, they are saying the same about BAM. They don't know the truth and believe all the propaganda. In the evening Nichepurenko reports what the students are saying about me: the platoon commander ought not to be at BAM, there must have been a mistake. Too right. A mistake that should be put right.

2 April 1936

Absolutely nothing to do. If I had a room it would be different. This one and that come and go on holiday.

I don't know what to do with myself. My only relaxation is going for a walk along the track. Spring is erupting ever more strongly but the mud is as deep as ever. An unusual wind has been blowing from the same direction for over a month. The divisional commander really does not deserve the bars on his collar, and that tells on the leadership and productivity here. Acting Commander Bezyaev of 2 Platoon is the deputy platoon commander for the regiment. He's barely literate, uneducated and completely incapable of providing the guards with leadership. These people are all Party or YCL members. I'll imitate the principles they work to, but the guards infuriate me. How is it possible to be too thick to string two words together and still exist? The only thing they are really good at is swearing. Take Sonkov. He's a great lanky fellow with a low brow and a stupid, vacant look in his eyes. He's so ungainly you wonder if he's actually an ape or an orang-utang. He's standing in HQ in a fur jacket with his hands in his pockets.

He's asked, 'What are you doing in here?'

'Eh, what?'

He gives himself a shake and the belt slides off his belly as if he were pregnant. He snivels loudly, wipes his hand up from his mouth, and sneezes over a room full of people.

'Take your hands out of your pockets!'

'What, something wrong with my hands?'

'Are you a guard or not?!'

'I am a guard. Course I am, why are you getting at me?'

He starts stamping the mud from his boots and kicking it under the table. His mouth turns down at the corner and he sticks out his jaw. Starts hopping from one foot to the other.

'Well, why are you standing there? What do you need?'

'Well, like, I'm here because of this business. What you going on at me for?'

How the hell am I supposed to re-educate these morons, waste my strength and health and get stressed out over them when they don't even understand human speech? They're not interested. Ask anyone and they'll tell you they've all ended up as guards by some semi-official route. The Gulag has strange ways of recruiting its workforce.

By 15 April the Second Track is to be completed as far as Khabarovsk, and I'll probably end up dumped in 1 Squad. Meanwhile the years are passing, taking my short life with them. I have to fight, take a risk, be ambitious.

Zavitaya is so quiet, the village all just impassable mud, puddles and pigs. What sort of life do the villagers have? The same as any other railway settlement?

What makes them happy, where are their goals and aspirations? There are young people growing up here.

Sometimes you take a newspaper, the army's *Red Star*, say, for 9 February 1936, No. 32/3279, and read 'Into the realm of science', and can draw your own conclusions.

The people sitting at HQ drawing up action plans understand sod all about our work or have no interest in witnessing it. It makes you wonder. These are Party members, people trust them and think everything is fine. I'm either a fool or a complete idiot, working my butt off trying to teach my classes in an exemplary fashion.

Lilin has just arrived from Moscow. It's best to say nothing. It pains me. For 300 rubles a month I could end up living half my life at BAM with as many rights as a stray dog, or I could be in Moscow living like a human being. Even so, I wouldn't work for a certain institution, not even in Moscow for 300 a month. Lilin is crafty, telling me I should urge the company commander to transfer me to the periphery, so he gets to stay in Zavitaya himself. We'll see who outwits whom. All the same, he's smart for thinking that out. None of the locals could have.

'Duty officer!' I hear someone say, 'there's no water, we've nothing to cook breakfast with and the cook's asleep!'

'Well, wake her up!'

'What's the point of waking her up if there's no water?'

No chance of getting washed, that's life. I went out without even a mug of tea. Nice. Great. Wonderful! I'd love to live like this for the next five years.

3 April 1936

Gridin is up to something in not appointing me anywhere. I'll bide my time. Pukhov: 'What is the Stakhanov movement? It is all about life becoming merrier, that's what!' The wind whistles straight through my room.

4, 5 and 6 April 1936

Secretary of the BAM Party Committee has arrived. There's been a delay completing the Second Track and the top brass are spitting fire. They threaten us. 'People who delay the work are enemies and we have laws for dealing with them. Those who are passive are enemies twice over. The Party knows they are there, relies on them, but they are not doing their job!' He beats all about the bush, but can't just tell us what to do. They issue quotas for how much ballast they want loaded without taking account of what is technically feasible. They call that 'tightening the screws'. I take out a pencil and calculate there is no way we can manage 250 wagons. They give the company commander responsibility for the quarry and he promptly delegates it to me. I'm not complaining! At least he won't be sending me to a squad and I should be able to get some rest.

Interesting news! The 'soldiers of the track' are to be paid between 2 rubles 24 and 6 rubles 40, depending on their work category. Work and earn as much as you choose. If you are a paid volunteer you are only forced to labour if you are being punished. If they really follow through with this, I'll have my discharge before you know it. For the time being, though, my only option is to hand in a really negative report and exploit the conversation that ensues.

How important clothes are! My leather jacket is enough to gain me respect, regardless of how many pips I have on my collar tabs. They deferentially call me the commissioner or the GPU agent.

Lots of positive things are said about the *zeks*, but about us? Not a peep. Don't they know that having somewhere comfortable to live raises productivity? I've had two nights without sleep now, at the quarry and at the track, carrying the can for Gridin. But it is all for the best. Slowly but surely I am doing the BAM thing, currying favour with the top brass.

I continue to lose at chess, flattering my superior's vanity, and he doesn't have the wits or the intelligence to recognize what a humiliating position he has put himself in. All I hear from him is, 'You've not done that right!' I confess my failing and do my best to show him how right he is, while in my heart of hearts I think, 'What an idiot!' There is no way he will ever understand how an excavator or the points on the railway work. He is, not to mince words, a ploughboy. How a plough works, that's the kind of 'machinery' he does understand.

He orders me all over the quarry: 'Go and see what sort of nonsense they're up to with the shunting engine.' The shunting engine is, of course, exactly where it should be. Or else, 'Why is the shunting engine jerking like that?' Because it's pulling forty wagons of sand and the poor little engine [illegible] to move it one metre.

Life is better for our senior colleagues. They call you on the phone:

'Provide us with such-and-such!'

'This is so-and-so speaking. Send me this and that!'

What are we supposed to say? 'Excuse me, you're talking to the platoon commander'?

They laugh. They already know it's me, or if they don't they will ask. We are not popular. When they find planks they panel their offices at HQ, while I have nowhere to live. I am bivouacked next to our headquarters, and during the day I just wander about. The devil knows what's up with the weather. In the sun it's plus 15, and in the shade minus 15. The north wind chills you to the bone.

And this is how the Stakhanov movement works: they certify Stakhanovites' statistics at a meeting in the Education and Culture Unit, and sometimes make them up there as well. At BAM anything is possible.

7 April 1936

Summer clouds are appearing in the sky. The larks are singing their hearts out, but it's still cold. I go to the quarry. No shuttles. They were all taken to Irkun yesterday evening.

I went back to my cold slum and gathered up wood shavings and bits of rotten wood to try to heat it. Now I'm lying about, writing these lines. Keep out of sight of the boss and all will be well. I still have no official job. The political adviser and storekeeper are trying to organize volleyball and football nets. They unearth one but can't work out what it used to be for. The political adviser asks me. I tell him it's a camouflage net. They agree.

8 April 1936

My commissar, as we jokingly call the political instructor from Phalanx 7, turns up. Tells us, 'The top brass are asserting themselves. Secretary of the BAM Party Committee Bachevsky is on the loose. One prisoner complained to her phalanx leader that the dog handler forced her to be his mistress, that the guards beat up the *zeks* and are no better than policemen under the Tsar, and so on. Bachevsky sets up a court hearing. He questions her in front of the phalanx leader and she turns to the man and says:

"'Do you remember, your wife turned up and she was crying and swearing at me for messing about with her husband?"

"'That clears that up!" says Bachevsky.'

What business has Bachevsky to conduct a judicial investigation without any qualifications, to undermine a volunteer guard's authority for no reason, and smear our unit? And then they complain about escapes. Still, what can you do? They've got the power and like throwing their weight about. Or perhaps he's hoping to get discharged too.

Gridin's adjutant, Kamushkin, was also there. I asked him how things were in Russia. 'Just fine! I had no wish to come back here!'

The civilian site foreman provided further confirmation of the general mood: 'If they say we can apply to be discharged, I'll be first in the queue. I'm a Party member, but work at BAM? No-o thanks. I've had enough. I value living my own life too much.'

It has got warmer. About time too. I've been assigned to command 3 Platoon but there's something they're not telling me. Perhaps it's nothing, but everyone is being terribly secretive. That platoon is a shambles. There are Party members all over the place, but they don't want to work. We'll follow their example.

Inyushkin is ill; he's not coming out of his house and nothing is being done about it. Bystrykin has not been out to the phalanxes once in the past forty-five days. As for the guards . . . What a collection of misfits!!! Divisional commander asks an orderly:

'Who are you?'

'The orderly.'

'Oh, a big shot!'

'And who are you?'

'The divisional commander.'

'Oh, another big shot!'

The orderly turns his back on him and says no more.

I've been elected, in my absence, to the trade union's inspection committee. I'll stick it out till the autumn, see what summer's like in the Far East Region, do some sketching, then get out. The company commander is letting me stay in his quarters while he's on holiday. Until then, the devil knows, I'm living like a dog.

9 April 1936

I take over 3 Platoon. It's a madhouse, a shambles. Three platoon commanders have come and gone with no proper handovers or reception. It's chaos and disorder. Everything is shrugged off, every disaster considered normal. I've noticed a change in myself, in how I received 4 Platoon in 1935 and how now, in 1936, I'm doing it with 3 Platoon. I suppose I've become an old hand, a savvy labour camp officer.

It's warm outside. The north wind is still blowing but it's no longer so cold. I sit in the company commander's office with Golodnyak and the political adviser, debating the transitoriness of life at BAM. We touch on the incident with Bansky in Phalanx 7.

Golodnyak says, 'I don't care if they kick me out, I'm going to alert the appropriate authorities to that case.'

To which the political adviser says quite openly, 'You don't think Golodnyak might come to regret that?'

I attach here Golodnyak's report as documentation of the deeds and misdeeds of the top brass and as testimony to the illiteracy and general educational level of the political supervisors.* Golodnyak needs to retain the support of the company

* It is no longer attached.

95

commander, and many others would do well not to knock the Guards Unit. The company commander gets paid 700 rubles a month. Outside the barbed wire I reckon his market value would be 120 to 150 rubles. Make of that what you will.

10 April 1936

My view and understanding of life are becoming more primitive thanks to BAM. That violin awakens memories of times past and my heart quivers with pain. This is such a bad situation. At least the sky is blue. Dusk. Compare the vastness and power of nature to you, a miserable worm. I may have little option but to take my own life. They will condemn but never understand another's soul, because nobody is interested in how anyone else feels. Where can I find refuge? Where can I escape to and how? Oh, violin, you tear my heart to shreds. I rage and I rejoice. The HQ staff guffaw oafishly, their shallow souls incapable of understanding the profundity of music.

Adjutant Kamushkin would like to get away too. He opposes the company commander and would be glad to see him, his old-fashioned ideas and loutish approach replaced. All I want is to replace my greatcoat for a raincoat. Kamushkin tries to scare me by telling me that once I'm discharged from BAM no one will give me a job. That is tripe, but needs to be thought about. Lavrov, the head of ammunition supplies, is a Muscovite and I sense he's finding things here heavy going. He'll get used to it.

I took out my pistol and put it against my throat. It would be so easy to press the trigger and then ... feel nothing. How easily it could be done, as if you were only joking. It's nothing to be scared of, nothing supernatural. It's just like supping a spoonful of soup. I don't know what held me back. It was all so real, so natural, my hand didn't even tremble. Oh, life! There are moments when that inner voice is silent. Instead I hear the voice of a would–be duty officer.

'Put me through to Phalanx 42 ... Who's that?'

'The tailor.'

'Don't you have a shoemaker?'

'No.'

'Pity!'

What I actually need is the phalanx's duty officer, not its tailor.

There's nobody to give my hand.[*]

Two *zeks* have bunked off from Phalanx 11: an Article 59-er and an embezzler of state property, in for ten years.[†] There's plenty of noise, but no effective action. They ordered a deployment of troops and allocated territories and districts, but couldn't actually follow through on any plans because there are simply not enough guards. I was summoned by the deputy head of the Third Section for a dressing down and warnings. I just thought to myself, you need to be realistic and actually do something rather than sounding off. There hasn't been a single conference on methods or any guidance. We know nothing, we have no background information about how to cooperate with the operational group. The man looked stupid, and looked even more stupid when he started trying to seem smart and issue a supposedly smart order. It all ended with a meeting, which began as usual. The top brass in the Third Section were up all night and decided to catch up on their sleep in the morning, but made sure we were all up. The meeting began at noon. My head is leaden. It's difficult now to remember, think straight and write anything down.

---

[*] From Lermontov's poem of 1840, 'Life is boring and sad and there's nobody to give my hand, to salve this ailing of my heart.'

[†] Offences under Article 59.3 included armed robbery. Embezzlement came under the Directive of the Central Executive Soviet and Council of People's Commissars of the USSR of 7 August 1932, 'On security of property of state enterprises and collective farms'.

11 April 1936

Everybody's political state and morale are dire, which causes an aversion to work, and hence escapes. Then, when the situation turns critical – and in the first ten days of April there have been twenty-eight escapes – they start ranting and threatening us with the Revtribunal. They blast us, and the political adviser offers his mite:

'Regarding the escape from Phalanx 11, the alarm should have been raised and everybody mustered.'

And who, pray, would provide security for a large section in the meantime, relieving the sentries, providing armed escorts? Those same guards? All right, the guards are seen as no better than dogs, which is doubtless why they serve no better than dogs. Another day has passed, so what? They're all shrieking, 'We were relying on you!' Yes, but did you manage to provide us with even the bare minimum, you Chekists, Communists and so on? No. Thank you for all the kind words, but out here in the Far East Region we don't need your bonuses.

They think they can improve political consciousness and morale by coming down hard on us, without wanting to know the circumstances or learn anything from our situation. People come to the political adviser's office to respectfully measure his collar size, but don't even get round to mending our uniforms. They go on and on about escapes and the Guards Unit's lack of enthusiasm or its inability to do its job, but did the operational group catch the escapees? No! Does that mean they're no good either?

For the top brass, a guard's life is cheap and I can tell you why. In the army, if a soldier gets killed they mourn him properly; the command don't have a ready-made way of acting or responding. But here? The guards are in danger, risking their lives every second of the day. They're ordered to prevent escapes but also not to kill anyone, and all the while they have to make sure they don't get their throats cut and their weapons seized from them. The brass choose not to take that into account. You need nerves of steel. A phalanx is filching railway sleepers to burn as fuel. The guards are responsible for the sleepers. They take them off the *zeks*, firing a shot in the air and causing the woman in charge of the phalanx to faint. Then it's the guards' fault for giving the silly bitch a fright. A vicious circle. It's all very well pontificating about this in your office with your bureaucratic thinking, but how are we supposed to predict how the Third Section will react?

The political adviser jokes, 'Platoon commanders get tired because of their work and the courses they teach, so they don't investigate issues.'

What brilliant wit! Commanders and guards are not human beings, why are they getting tired?

They're completely unfair to the guards. We are now practically ordered to do our supposedly voluntary, out-of-hours service for the community. Meanwhile, what has happened to the instructors in the Education and Culture Unit? They complain the guards don't help them enough. We don't help the operational units enough. But when do the operational units help the guards? The *zeks* run away because their living conditions are terrible and that causes lots of concern. I wonder how they'd take it if I ran away from my living conditions!

The devil himself would be hard pressed to make sense of this place. Some are saying we should stop guarding the 59-ers completely and then they would work better. Others yell, 'What are you thinking of, letting former armed robbers loose without any guards?'

Actually, Political Instructor Golodnyak was to blame for the Bachevsky episode. Khodzko, the head of the Third Section, mentions my education, and Bachevsky agrees that I'm politically well trained. I have a pain between my eyebrows. 1 Company has

Zeks checking the laying of sleepers on the track. *BAM – the Second Track*

Backfilling the track with aggregate. *BAM – the Second Track*

degenerated, 10 Company has degenerated, and there are hints from the two of them that my company commander, Gridin, is a troublemaking one-man disaster zone. In a place like this, everyone degenerates. Me too. Nobody wants to be serving at BAM.

12 April 1936
Tsimmes weather.* No wind, steaming hot, too warm in a greatcoat. Today is a holiday in Moscow and, if they are having the same weather, there will be excitement, laughter and joy at the stadium. Here our drunk cook ruined breakfast and no one got anything to eat. Now he's got five days' in the cells to chew on, and has lost three months' remission.

Promotion can come quickly at BAM. Tsigankov had no Party documents but was the political adviser of a company, and now he is the commander of a section. The political adviser of 1 Division, on the other hand, used to be a squad commander.

My first spring not spent in Moscow, apart from when I was in the Red Army. People are being released in batches. Five hundred are due to leave on 15 April. But when will we be released?

13 April 1936
They've stripped the platoon down to the point where the deputy commander is on night duty. They are transferring and redeploying zeks† and expect us to provide guards to escort them. The section head rings to say, 'Send us an armed escort'; the Third Section rings, 'Send us an armed escort'; the division rings, 'Send us an armed escort'; and so on. Send them to us, even if you have to give birth to them yourself!

---

* A Jewish stew of sweetened vegetables, sometimes with fruit and/or meat. Here the meaning is 'weather to enjoy'.

† On 1 January 1935, 153,547 prisoners were working at BAM; by 1 January 1936 this had increased to 180,067. (*Sistema ITL v SSSR. Spravochnik* [*The Corrective Labour Camp System in the USSR A Guide*], comp. M. B. Smirnov, Moscow, 1998, p.153.

Political Instructor Lykov's wife is giving birth and asks for a horse to take her to the hospital. It's urgent, but our bunch aren't sure whether or not that's allowed; how will the top brass view it? It doesn't matter if somebody dies, as long as you don't contravene the regulations and remember to get all the necessary permissions.

The cleaner comes bursting into the office at HQ from the kitchen, shouting, 'The guards are turning the air blue with their swearing. What sort of job is this? Aren't we human beings?' She went on and on and, in her indignation, started swearing herself.

The witches get so indignant, but while they yammer on we just have to put up with it. In fact you can get a flea in your ear if you respond less than diplomatically.

14 April 1936

Every day there's some new freakish incident that should have consequences for someone. Gridin is throwing his weight about. He didn't show up to work in the morning. He was sleeping. Then he stayed in the office till midnight and the clerks were all stuck there. At two in the morning he comes out of his office and says to his adjutant:

'Anyone who doesn't work out of fear but for a clear conscience can leave!'

Taisumov, not well versed in Russian idioms, asks, 'What does chief say?'

'I said you need to work at the prompting of your conscience, not out of fear.'

Terrified, the lad squeals, 'I work out of fear! Only out of fear!'

I try pressuring the maintenance manager about my room and have him spinning like a top. 'There's only me and a few others, and we'll do it, and you can see for yourself how busy we are.' They're so busy that the company commander's food ration cards aren't ready yet; the adjutant still needs his shelves fixed, and the company commander wants his apartment whitewashed.

Nature is awakening. The geese are flying north, the rooks are on the cornfields, the larks are singing. A spider rushes in a terrific hurry, a fly buzzes noisily. I feel hot in an overcoat. There's a haze on the horizon. I don't remember anything else.

Oh, and then the *zek* leader of Phalanx 11 lodges a complaint with the section commander and Bachevsky, claiming that the guards are behaving outrageously, not allowing him and the instructor and all the rest on to the work site. The guards are sabotaging the project — we just desperately want to work, etc. We check it out. The instructor is only allowed to move around under guard, and the rest of the *zeks* had proceeded through the camp zone. Does he think the sentry is a bumhole? It is his duty to stop him. He'd stop us and give us a tap with that truncheon if need be. But it's noticeable how very swiftly the section head responds to a complaint from a *zek*. We are to investigate as a matter of urgency and report back. What about our version of events? They don't want to hear. Well, we'll investigate the matter.

15 April 1936
I draw a plan for an ammonal store. The sun is blazing hot. I dream and believe I am in Moscow, in Sokolniki Park. There is gymnastics in the stadium and I am training as usual alongside everyone else. They say they stiffen the discipline here with Muscovites, but the opposite is true.

Are we going to have an easy time, after the bustle of the capital, in a hole like the Far East Region? They demand a lot of us: we work eighteen hours a day, live in conditions only fit for a dog, and get paid less than we would in the army. We have a higher likelihood of getting sentenced here than anywhere else. What on earth is the point of it all? Platoon Commander Nikolenko is off. To where we all want to be, away from BAM. Party members, where is your sense of duty?!

He confirms that the political adviser himself would be only too happy to resign. So much for our political motivation and morale. You should just hear the way he shrieks at us, the bastard. What can you say? He's a time-server.

16 April 1936

Impenetrable darkness, my eyes hurt from straining to see.

3.30 a.m. To arms! Four *zeks* have escaped from Phalanx 11 under fire. I take five volunteers and we fan out over land, swamp and water. The 15 km forced march warms us up but to no avail. The fugitives are picked up in Zavitaya.

I'm called in to the Third Section by Khodzko and carpeted. He speaks quietly, tactfully, even, but could let rip at any moment. They consider me tantamount to a Party member and promise to discipline me like a miscreant Party member. And prosecute me as a commander. I feel like pointing out to the esteemed head of the Third Section that the escape happened just two hours after his pep talk, but refrain. I need to be diplomatic and not ask for trouble. In the afternoon I photograph an [illegible]. It's hot. The skylark trills joyously as it rises in the sky. It sings its heart out, rejoicing in the sun, the springtime and its life. I am not rejoicing in my life. I'm dragging out an existence, wasting my life for nothing, for 300 rubles a month. Called to the phone again.

'Comrade Chistyakov! When is all this disgraceful behaviour you are presiding over going to end? You've posted guards at the station and they're dozing off! You need to choose men with more mettle!'

The guards are not mine, what does this have to do with me? Where am I supposed to find these mettlesome fellows who don't exist? The Third Section keep trying to lumber us with their work. They have no staff of their own to process arriving and departing prisoners, but soon find people when they want to cause us trouble.

17 April 1936

Walk 15 km to Phalanx 7. Beyond the switching track the railway changes markedly, turning sharply into the hills. It snakes through the slopes in a narrow cutting. The line of the subgrade briefly slices through the hill but then proceeds over a terrace to left and right. To one side is a drop, to the other sandy landslides where the slope has been cut into. There are layers of coloured sand, the roots of trees and bushes, gullies, and telegraph poles which, as you look along the line from above, have the appearance of the teeth of a huge saw. In addition to all this, woodcocks flock in clouds, causing the most amazing commotion in the air.

At Phalanx 7. Clean, bright premises. It's warm and cosy. I meet the renowned leader of the phalanx, Viuga. Someone locked Shakova in a cupboard and kept her there for two days after sending the guard with some people to Bureya on a fool's errand, and in the afternoon she turned up, shrieking:

'The guards are victimizing me. I'm afraid of them, they want to kill me!'

Another incident. Squad Commander Zakharov got TB in the guards and is no longer needed, so he is being fired. While you're healthy, you've got a job; if you're ill, away with you!

My foot hurts. I got a blister and it spoiled my mood. I had a wash in their bathhouse and felt I was in paradise. After that I would have loved to just go to bed, but had to sit up even though nothing needed to be done. My thoughts broke off, or rather, were broken off. I have to transfer a group of released prisoners to Phalanx 9.

18 April 1936
Went to Phalanx 11 and my head is in such a muddle I don't feel like writing anything. Sky overcast.

19 April 1936
Escapes from Phalanx 11. Two people today and no reaction from the Third Section. Barbed-wire enclosure with lamps not completed. Neither we nor the Third Section can order or compel that to be done. Why should I want to draw attention to my own powerlessness? Somebody evidently finds it more expensive to construct a secure camp and cheaper to let a few people go missing. There's a shortage of guards to take prisoners out to work. The guards are accused of failing to provide an armed escort. They are being scapegoated.

How does the camp administration react to the escape? They don't. It's nothing to do with them. Our job is to watch them escape and your job is to catch them! Our job is to insult the Armed Guards Unit and yours is to put up with it. Company Commander Gridin rants at Divisional Commander Inyushkin, who doesn't give a damn. He sticks to his guns and stays at home.

20 and 21 April 1936
Stomach ache. Nausea. I go to the hills with Lavrov. It's overcast. I regret not bringing a gun when a couple of grouse take off under our noses. No matter what we start talking about, we always come back to how to get discharged from BAM and how much we don't want to serve here.

The lads are trying to form a jug band, but when will they find the time to rehearse and play in a day that runs from 9 a.m. to 4 p.m. and is already overloaded? We have a break from 4 to 8, and then we're back at it until 2 a.m. Gridin has said that by 10 a.m. tomorrow the volleyball court will be ready. I will come to play.

'Why are you here so early, Comrade Chief?'

'What else have I got to do?'

He is right. What else can he do? He can't talk to anyone because of his rank, and if he starts hanging around at HQ no one is going to be too thrilled. My platoon has been declared 'special', which is doubtless a slight advance.

22 April 1936

I just want to forget everything. I have a talk with Adjutant Kamushkin, which makes me feel a bit better. At one point we talk about how erratically the telegraph works.

Political adviser telegraphs: 'On Thursday daughter all well'. Arrives as: 'On Thursday doctor farewell'. Another day of my life passes, remarkable only for this incident.

Khodzko calls the political adviser: 'We need at all costs to hold on to those guards who are trying to resign.'

Response from the guards: 'Prosecute us if you like, we will not serve.'

Many people imagine serving at BAM must be the happiest time of your life. It just shows how much they know.

I have cramp in my arms and legs. It's as cold in my 'room' as it is outside. I'm forever transient, living this nomadic existence, eternally unsettled. Going to bed preparing to be woken up over some alarm in the night is just great. Rain and hail. Is it really going to be like this for long, for a whole lifetime? The hairs stir on my head.

23 and 24 April 1936

Days flying by, leaving a bad trail in my memory. One day is so much like the next. You know that tomorrow the machinery will start up again: escapes, arrests, pressure from on high. I can't think what to do in that useless four-hour lunch break. Mud and cold. They're trying to play their own home-grown jazz, which is more noise than theme or art form. There's nobody leading, so whoever fancies it beats the tambourine, rattles, chimes and so on. It's cacophony, like the jangling in my heart. From time to time you forget, but then BAM comes crashing right back like a wedge in your brain. I chat with Lavrov. I've found someone I can exchange a few words with.

My chess game with the company commander is interrupted by phone calls and commanderly swearing.

25 April 1936

Lubochkin comes to Phalanx 11 and starts threatening: 'Any more escapes and I'll have you in court!' The lads are on edge and angry. Very angry.

You can't help becoming ill. You aren't allowed to shoot or beat people to death, but you also aren't allowed not to shoot. Every professional criminal is just looking for a chance to escape. Last night I was even colder than during the winter. You live in fear that someone may nick stuff. You are alive, but not enjoying life. Or anything else. You live in anticipation of lunch, the lunch break, and the night. You are waiting for something unknown and ill-defined. But the one aspiration you can't shake off is to get away from BAM and that badge of rank.

We are making preparations for May Day, only there's no sense of celebration. No escapes, which is a relief. All lunch break I conduct the 'orchestra'. It's ridiculous, of course, but what else is there to do? In the evening, frankly, I was half out of my mind.

Gridin reprimanded me: 'Why don't you know what is going on at Phalanx 7?'

I snapped back at him: 'It was twilight and they said it was being disbanded, but when and where they'll be going no one knows.'

Driving snow. How can I sleep at night? In my room it's so cold my teeth chatter. I don't even feel like sleeping. I am sitting in the project office next to a stove, trying to store up some warmth for the night.

'How is it in your room?' Adjutant Kamushkin asks.

I reply, 'It's warm in the company commander's room, so it must be warm in ours too.'

Laughter. The adjutant's room is not cold either; he can laugh.

26 April 1936
There seems to be nothing to do, and yet in the course of the day you get worn out.

'Send a guard escort!'

I do so.

'No, in an hour's time!'

This goes on all day.

I attend a meeting with Kalashnikov present. We're given a talk featuring all sorts of Japanese gangs and saboteurs. It's only too obvious this is to make us all sit up, and it's very crudely done.

The descriptions of the saboteurs are just absurd; they have commonplace characteristics. One sounds like the political adviser, another resembles me, and we're supposed to go out and catch them. Somebody is playing games with us, but Gridin, who can't see this, starts barking. He rounds on me:

'Here in your Phalanx 7 some Tarsky is deciding where to post the guards. Is that any way for you to be working? Have you taught your commanders how to do their jobs? No! If need be, I'll have you in the cells!!!'

Political Adviser Khrenkov backs him up, scared for his own skin. I try to object but the chief cuts me short:

'Silence!!! Just keep quiet!!!!'

'Fine,' I think. 'You're going to add me to your collection, along with Maikher, Golodnyak and Novikov.' Perhaps nobody told him anything directly about it because of the kind of commander he is. For instance, if he says, 'I beat you but can't beat anything out of you,' what is going on in his mind?

Apart from berating us he probably can't think of anything else to do, because it's all he's capable of. The commanders don't work well because nobody works with them. And commanders sent from Moscow consider it little better than a prison sentence to be sent to BAM.

Our company commander has been planted here to sit in his office and press buttons, but he only presses one useless button all the time. Karmanchuk passes on some interesting information about my superior. At a meeting in Svobodny, Company Commander Gridin was agreed to be the most useless of the lot, and there were no training courses before because there was no one to run them. That was the level of Gridin's commanders. All he manages is to antagonize them. This is what he's like:

'Go to Phalanx 7 immediately.'

'There are no trains.'

'Then walk!'

I walk there to confirm that the phalanx has left. He considers this perfectly normal, and checks five times that I am going. Karmanchuk mentions Divisional Commander Inyushkin too. Turns out he was a platoon commander in the sapper section of a reserve regiment in the army.

27 April 1936

I walk at night. Along the way I check the sentries at Phalanx 11. There are many beautiful spots, but they no longer move me.

I get back from Bureya on the 43. There are people on board, travelling with nothing on their minds. Travelling by train without a worry about escapes. Travelling, structuring their lives. We can't do that. We see things completely differently from people without collar tabs.

One of the *zek* armed guards has shot himself. The report claims he was afraid of being sentenced to a new term, but the reality is probably different. They write these reports to keep up morale. What will they write if I top myself? I am going out of my mind. Life is so precious, and wasted here so cheaply, so uselessly, so worthlessly.

28, 29 and 30 April 1936

No time to write entries. I'm being hauled in every couple of minutes by HQ. Preparations for the May Day holiday.

The big boss is jumping down my throat. Ranting and raving: 'Bring me the sentry duty schedule for May! You have thirty minutes!!!'

Done. The squad commander turns up without his belt. I get blamed for that too.

'There! The platoon commander's example is followed by his subordinates! Twenty-four hours in the cells!!'

Next he goes for Slenin, a courier.

'What are you staring at?'

Slenin later remarks, 'He yelled at me and I just thought, "Get lost!" and left him to it.'

I'm doing my paperwork. Boiling with anger and bitterness. I'm aware that I count for absolutely nothing. They treat you like a child. They act like you're just the same as all the others. They say, 'The same type!' It's mind-numbing. You look at things differently. For instance, it's evening and they're screening a film. I'm standing by the door in uniform, leaning against the door jamb. Enter Gridin, who asks:

'Has it been on for long?'

I reply, 'No, Comrade Commander.'

But what I am thinking is, 'He must see me as a soldier standing to attention with his eyes fixed on the ceiling.' Hell, when will all this end?

And what about the audience?! They love the vulgarity of *Another Man's Child.** They don't empathize with it or understand it. They talk, stomp about, slam doors. They dress garishly. They have expensive clothes but don't know how to wear them stylishly. I don't think they're capable of it. I wonder how they occupy themselves at home, what their outlook on life is. Gridin has insomnia and stays up till 2 a.m., but why do we have to? I don't suffer from insomnia like that.

1 May 1936

So, uselessly, pointlessly, meaninglessly, life passes. Today is a holiday, but not for us. We have turmoil and muddle. Everyone confined to barracks. We can't go anywhere or do anything. We played volleyball in the yard. Oh, these muttonheads! They can't shoot, can't play volleyball. Warm day.

Very soon I will be a complete dunderhead, because my mind is filled with escapes and thoughts of discharge and nothing more interesting than that.

2 May 1936

I really will have no option but to earn myself a prison sentence and get out. It won't be that bad. I certainly won't be the only person in the USSR with a criminal record. People just get on with it now, and will in the future. That's how BAM has re-educated me, how it has refined my thinking. By making me a criminal. In theory I already am. I'm quietly sitting here

* A comedy by Vasiliy Shkvarkin popular in the 1930s.

among the 'soldiers of the track', preparing and resigning myself to that future. Or perhaps I will top myself. I've been working here for months and there will be more months, miserable and depressing just like those. And beyond that, more of the same. This job leads you to crime.

'My soul is torn apart and my heart is racked with pain. The past seems but a dream.'* I can hardly believe I actually lived in Moscow and was free. That I ever built a future for myself or made plans.

The second day of May is over. Although it was a holiday, I felt no freedom. I couldn't go anywhere, we were confined to barracks. You lurch along the track with thoughts you can't dispel. There's nothing to distract you and nowhere to escape to. You find your hand reaching for that revolver. If death is unavoidable, let it be sudden, not a slow process of decline. Isn't it better to force the natural course of events? The company commander probably suffers from insomnia, hanging around until 2 a.m., but why do the rest of us have to? I don't make such an issue out of not being able to sleep.

No letters yet, I wonder if something is wrong. Although I haven't written any either.

3, 4, 5 and 6 May 1936

I have to start every day like this, because this is the way the days are: every day is a tombstone for my life.

We despatch 177 to the east. There's muddle and disorganization – it's a disgrace. We have no wagons, no essential equipment, no tools, no one supervising the departure. The guards are being given dog's abuse. 'Send an armed escort to take prisoners to the bathhouse at midnight or we'll lodge a complaint.' How are you supposed to organize people when no one knows what's going

---

* Allusion to a popular ballad by Nikolai von Ritter, 'Coachman, do not whip the horses!'

on or wants to find out? Everyone is trying to shuffle off the responsibility, and who cares what the end result is? It only has to matter to the guards. The guards will look after everybody, the guards will make sure everything is done in a civilized manner, the guards will take care of training, the guards will sign up to the industrial business plan. Platoon commander, deal with escapes! Deal with fires! Deal with armed escort duties! Deal with everything. It's just such an amazingly important job. The *zeks* in Phalanx 177, climbing into wagons carrying manure, are quite right when they complain indignantly that livestock are transported in better, more hygienic conditions than prisoners. The boss yammers on for good reason and for none.

'What about your Squad Commander Pasenko, is he married?'

'I'll find out, Comrade Chief.'

That sets him off.

'You don't know your own men. What way is that to work? What sort of commander are you? You ought to be taught a lesson.'

I wonder whether Comrade Chief knows my marital status.* I'm quite sure he doesn't. A political instructor has been dismissed after being held under investigation for six months. They wanted to pin sabotage under Article 58.14 on him but didn't succeed.

The lad didn't show any fear and told them, 'You forced me out to the *taiga*, but I want a life,' and so on.

Bystrykin said quite openly, 'Why are you creeps breaking your backs? I just used to glance at the platoon from a distance and head back home.'

He explains his serenity is due to the fact that the top brass made him so fed up his nerves ceased to function, which is why

* As far as we can tell, Chistyakov was single.

he's so relaxed now. He is nerveless. Company Commander Gridin is being 'nice' to me again.

Contact with the phalanxes is abysmal or non-existent but there are, in fact, things we need to communicate. We have no means of transport as the trains don't stop, and 40 km on foot is not my idea of fun. It simply won't do if there are things to be delivered.

Comrade Chief rants, 'Where are your men? You just sit around and do damn all!'

It costs me a great effort to hold my tongue, and I will snap in the end, probably sooner rather than later. It's good that I have Lavrov to talk to, at least. We joke and laugh, but there are tigers clawing at our hearts. Nichepurenko looks in on us and starts going on about how great life at BAM is, that no one could possibly want anything more or better, that he hopes to serve another five years and more, that he has come into his own at BAM.

It's certainly true he has come into his own here, but the stamp of BAM is upon him. He knows nothing about life, he's pig ignorant. He gets by on cliches like 'The worthiest workers are those not afraid of difficulties', 'We must sacrifice our own lives', 'The Party and Soviet power know what they are dictating'.

Meanwhile, the boss is on the rampage again.

'What sort of communications do you have? Just make sure Bezrodny is here to see me tomorrow morning. Go and look for him yourself.'

What a man! Is he ever in a good mood? How can someone like that exist? How can he fail to understand that it doesn't strengthen his authority? That none of his subordinates come near him if they can possibly avoid it? Whether or not they're afraid of him, to a man they hate him and do their best to steer clear.

But why is the political adviser taking no interest in our life? Why is he no longer monitoring our political consciousness and morale? He hasn't called me in for questioning once. It's a mystery. The devil knows how he meets anyone. So much for the working relationship between commanders, subordinates and superiors. These people are the Soviet Union's Party vanguard. This is how our leaders exercise influence. It's unbelievable.

7 May 1936

The clouds have gone and immediately it is warm. On my way to check the explosives storage facility, I sit on the track. Spring is all around, but there are blizzards and demons in my soul. No, I am not a happy commander! Rogovenko, commissioner of the Third Section, is in the guardhouse for going on a drunken spree and threatening to shoot himself. This is becoming a habit: Maikher, Golodnyak, me, Rogovenko, and many more are staying quiet about it. People don't come to these decisions lightly. Life is not much fun. Is it worth the effort? I can't live on hopes, I just can't. Here at BAM the only place that does seem to operate in accordance with the regulations is the Revtribunal. They hit you with Article so-and-so on the basis of such-and-such. It's the law. Tough!

8 May 1936

Every day some new truth is revealed. Here is one. The Stakhanov brigade of Phalanx 4 earned 2,000 rubles in twelve days, demanded decent living conditions, food and so on. The section responded: 'Sort it out for yourselves as best you can.'

What can you say to that? It's the same for us. The Stakhanovites officially have today off. The Armed Guards Unit doesn't get days off. We work eighteen-hour days. Do we get paid for that? Not a chance! What sort of incentive is there?

People who chose to come and work here have only themselves to blame, but what about me?

There is no water. You need to kick up a fuss and beg for it. Issuing orders and demanding it doesn't work. Everyone is so slipshod, everything is such a godforsaken mess. They brought *zeks* from Phalanx 6 to 4 on the basis of an order from the Audit and Distribution Unit. Phalanx 4 wouldn't accept them so the guards were left standing there: 'We don't need them.' What sort of infernal chaos is this? Nobody knows what's going on. Was it sabotage or what? They pull me to and fro throughout the day, like a deaf commander tugging at a bell pull. I need to bring this to an end. A railway engineer applied to resign and was told that, without exception, we are assigned to this project until it is complete.

There is a ray of hope, but we will need to take our own measures too. What about the YCL organizer? He's self-taught, attends the village school for three months then gets sent over here. Then they wonder why the YCL is inactive. Golodnyak, in charge of financial matters, is like a bull in a chemist's shop. I try to explain things to him.

9 May 1936
You rush about all day, trying to forget time, waiting for it to be evening. Come evening you're exhausted and just want to go to bed. One day follows another.

The political adviser, when I say, 'No report for January, February and March,' replies, 'I write a lot of baloney, and you need to do the same.'

All right then.

I went shooting with the head of combat training. Some boys about twelve years old are collecting cartridges, running about, laughing. They roll themselves up in a ball and somersault down the slopes and sandy cliffs at the quarry. Carefree boyhood! How I'd love to join them.

The snowdrops are out.

2 a.m. Call from the Third Section: 'Send an armed guard!'

The political instructor sends one. A quarter of an hour later the guard is back. No sooner has he taken off his boots than they're phoning again. Political instructor goes to the phone:

'What sort of a shambles are you in over there pestering people? What nonsense is this?'

It goes all the way to Khodzko at the top of the Third Section. He phones, demanding to speak to the duty officer, but gets the political instructor.

'I demand to speak to the duty officer. Pass him the phone.'

'Well, this is the political instructor. I'm senior to him. Tell me the problem.'

'I said I want the duty officer!'

'Are you saying you don't want to talk to me?'

'Yes!!'

'Well I don't want to talk to you either.'

'Get yourself over here, now!'

'I can't!'

'Why not?'

'I've hurt my leg!'

'Have you got a medical note?'

'I don't want to take time off, so I'm working to the best of my ability.'

'Bring me a medical note tomorrow without fail.'

10 May 1936

In the morning we hear the following conversation:

'I apologize, Commissar, I've had enough sleep. I'll get up now and go to the holiday home* for three days. I've been promised a place there by the head of the Third Section.'

---

* The guardhouse.

'What for?'

'Because I didn't want to talk to him.'

'That was silly. You should consider it an honour to talk to a chief.'

'He wasn't talking to me, he was swearing at me.'

'But our senior officers are supposed to swear, otherwise what sort of bosses would they be?'

'Well, he's the head of the Third Section, so he should do his swearing over there, but I'm in charge of the platoon here, so we're both bosses. I can swear better than him, too, but I didn't say a word.'

The weather is foul. Rain and cold, mud up to your knees. I walk through Zavitaya with the head of combat training, squelching, not bothering to pick our way because everywhere is equally muddy, and we debate. I bet it's not as wet as this in Moscow. What wretch had the bright idea of dumping us here? Why didn't they ask us first?

The May Day bonuses have been announced, rewarding both commanders and guards. Not me, which I am glad about. The boss has gone off to the line at Arkhara. Afanasiev is enjoying a good shave, and it's good for a chief to get a breath of fresh air. They've put together quite some division. The divisional commander is barely literate, and the same goes for the platoon commanders and political officers. Doronin, Karpenko, Sergeyev, Soloviov . . .

One was a squad commander, the others are former guards. How amusing.

11 May 1936

There's never a day without some new miracle. Today is supposed to be a day off, but the boss is short of things to do at home. He is poking around HQ. He calls me in:

'What have you got going on at Phalanx 11? You just sit there.

Not a damn thing is getting done and you are doing nothing about it! Get out there now! How many times do I have to tell you? When are you going to start working properly? There's the divisional commander himself going to inspect the phalanxes, sorting things out.'

I can barely contain myself, and at some point I'm going to snap. There will be a clash.

A great day off that proved to be, stomping 34 km out there.

The *zeks* are having their day off. Company Commander Gridin has ruined mine. I don't make it to the cinema or the bathhouse. He must have insomnia again and needs to bark at people to work up an appetite.

Outside, rain, mud, filth. We are so used to living in a shack now; we're used to everything being makeshift. It's just best not to talk about it. It's the same in all the Armed Guards Unit camps. The guards are on duty every six hours, like clockwork. For those on contracts, it lasts two years, and for *zeks* the full length of their sentence.

We now have our own academicians out here and don't need any more throwbacks, but still they keep on sending sundry Gridins. The commissar tells us caustically: 'Gridin is thinking, those bastards are glad I'm being sent off on vacation!'

We are glad. We're looking forward to being able to breathe. All we need now is for Political Adviser Khrenkov to go too. Life will be a bed of roses. Golodnyak instead of Khrenkov, Chistyakov instead of Gridin. That would instantly bring us five metres nearer to socialism.

'We are building socialism together, so why does Gridin take offence all the time?' the commissar wonders ruefully. 'The May Day order got lost, the secret order about Dovbysh got lost, the secret order about developing the Armed Guards Unit got lost. What's going on here? You lot are incapable of rallying the commanders round you. This is an abscess waiting to burst. Why was my ticket held up for twelve days with the company commander? What sort of nonsense is this?'

12 May 1936
With every day that passes new facts, appalling but true, come into the open.

Karmanchuk tells us, 'I was travelling with Shishov and Gridin to a meeting. Gridin is grumbling, "If they gave me good squad commanders, I would make them acting platoon commanders and they would work. But all these miscellaneous platoon commanders are a waste of time. They just give me a lot of bad blood."'

That's the truth. Gridin's unwillingness and inability to lead is the reason why our existence and our relationships are so foul. We touched once again on killings. If a guard gets killed in the army they don't know how to account for it. But in our unit? If someone gets murdered, they file a report and that's that. You chose to come here, so what more do you expect? Another technique: you give someone belated instructions, force them to sign for them, and instantly shed all responsibility. Officially, you are now in the right, and what happens to the other man is no concern of yours. A guard is prosecuted and sentenced, and it's of no interest to you that he has a family and so on. He took the pay so he has to be prepared to take the rap. We don't have enough guards, which is why they have to work eighteen hours a day, with one platoon commander in charge of thirty of them. If there's an escape, you lose your work credits or end up in court.

My brain aches. A shudder runs through my body. Despair! How, how do I get discharged? I need to get sentenced after a year of service. I rack my brains over it from morning until night. You never know where you may be going from one day to the next. Every day brings new torments, driving home your insignificance and emptiness.

I start looking back over the days and find there's nothing worth remembering. Everything is just vile. Where can I find solace? Nowhere. We'll just have to get through the next four months somehow.

Divisional Commander Azarov resurfaces. He's going to appear in court, but how can they prove he was stealing the food? Where and how was the shortfall registered? That will be the situation if Azarov denies everything. He'll have compromised himself in the eyes of the guards, but that's it. They'll just transfer him somewhere else. Only at BAM could someone like him find a job. He won't resign of his own accord. He'll beg to be kept on. Unlike me.

13 May 1936

Even Pavlenko the autodidact has recognized the nature of the training and re-education he's received at BAM. He is growing, learning, getting the picture. He applies to resign, adding, 'If necessary, I'll bypass the company commander.'

Everyone suddenly remembers us when there's an escape. This is how it goes: there's this son of a bitch wants to resign, let's give him a surprise and send him across to 1 Squad. You'll have something to complain about there! We'll arrest you! Throw you in the cells!! Have you in court!!! That's how they look after a commander. Oh, joy and jubilation!

14, 15 and 16 May 1936

I'm making a billiard table. On the 15th, I trek to Phalanxes 7 and 11 in the afternoon. I come across some tin cans on the way and shoot at them with a small-bore. It's warm in the afternoon but so cold at night my hands are freezing. My legs are really bad; I have cramp so painful I could cry out. Another year of this and I'll be a cripple. They won't need me then. And what am I sacrificing my health for? Four hundred rubles. Not a good bargain. I wouldn't want to stay here if you paid me 1,500 or 2,000. Billiard table just about usable, and there's a queue of people wanting to play. Adjutant, standing in for the boss, fancies a go at winning after 8 p.m. (during his working hours). Rain, rain, rain.

17 and 18 May 1936
Back to 11. The bloody phalanx leader has contrived to select the worst villains, Tsuladze and the like. He sent Ivanov out for milk. Here they come, drinking it, while we can hardly stand. I go out after escapees with Lyashenko. We climb the hills in the dark, through the swamps and mud. I fall into a pit, probably sprain my ankle but press on. We wade through water, climb places we'd never tackle by daylight. At 2 a.m. I lie down to sleep, my legs wet, aching and cramping. There's nowhere to dry off. When I return to the search party, I take a rifle but find no one. I'm barely able to move. Trekking 40–50 km every day wears you down. If I take the boss's horse, the political adviser sounds off. For them, a horse matters more than an escape. I have a lot to write but my head is spinning.

19 May 1936
I'm thoroughly ill. My chest aches and I can't bend or breathe properly. Maybe it's pleurisy. Enthusiastic army careerists go chasing after ranks, even those in BAM. Fix those bars on their collar tabs and they strut around feeling superior. Proud, smug. Golodnyak shows up. How do you get discharged? He's probably another informer. Hard luck, laddie, no dice. The guards are being torn to pieces. I go to Political Adviser Khrenkov and show him the instructions they've been given. He can't make head or tail of them.

20 May 1936

Green meadow covered in flowers. Covered in flowers! It's a lovely summer's day. The vault of heaven is so blue, so fathomless. Against a background of dove-grey haze on the hills the trail stretches like an emerald ribbon. The song of the larks pours out from heights unseen. The air is still and pure, with only the buzzing of flies disturbing its silence. The wall of a hut on the horizon looks like a white sail. Smoke from a campfire smoothly ascends and dissolves, dissipating. And the colours, yellows, lilacs, blues and darkest crimson. The flowers rejoicing in the sun. Birds rejoicing in the sun. The cows, stretching their necks, lazily flicking their tails, content. The sheepdog, stretched out on the ground, blinks in the sunlight, his tongue lolling to one side. In another part of the picture, meanwhile, *zeks* are toiling on the railway, the very sight of which is enough to make you loathe this project, to sense your insignificance in this scene and the vacuity of the life we live here. The stillness is violated by the sighing and the wailing siren of a railway engine. The thought is inescapable, reflecting as it does reality: I have been robbed of everything.

21 May 1936

My day off. For the first time in my life I paint with oils. I am not, however, allowed to spend the day as I please. A meeting has been called, and quite some meeting it is too. Company HQ are not coping. There are delays everywhere. The Plan is not being fulfilled and the project is jeopardized. They resolve to conduct a ten-day Stakhanov shock-working campaign which, of course, will be a job for the Armed Guards Unit. We are the scapegoat, considered bone idle and so on. The commanders and political officers are given full authority over the phalanxes. We are to do the job someone else ought to be doing, and need to remember: 'How you work reveals your attitude to the Stakhanov movement in general. Fail and you will earn yourself a sentence.'

They mean 'be guilty of sabotage'. Golodnyak quips, deciphering OGPU: 'O God, Protect Us'. That is the prisoners' version. We think it stands for: 'Our Goal, Pulverize the Uppity'.

22 May 1936

Living conditions, educational recreation, diet and other matters have come under discussion. Don't worry, no need to be incredulous, they're not worried about us, they're worried about the *zeks*. The workforce is in the wrong place, there aren't enough essential supplies, and this obliges us to shift people around, 'disrupt the Plan', fail to reach the quota. What does the company do about it? Send in the Armed Guards Unit! Delegate all responsibility to the platoon commanders! Let them sort out the bungling by company HQ! That's how it's done.

The section head admits the twenty-four-hour worksheets are nonsense. The intensity of the work isn't quantified and there's no allowance for permafrost in calculating the time for earthworks. Doesn't that sound like fun? What responsibility do these people take? None! The project leadership barks, everyone runs around, and we take the brunt of the work. Efforts at 'rehabilitation' continue. First it was Viuga's turn to clown around, now it's Arkhipov, and they think that's only fair. Platoon commander Ogurtsov replies for all to hear that Political Instructor Novikov has not appeared because he was feeling lonely and has gone to see his wife. He wasn't doing anything useful anyway.

Pavlenko complains, 'The company commander had such a go at me! "Do you understand the situation in the Far East? No leave!" Then off he goes for the whole summer.'

23 May 1936

In every age and in every nation, the only thing that has ever really mattered is who you know. It is no different here. The company commander, political adviser and divisional commander get expenses for their travel, but do we? No chance. Yet who does the most travelling? It is puzzling. A fair solution would seem to be for anyone who travels for work to get expenses. The *zek* guards don't want to work in security for 15 rubles when the *zeks* on the track are getting 250–300. That's quite a difference.

Dubrovin is behaving strangely. On the train a guard asks him, 'Where are you going, Comrade Political Instructor?'

'Abyssinia!'

'Is that far?'

'No, we'll go about a hundred kilometres, then another fifty and the same again and we'll be there!'

'Why are you going there?'

'I need to see the king of the natives!'

The guard believes him.

24 May 1936

Dubrovin again: 'I open baggage wagon No. 1 with a skeleton key. The conductor appears.

'"Where do you think you're going?"

'"Do you have any idea to whom you are talking? I am the commander of the YCL's Far East Region regiment and commander of the Tamarchukan Armed Forces. Stand aside, my friend, stand aside, I say."

'I go to the restaurant. I'm sipping a liqueur when Khopersky comes in and sits opposite me. I slip the glass behind the curtain and concentrate on my coffee.'

Training courses. One man doesn't show up for morning gymnastics. He's sitting it out in the toilet and invites Dubrovin to join him. Regarding this, Dubrovin states at a meeting that evening, 'No one's going to lure me into that. I would never choose to sniff a stench for forty minutes instead of fresh air.'

25 May 1936
They yell at us, and force us to shout, 'Stakhanovites!' while there's no tobacco in the phalanx, which is valued there more than gold dust. It is measured out a strand at a time. No one ever finds cigarette butts.

26 May 1936
Rain, sleet, darkness. I trek from Phalanx 11 to Zavitaya. Night.

27 May 1936
I went to Phalanx 24 with the head of combat training. We sat on a hill to sketch and write letters. In the evening, I watched *Without a Dowry*.* I'd be better off not going to the cinema, it reminds me of going to the theatre in my old life and just makes me angry and upset.

The guards unit is degenerating, or rather, more accurately, has degenerated. The report from 14 May is full of suicides, alcoholism, nobody doing their job. Why? Because life was better in the past and everyone wants things to improve, while BAM, well, it can go to hell. I'm going to behave like all the rest of them: it's summer, time to take a break. If nobody asks questions, fine. If they kick up a fuss, we'll work.

28 May–3 June 1936
Another Stakhanov ten-day shock-work campaign has been declared, but how is that going to happen? Perhaps I am failing to understand the actual situation and what really needs to be

* *Bespridannitsa* (1936), film from a play by Alexander Ostrovsky, directed by Yakov Protazanov.

done. What I do understand is that they are using us to pull their chestnuts out of the fire. Your job is to travel all over the place and actually do the work, they say, while the five of us will pass judgement on what you are doing. Yershov is just the same. Sod being useful. Without pausing to think or understand, he yells and issues instructions. A typical desk worker. If I'm dealing with some pipsqueak who won't listen or try to understand and never will, I just keep my head down. Why waste time on him? These people lord it over their subordinates, but only have authority over the lower ranks. Their equals regard them as complete dopes. The hired volunteer staff at company HQ are failing to cope so it's decided the guards should be sent in and, to make them work harder, threatened with prison sentences. The guards can be dragged before the Revtribunal, but the hired workers get away with anything.

A *zek* bugler signals a warning of explosives detonation.
BAM – the Second Track

I am called in by Political Adviser Khrenkov, who demands, 'Why aren't you at Phalanx 11?'

I tell him, 'If you are going to get funny with me and say I only spent six hours at Phalanx 11 and threaten me with a trial, I'll pack in working completely.'

This is supposed to be voluntary work, for the good of the community, so if I feel like doing it, I will, and if I don't, why should I?

I went to see Khodzko, the head of the Third Section, about withdrawing the armed guard and he called in Kalashnikov. It was all very silly, there was something obviously not right or relevant. Suspicious. In addition, some character, a track worker, comes barging in and settles himself on the sofa.

One thought bores relentlessly into my brain. When? When, for heaven's sake, will I ever be free? Even Party members like Ogurtsov and Nichepurenko treated the review as a formality. There was an attempt to intimidate them with a telegram from Krylov at BAM HQ, but it seems to have been hot air. Intimidating, criticizing, cursing is something anyone can do, but nobody is capable of teaching or supporting, nobody. That is the BAM mindset.

Once again I tramp back from Phalanx 11, on a warm, bright, moonlit night. Right now in Moscow, from 7 p.m., people are out strolling with never a worry about escapes or *zeks*. They don't know we exist, and might only laugh if they did. No, I can't write, my soul is in tatters. I'm going insane. What a life!?!

Weather brightened up today and everything seems happier and easier. But life, life! Should I force the course of nature? The ten-day shock-work campaign took away all my personal life. When you're playing volleyball you can forget everything, but afterwards our shambolic life comes back to haunt you in all its glory. The contrast with civilian life is stark. Everyone at BAM is mired in escapes and hopeless stupidity. Some people are angry about the working conditions, others have found this is an area where they can get by and throw their weight about, and that is how they live.

They have some original customs in Zavitaya. In a front garden the ladies who live in the house are sitting on the earth mound by the wall. Their small talk is suggestive and their husbands walk or stand about in their underwear with their hands behind their back or folded like Napoleon's. They make jokey remarks like:

'Did your wife sew those trousers for you? Look at the crotch! Is that in reserve in case you get a hernia?'

Nichepurenko bursts out: 'I didn't know the company commander was holding back my leave, that they wouldn't let me resign, and all that time I was busting a gut. Not any more.'

The evening is velvety, pink and warm. The sap is up in the trees, they are fresh, leafy and emerald green. The only entertainment for the residents and young people here is to go down to the station, see the train arrive, and mill about.

But again, what do I need to do to get out of this place? I've seen enough of summer in the Far East Region. It's nothing particularly remarkable or unremarkable. Emptiness, ugliness. A government commission is coming to declare the Second Track open. If I can stick it out till October, something should happen. Either to me or to BAM. I fear my patience may run out first. Perhaps things might even get better. Political Instructor Golodnyak is heading east to Phalanx 19.

4 June 1936

Today is summer. Hot. They dismissed Azarov and that's the end of the matter. The chief sits there listing escapes.

He was holed up in his room for the winter to keep out of the cold. He's doing the same in the summer, but to keep out of the heat. If it's cool he goes out to bask in the sunshine. I spent till 2.30 a.m. yesterday playing billiards and overslept till 10.00 today. Went out to sketch at the quarry. There's been an escape in Phalanx 11. Who the hell cares! When you look back at everything you did in the day — everything you coordinated, agreed, investigated — you could almost believe it was calm and wonderful. I'm morally dead. Here's an example of the way BAM functions: they've relieved me of command after a month of service standing in for Gridin and I haven't received a kopek. BAM has its own way of doing things.

5–6 June 1936
Two days and nothing in them worth writing about. On the holiday I went to a so-called sports field of the District Department of the NKVD for a competition. All I did was upset myself.

When I was wearing shorts and a vest and spiked shoes I remembered the stadium in Moscow, remembered being alive. Best not to. Told Adjutant Kamushkin I would serve only till autumn or opt to face trial. Political Instructor Sergeyev·came round again. Also asked how I was finding the work. I told him, no later than autumn. He said I would get my discharge, they wouldn't try to hold on to me. I don't know how true that is, but it cheered me up a bit.

7 June 1936
They expect leadership from the likes of Pakhomov. Nanny Pakhomov is a bootlicker who's in with the company commander. He wants to pick up shock-work credits and get back home as soon as possible. Gridin gloats, 'See how I make them knuckle down!'

Got sent *Red Sport*, which was unsettling.* That's where life is, so nothing new. I went to the office with Sergeyev and found

* *Red Sport* was a newspaper published from 1924 until 1946, when its title was changed to *Soviet Sport*. Its first editor, Aron Itin, was shot for treason in 1938.

them playing cards. That infuriated me. That sadist G[ridin] will be back soon, so I need to make hay while I can. Kamushkin and Khrenkov are not too devoted to the service and roll in at 11 or 12. What can I do about it? Nothing! I've learned to deal with it Cheka style, as they say. The Third Section are bastards, though. They're bringing a case against Platoon Commander Ogurtsov over Baranov, because someone informed that Baranov had lived for a month with the guards, eating and drinking and not paying for it.

Are there really people who live in freedom? I am going to win mine no matter what it costs. I'm not having some group leader try to teach me the rudiments of political literacy. What a joke!

8 June 1936

The touching concern for the Armed Guards Unit is evident everywhere. Take the canteen. So off-hand, and should you ever ask for anything, you're finished. You won't get served for an hour or more. Not only is there no choice of food, you don't even get two courses. Pilaf today, with dried-out rice. Whether you consider it edible and whether you want to eat it is entirely up to you. Take it or leave it. You want some white bread? Should someone organize that for you? No one does. The canteen workers don't give a damn, so there is nothing like that. There isn't even anything to buy. If you are not full after one helping, too bad, because you won't be getting a second. Fancy some ice cream or cranberry juice? You must be joking. As for queueing, no problem. You can queue for an hour or more because how you spend your time during the four-hour break is your affair.

9 June 1936

These are the sort of people we need:

'I got there with 2,000 on me. The whole village comes

132

running. Girls! I put three quarters of a litre of vodka on the table straight off. The women are looking at me, but I don't turn a hair. I walk out the next day, hands in my pockets, and anyone who hadn't seen me yesterday is asking, "What's going on?" A commissar from the political section? I walk along looking like a collective farm director. Drunk out of my mind every day. Thought I might have stayed there, but what is there to do in a village? Can't earn anything worthwhile, picking away at the soil! No, I thought, I'm off. And here I am.'

I notice HQ are having meetings, taking decisions, passing resolutions, drawing conclusions. They'll be announcing whose work was exemplary and who's to face the court. Platoon Commander Nikolenko comes prying and asks how I'm doing. I tell him, I'm here till October and then either they let me leave or I'll choose trial. I do seem to have accepted the idea of facing trial.

During the night there's an escape from the Third Section. They told Goryachev and ten people ended up in the punishment cells. When it's dark, people run away. There are houses all around, so you can't shoot. You can't beat anyone or you might get time yourself.

The weather's nasty. One or two days warm, then five or six days of rain at the Far East Region holiday resort.

10, 11 and 12 June 1936

Emotions, moods and so on blunted, leaving only criminal inclinations. Sometimes I feel a spark of life, but nobody here can fan it and give my thoughts some focus. It's turning me into a bloodless creature. But my emotions still proclaim their existence and demand proper sustenance. I'm not sure what it is best to compare the unit to: is it more like a monastery or a coffin? Perhaps a bit of both. It's like a monastery because there's nothing culturally Soviet about it, and a coffin because a person slowly dies, and with him all sign of life, except that people escape. But my blood is still pulsing, and with it thoughts swarm and pour in a rushing torrent and, interrupting each other, rise, rise into consciousness in a disorderly mob, then take a certain course and I can relax into thinking about the situation calmly again. My old life is becoming history, as if it had been lived by someone else.

So even my inner world recedes day by day into eternity until it reaches freezing point. You start believing they can make you lose all emotion. Yet every day brings you nearer to freedom. Only, what kind of path are you walking to get there? A path of defeats, misery and rage. A path that makes you even more contemptible, a path humiliating to the humanity in you. Sometimes, though, you try cold-blooded analysis and much of that peters out for lack of fuel. There have been prisons throughout history so why, ha ha ha, shouldn't I be in one rather than only other people? This labour camp existence is necessary in particular historical circumstances, hence necessary also for me. As time passes, memories of that other life, which everybody except the camp inmates and me is living, will cease to be painful. I will be able to gaze levelly at it.

They will give me no option but to do that, by deducting service credits which might have shortened my stint here. I will walk over the sand and the hills, through the swamps and the permafrost, through the dense Siberian forests and the quagmires. We are everywhere. And everywhere life springs eternal. I will learn the laws of life and its particulars. If only in my imagination, I will see live people, witness the things they do, and be among them, live among them. But what of reality!!! My thoughts break off, and where is my right to life? What have I done, what kind of criminal am I? Am I even a criminal? Perhaps this is how it has to be. Perhaps I am not supposed to live my own life. That would explain everything. Here you are presented with the sight of what you were, of what you had stored up, and that is all you now have to live on.

13 June 1936

It looks like they've invented a way of punishing people by forcing them to live a different life while still being fully conscious of their old one. From the perspective of history you don't count, so just stay where you are and keep your mouth shut.

But the reason we have education is so we can be objective, and the reason I have consciousness is so that I can feel.

It's easy to switch off from everything for a moment and rush headlong after horror, but you can't do that every hour, every second, for long years. There are times when you have to seriously ask yourself whether you should win by dying. But there are more moments when you feel you are almost being forced to live, in a way and in circumstances designed to make you see how completely contemptible you are.

Here is Yershov's political rhetoric:

'Preparations for the May Day holiday were a disgrace. An incorrect direction was given to the Stakhanov movement, which started from the top down rather than from the grassroots up, a political minus.

'There was an under-appreciation of the review, an inappropriately convivial approach to work by the acting company commander. There was no leadership of the phalanxes by the company's units. Obligations were taken on but carried out in a very basic manner.'

Political Adviser Khrenkov summarized admirably: 'Give him a quick punch in the face and kick him out of the People's Commissariat of Transport.'

They were pleased: 'Your reports are documentary evidence of your social profile which, it must be said, is poor.'

How can they not wince when they harp on about my social

antecedents? It's obvious that they want to crush me morally, but what the hell. The result: it's all over. The acting company commander did a job but it is not being registered – he blew it, and that's that!!!! And here's the clincher. The head of the Third Section, after beating about the bush, comes out with:

'You need to quit the Armed Guards Unit.'

? !!?! ???

(Delighted to. Perhaps from tomorrow?)

'Were you recruited directly?'

'No, through the Gulag.'

'Well, that is more difficult. You will have to stay until the end of the project.'

That's the answer to how long our service is to last. There is an opportunity there, though, not to be missed. Nikolenko, my successor as platoon commander, is in a worse situation than I am. He is a member of the All-Union Communist Party (Bolsheviks).

I need to get out of here, and the sooner the better.

16 and 17 June 1936

Two days of meetings. The first is once again about the Stakhanovites and the acting heads, including, of course, me. Why are you undermining, misunderstanding, misrepresenting, etc. the Stakhanov movement? We'll let them go on at us for now. Krivoruchko refuses to supervise us.

'Not my kind of work, I couldn't cope, and I can't neglect my main work. I've only just taken on the platoon! I don't know the people, there's the escapes ...'

They cut him short.

'So you're refusing to work? Admit it!'

They are working on him as a YCL, and criticizing me, although not by name. That in itself is an easing of the situation, or a victory for me. A meeting with the political

136

commanders. My nerves are at breaking point. After Political Adviser Khrenkov's report (who kept butting in while Adjutant Kamushkin was speaking), someone remarks: 'We don't have enough guards.'

That is the nearest we get to support and a boost for my morale. Regarding my non-accommodation, they wriggle out of answering: 'We found him four places but he wouldn't accept any of them.'

Thanks for that. By then I was ready to weep. No point appealing to Company Commander Gridin, the political adviser or anyone else. My only option is to commit some crime.

While shaving, blood spurts from my face. I have no appetite and I feel nauseous. Every day brings new demonstrations of BAM virtuosity. Ogurtsov gets a bonus, which leads to a drunken binge and denunciations of him for failing to repay money borrowed from *zek* guards. Here I detect the hand of the political adviser and Gridin. Afanasiev is eager to join the Armed Guards Unit and is working at it, giving speeches the top brass like to hear and engaging in mild self-criticism. Everyone is very tense but afraid to speak out, which is probably diplomatic.

The 'soldiers of the track' are trusted more than us. If one of the prisoners makes a denunciation to the Third Section, they drag us in. One bitch got fired from the kitchen, claimed Afanasiev raped her, and now the lad is facing a court hearing. While she was working in the platoon kitchen, everybody used her. The political adviser of 1 Division denounced me, claiming I had said something out of turn. It's clear they are dumping non-Party members. There are three of us in the company. Have they made Bolsheviks of us? No. They cheered us up no end by noting that Brench was improving. Yes, he was developing from someone barely literate into a political instructor and then a divisional political adviser. What sense does that make? They could have made something out of me. That might have made sense.

18 June 1936

The latest joyous tidings: mass escape of five *zeks* from Phalanx 11. I feel like topping myself, but the cold light of reason tells me to wait. Sooner or later I'm going to get convicted, preferably sooner because then it will be over sooner. I am now openly on the warpath, cocked and ready to fire. Devyatkin just wants out too. He let a criminal group loose without a guard, despite earlier warnings.

Went to 1 Squad. There's something wrong with the way they work. Yershov says it's better to let five escape than not allow a brigade out to work. They have no transport to shift turf 4 km and their food is appalling. Of course they're protesting. I feel terrible, my thoughts are totally confused.

19 June 1936

We are being blamed for everything. Political Adviser Khrenkov hasn't been out to Phalanx 11. The guards are offended. The mass of the 'soldiers of the track' don't know him either as a Communist or as a political adviser. HQ hand down orders to complete this and that. Political Instructor Sergeyev confirms that the guards of Phalanx 11 are dissatisfied with Khrenkov. Sergeyev is also cheesed off that he is not getting firewood and that Pakhomov spends his time playing with the chief's children and does damn all else.

20, 21 and 22 June 1936

Life can't get back to normal because we don't have normality here. My legs are sore, rheumatism. At night I feed bedbugs. My memory is playing tricks, I can't remember what happened yesterday, the 21st. I went to the theatre. It was the usual provincial stuff. They changed costumes in a couple of seconds. It was complete ribald gibberish; for example, 'orders taken for children's felt boots made from their parents' hair' generated mirth and wild applause from the populace of Zavitaya.* That's the local culture for you, their understanding of high living.

Adjutant Kamushkin tries to make amends by asking, 'Well, did you jail drunken tailors and did my hypotheses prove correct?'

I reply drily, 'Yes.'

Things are no easier yet. I sat on the earth mound by the theatre and Kamushkin and his wife installed themselves opposite, talking to Lavrov.

Kamushkin commented loudly, 'Well, I don't think he is going to last long.'

He was referring to me. We'll see.

Escapes from Phalanx 11, and none of the top brass do anything other than talk, paying barely any attention. The unofficial reason was let slip by Khrenkov's wife.

'My husband and I should be in Moscow for the 7 November holiday.'

That's how it goes here, but what about reality? Khrenkov: 'We support shock-work tempos!' Khrenkov: 'We support all the camp activities!' He's a wolf in sheep's clothing.

You get so tired of this. It would be good to get away from the top brass by riding out round the phalanxes. Peace! Quiet! What a joy that would be!!!

23 June 1936

I went out to Phalanx 11, took the 44 as far as Bureya. The local operational group were nice to me. Nine *zeks* have taken off

---

* A joke classified advertisement circulating in the 1930s.

from Phalanx 6, Articles 56.17[*] and 59.3. Everything is upside down – the Third Section, the operational group, and we are all pulling in different directions. Choose one of two holes: a prison term or the grave (shoot yourself).

I catch a ride with a one and a half ton truck driving along a track between villages. It's lurching so much the only thing I can do is to lie flat. It's murderously hot and there's dust in my underwear. When it mixes with sweat, a thick layer forms on your face and stretches the skin. We go up hills, speed round bends in all directions, crazy. I'm so thirsty I feel sick, but there's no water anywhere. A stream provides relief. We drop off two agents, Kasumov and another whose name I don't know, and then arrive at Rodionovka.

I eat bread with milk. Morozov goes back to the truck. There are two agents to search, and me on my own.

Strange, charred trees. A hunter's lodge, a second, third, fourth. Two men move away but come back and sit down. I go over. They're agents. The road must lead to Tyukan but forks in two directions. Which to take?

Blyukher Collective Farm. Traditional Chinese huts. The stove chimney goes underground and leads to a dry tree smeared with clay 10 m away from the huts. In the hut, the top of the stove takes up half the room and serves as a table, bed, and anything they need. In the left corner is a pit with a firebox in it. No mugs. The only crockery is shared bowls.

It starts raining. It's 12 km to Tyukan and it's ten at night. We're soaked through, but we're marching at speed so still feel warm. I'm furious about everything. If we catch them, I'll kill them. We reach the track, but don't know where we are. From Irkun to Tyukan is 6 km + 45 km and the rain seems heavy enough to make your bones go soggy. Tyukan. The signal is

[*] Article 56.17 covered felony.

green. Oh, don't let me miss the train! Will it stop, or even slow down enough for me to get on? There's coal burning on the platform, someone will put it out. I hear whispering in the bushes.

It must be who we are looking for. If I go over and try to arrest them they will just run away and I can't see in the pitch-dark. I look out for a wagon. There. Open, loaded with coal. I climb in, listen. The train whistles. One climbs in, a second, a third. I stay silent, climb up higher, and get my pistol out. A guard shines a torch round the inside and I see them. They might be the ones from Phalanx 6.

So, no sleep tonight. Cramp and aching in my legs. I'm black from the coal and can feel the dust working into my pores. The *zeks* sleep soundly, snoring, but I'm on duty. I get out at Zavitaya as black as the devil, go to the operations post and they muddle the names. Sure enough, they're from Phalanx 6. It's 4 a.m. All thanks to the Third Section. It happens.

The phalanx leader requests permission to transfer *zeks* from Phalanx 17 to 6, presents a list. Toryaev on reception authorizes it, Yepifanov confirms, and off the villains go without a guard. We, meaning the Third Section, 're-educated' them and there's the result. Ten scarpered. The episode doesn't strengthen my position, even though I warned the divisional commander about the contingent the day before. What action did he take? None.

24 and 25 June 1936

I spend half the day waiting at the station for the express bringing firewood and timber then go to Phalanx 11. I walk, photographing the scenery along the way. At the phalanx I run into the section head and Gridin. I spend half the day walking round the huts. There's a lot of talk, noise and hot air. Brilliant ideas and hopes abound, and all the while the place leaks *zeks*. Adjutant Kamushkin tries hard to persuade me I am wrong to think everybody is out to get me, and says I should stop scowling. In parting, he shakes my hand firmly, communicating friendly concern, and adds, 'So everything's all right, then?'

I'm not getting enough sleep. Not a single escape today. Incredible! That is good, but I feel no inner peace. I don't manage to do any sketching; trek from Phalanx 11 in sheeting rain.

26 June 1936

I'm sick at heart. Everyone is talking about the end of the project. The hired workers are gradually being dismissed. I'm so envious. Kamushkin is surprised that I have learned that it makes better sense to let twenty people leave without a guard than enter 'Task delayed' in the Armed Guards Unit's work record.

I had quite a conversation with Torpan, recalling escapes and killings. We went out into the *taiga* looking for escapees and found scattered corpses. Who killed them? When? Nobody has any idea who these people were. If someone gets on your nerves and you take a shot at them, you just leave them where they fell. If someone finds them, fine. If they don't, they're dead anyway. Here's an example:

'Bugayev went out to the forest and brought back one that he caught. The other one he shot. The one he shot, clean through his chest, crawled back 35 km. We didn't go out looking for him, of course. He rotted out there for twelve days.'

27 June 1936

The guards sometimes deliberately let *zeks* escape, saying [illegible] officially that they'll live and get paid better as forced labourers than they do as guards. The top brass just can't, or won't, see that. So far we have peace and quiet in our company, but in 12 and 13 they're losing fifty to sixty people a day. You reread these lines and wonder: was that all life had to offer today? 'Fraid so.

Great sunset, but it's not for us. It's just unsettling. Its beauty doesn't inspire good thoughts and reflection, but bad. It's good that the head of combat and I have the same rank. Makes it easier for us. Otherwise we'd do ourselves in.

28 June 1936

What have I had to celebrate today? The one high point is that I have moved in with the head of combat from my storage cupboard, and my head aches because it feels so amazing to be in a real room where it doesn't leak and where I can feel at home. I can hardly believe it's possible to live so well.

My heart is still coated in a residue of disgust and the room only emphasizes the sheer nastiness of living and serving at BAM.

Outside there's rain and mud up to your knees. The clay sticks to your boots and you can barely lift your feet. So that was my day, but it is also worthy of note that I got no supper. The guards are saying that the project will actually take about another twenty years. Grinevich. Adjutant Kamushkin reports through the head of combat that they've now found me a room. As unacceptable as the others, I expect.

1 July 1936

For some, this is their day off but I am deputed to trek out to Phalanx 11. You have to talk the same nonsense every time. People ignore you, snap back at you resentfully, and that's how I feel too, completely fed up with everything. Everywhere there is moral exhortation but no practical help. The same old mistakes and shortcomings are repeated year after year and nothing gets any better.

I'm sick, sick at heart, completely worn out, at daggers drawn with the top brass.

2 July 1936

If only the weather would clear up. It's as dull as autumn, and cold at night. Summer is passing unnoticed, just like life in this place. The days are empty, and filling the emptiness with work, BAM work? No, I just can't do it. To wish on yourself something you can't bear to see and hear, you would have to be an idiot.

Queues in the canteen. Spent forty-five minutes today waiting. Yershov comes barging in, helps himself and that's all fine. Will that be all, sir?

Khodzko jumped when I asked, 'Who's in charge of this queue?'

Gurko is quietly beavering away, making suitcases and beds, presumably for the brass. Just try saying anything about it!

3 July 1936

Well, here's a joke. Tsvetkov, the secretary of the Kamchatka Company, shares his impressions of the work of a commissioner:

In Phalanx 4 all the workers are Stakhanovites, working seventeen hours a day. Even more original is Phalanx 18, linked to 4. In Phalanx 18 they have savings amounting to several thousand rubles, direct costs are low, and the Plan has been overfulfilled 107–140 per cent with only thirty Stakhanovites. The five-man committee has castigated the commissioner for this. Phalanx 4 has overrun its budget, has high direct costs, and has not fulfilled the Plan, but there are lots of Stakhanovites, so everything is fine. The foreman of Phalanx 4, a Tatar, took due note of the situation. Tsvetkov bumped into him and, when he asked why he was in such a hurry, he said:

'You don't get criticized for failing to fulfil the Plan but you do get into trouble for not having enough Stakhanovites. I'm

144

rushing to make more of them, every one of my people will be a Stakhanovite.'

Four more *zeks* have escaped from Phalanx 11. Divisional Commander Inyushkin, on behalf of Company Commander Gridin, has ordered me to go and live in the phalanx. He can forget that! Devyatkin doesn't want to work and deliberately drags his heels, and the company commander doesn't cancel the *zeks*' credits because he's afraid the head of security will find out the actual situation in the company.

There are rumours we'll be here until May 1937. Wonderful! And Khrenkov's wife will be here even longer.

4 July 1936
There's no electricity. We sit by candlelight.

There are rumours we'll be here until May 1937. In Phalanx 11 everything is shambolic. The site foreman has no idea what he's doing and the workforce are in total disarray.

Yesterday I sent twenty-nine workers to Tyukan and it turned out there was nothing for them to do there. Meanwhile, at the turf site there's no one to cut the turf and people are standing idle. Foreman Gusarov is drunk all the time. They are deliberately disrupting the Stakhanov movement. In the report they wrote nothing about intending to fulfil the July Plan. People are being eaten alive by bedbugs. The medical unit does nothing about it, and Yershov's tone seems to have changed.

The fact that we took the billiard table has so incensed Adjutant Kamushkin that he has conveyed, through Lavrov: 'Now I see the true face of Chistyakov. What kind of petty bourgeois ideas and actions are we getting from him? He made it out of BAM materials, used the workshop, and paid for none of it.'

Came back from Phalanx 11 on the Young Pioneer railcar. It moved at speed, catching up with a freight train. You get a

145

pleasant breeze. The twenty-minute ride distracted me, but not for long. Even in that short time for reflection I was mostly pondering how to get discharged. That's the life I live.

5 July 1936

Pasenko, the divisional political adviser, had us in stitches telling us how Brench explained the word 'aggregate': 'It means the chief of all the combine-harvester engineers.'

Trusting his definition, the group leaders left to pass on this heresy to their squads.

Afanasiev is in raptures over how the propaganda brigade's balalaika player renders 'The Moon is Shining', drumming on the body of the instrument and twirling and twisting it:

'I've never seen a musician to rival him!'

Well, where could he? Unless he saw one at the annual village fair. Such is the sophistication and education of divisional commanders and political advisers. In the evening he will be reporting to the five-man inspection committee.

In the canteen, Kamushkin, speaking loudly to make sure I hear, tells Yershov, 'If he's not prepared to work, he must be removed.'

I write a letter of resignation. Let's see where that gets me.

I sent someone to his apartment to invite Lavrov for a game of volleyball. He's missing his wife. No word from her for a month, or maybe ever again. She doesn't fancy a trip to the Far East Region, and is perfectly able to remarry.

My letter is being talked about: 'He wants to get back to Moscow!' says Kamushkin. 'He can earn 300 rubles there and have a good time.'

Paskevich replied, 'We should invite him to play volleyball. Is he a Party member?'

Political Adviser Khrenkov pipes up, 'He was expelled from the Party.'

6 July 1936

I went to confession today. Khrenkov and Kamushkin have decided to sort me out, and how. Political adviser:

'What's this? Your latest tantrum?'

I asked what he was talking about.

'Your letter of resignation, of course. First you call your bonus a bribe, then you tell the guards you'd rather face a court hearing than serve at BAM. You are revealing your class allegiance. I look at your face and don't like the allegiance I see there.'

Then Kamushkin piles in: 'You are disrespectful of your superiors. You leaned your elbows on the table and didn't even stand up when I gave you an order.'

Khodzko, head of the Third Section, denies he ever suggested I should resign.

Lavrov wriggles, insinuating that I tend to exaggerate. They have probably already been briefed on how I am to be dealt with.

Khrenkov adds, 'You are conditioning Lavrov to your own way of thinking. The definitive response to your application is this: you were conscripted into the army. If you had not been drafted into security you would have been enlisted into a regular unit. We will therefore not accept your resignation, and you will not return to Moscow.'

Sergeyev has been in Zavitaya since lunch but does not visit the platoon, saying something about Phalanx 11. But who is the stool pigeon now reporting to the political officer? Perhaps Sergeyev, or Pasenko, of course. An ambitious commander or someone else? Perhaps even Lavrov? I feel like shooting myself. My head is splitting and my rheumatism is acting up. The weather is diabolical, rain, mud, devil knows what.

But what a bastard Khodzko is! He denied everything he had said about my resigning.

7 July 1936

Two more gone from Phalanx 11. When will this ever end? If I'm supposed to be here for the rest of my life, the only way out is to get a criminal conviction. Company commander Gridin has replaced some of the guards at Phalanx 11 and it's made damn all difference to the escapes. I go with Nikolenko to receive Phalanxes 3 and 25. He asks, 'How's it going?' I feel really ill. After lunch I have to slog, sort things, find things out. The guards must be laughing at us rushing around, knowing it won't make the slightest difference.

8 July 1936

I probably will, in the end, like it or not, have to take leave of life by myself. Seven escapees from Phalanx 11. Spend all day trying to catch them. My nerves are so stretched I don't feel the rain or the branches hitting my face. Everything seems unreal, including life. I pass my days under intolerable strain, waiting only for the next disaster. I'm dog tired after walking 50 km, and when I get back to HQ the top brass have a little surprise for me.

Divisional Political Adviser Rodionov calls me in and demands, 'Do you even know what's going on at your Phalanx 11? What are you doing here?! Go straight back.'

Night, 11 p.m., rain. I'm mentally exhausted, endless quizzing. How about jumping off a train in the dark? I could maybe break my limbs, cripple myself. No. I reply that I am not going back right now.

Divisional Commander Inyushkin, standing beside me interjects, 'I'm just back from Phalanx 6 and the mood there is exactly the same, everybody says we'll be in court soon.'

That's down to the influence of the platoon commander. Rodionov orders me to accompany Inyushkin to Phalanx 11, but he too refuses to go there in the night.

To me, Rodionov adds, 'You are not educating the guards, you are not doing your job.'

I wonder what the political adviser is here for if not to educate the guards. I got so angry I thought I was having a heart attack, didn't want to eat or sleep. So what has today brought? A declaration to the Armed Guards HQ that this platoon commander is a class enemy, doesn't obey orders, and that his crimes have been witnessed by Divisional Commander Inyushkin and Divisional Political Adviser Rodionov. That's the legal situation, and the way the court will view it.

9 July 1936

Like it or not, whether it makes sense or not, 'Get back to Phalanx 11!' So I do. Rain, cold. The divisional commander, political officer, me, the whole gang. I am summoned to Zavitaya, to the Organization and Staffing Section. I wonder what Inyushkin's going to come out with there. Escorting the political officer to Tyukan, I hear him say:

'I am a Communist, do you think I enjoy working in security? You are all the same. If you were allowed to resign where would you go? What are you capable of?'

10 July 1936

Endless meetings. They're scheduled for 9 a.m. but Naftaliy Frenkel arrives, or rather just puts his head round, so we're kept waiting till 1 p.m.* Reprimands and political rhetoric.

After dinner another meeting and a movie, *The Tailor from Torzhok.*†

Only, oh, silent horror, the movie has more breaks than film.

---

* Naftaliy Aronovich Frenkel (1883–1960), convicted in 1924 of fraud, released early. From 1927 worked for the OGPU–NKVD–Ministry of Internal Affairs. He came to prominence during construction of the White Sea Canal in 1934–7 and was in charge of the Baikal–Amur Mainline railway project. See Irina Shcherbakova's Introduction, [p.xiii].

† *The Tailor from Torzhok* (1925), Soviet silent film. A comedy directed by Yakov Protazanov.

Orlov is doing his best for us 'active' non-Party members. I ask for a funeral march to accompany the film and suggest it must have been shot during a solar eclipse with the tailor cutting the film himself. Nothing helps. There's a general sigh of relief when the lights finally go up again.

11 July 1936

You have to authorize your own days off or do without. I sketch at the quarry but my soul is full of gloom and garbage.

After lunch, Political Adviser Rodionov from 1 Division comes into the room. Oh, these subtle approaches. He's an envoy. Well, sniff out what you've come for. I get a pep talk about the need to complete the Second Track, after which I can leave, and: 'You'll go back to Moscow, go to the movies and Park of Culture.'

In order not to say anything unwise, I greet him by expressing surprise a divisional political adviser should call in on a mere platoon commander.

Are they collecting evidence against me? Life is rife with paranoia. You can't help losing your balance and going crazy. Your head gets muddled. It's chaos.

12 July 1936

Read yesterday in *Izvestiya* about the errors of paedology in educational research. The other commanders gradually move away from me, unable to understand what it's all about.* Fine commanders!

A lot of what is said in an article titled 'Ignorance' is directly applicable to Rodionov. Yershov admits he is at fault, not having opened the complaints boxes for the past two months.

* The reference is probably to a 1936 decree of the Central Committee of the Communist Party, 'On Paedological Perversity in the System of the People's Commissariat of Enlightenment'.

These commanders have a job for life. There are still plenty of opportunities in the USSR where young professionals are put off by the working conditions and nobody else wants to work there. Still, how come a platoon political instructor, a divisional political adviser and a company political adviser have between them failed to educate the guards of Phalanx 11?

13 July 1936
This is a brilliant place to put a penal phalanx. The train slows down when it has to go uphill, so any number of people can pile on without it stopping. Where it does stop, it doesn't take on passengers. For example, after I've been playing volleyball, when my entire body aches and I need some rest, I still have to trek on foot all the way to Phalanx 11. My boots have lasted 0.5 months and are wearing thin. Rodionov, travelling with me on a goods train, volunteers his opinion:

'I've written to Krylov and Shedvid and the Centre about how we are treated and all the disgraceful things that go on.'*

He starts wondering aloud whether we will finish soon. That suggests he has no information.

Then he says, to encourage me, 'It will probably all be over by November.'

He would like to get back to Moscow as well.

Political Instructor Sergeyev decides to put his foot down: 'Either I play volleyball right now or I never will again. What's the meaning of substituting Tishchenko, who's a guard, for me?'

The meaning is that Sergeyev is totally useless at volleyball.

14 July 1936
This is how they classify people: 'Obedient, carries out orders unquestioningly, docile as a calf', in other words, just the kind

* Oskar Vladimirovich Shedvid, head of the Third Section of the Gulag, deputy head of BAM, was executed by shooting on 28 August 1938.

of commander that's needed. They could have added 'terrified of the top brass'.

15 and 16 July 1936
I keep forgetting everything. My head is bursting because of the escapes and general disasters. I ride to 6 but then walk from Bureya to 8 and back. My legs hurt. I'm continually being followed. Bezrodny lets slip that the political instructor is asking when I became a platoon commander, what courses I taught, and so on.

Fine, spy on me to your heart's content.

I'm drenched to the skin.

I get the impression the company is literally falling to pieces. The guards are degenerating, the *zeks* and hired workers too, and injections of indoctrination soon wear off. They've stripped Chaika, stripped Tsirkunevich. [Illegible] Zhusov is in the cells, Pakhomov is said to be short of 10,000 rubles for uniforms. The top brass haven't gone unnoticed either.

In *On Guard at BAM* they've written that Political Adviser Khrenkov is taking things too easy. Whichever newspaper you pick up, whatever you read, you find people learning new things, motivation, life. But here? The devil knows what kind of people we select, just illiterates, which is why the top brass are the way they are. So, they are collecting evidence against me. Meanwhile, people keep escaping from the phalanx. Neither the company commander or divisional commander have managed to do a damned thing about it. I'm so used to the idea of landing in court and living in a phalanx as a *zek* that it seems a natural and inevitable progression.

17 and 18 July 1936
At Territory 11 I give a reading of Kalinin's speech about the new constitution. No interest from the *zeks*. They heckle me:

'We never get any time off, if it's not talks it's meetings and we only get paid 200 to 250 rubles.'

The guards look at the prisoners enviously, and sometimes say openly, 'We'd be better off doing the labour than walking around with a bludgeon. It's less hassle and you aren't responsible for anything.'

There is a meeting at the divisional commander's. You look at all those political officers and remember what Meshkov [illegible] said:

'Hell, what's left!? I might as well go into security.'

Who else would have you? Your market price would be 100 rubles.

Here's a picture of the barber's at BAM.* They shave you and use eau de cologne, sprinkle it up your nose and over half your face, but at least you get to appreciate the scent.

Armed Guard Vedernikov from 1 Platoon also says, 'Damned if I'm going to stay in security – send me to court for all I care, I'm not playing this game any more.'

In the evening I'm back at Phalanx 11.

The *zeks* are not stupid, they're beaten and intimidated by admin. The staff only have to threaten to cut their quota fulfilment record, deny them the credits they're due, and they're reduced to animals. The top brass are cold-shouldering me. They'll cook something up, and the sooner the better.

Legs ache, rheumatism. Every day I cover a good 15 km. I can't bear to think that this might go on for a lifetime, or even a year. I'll just keep going and do what it takes not to get stuck here in security. *On Guard at BAM* confirms how Khrenkov works. He is 'taking things too easy'.

19 and 20 July 1936
No, I have to get out of this life, and the sooner the better. I suffer from incessant nervous tension, an eternal emptiness.

* Unfortunately, the photograph is missing.

Being stultified to the point of disability makes staying in the Armed Guards Unit worse than going mad. Time to terminate this slow, inquisitorial invasive mental murder, to end it instantly. Guard Voznyuk, though once a *zek* himself, has taken to battering prisoners with his rifle butt in full view of everyone. They're too soft with the *zeks*. The materials the educators use are too difficult, and they research and re-educate the many 'soldiers of the track' from the safety of their offices, without knowing the reality.

Here's an opinion from Valyi: 'Your commanders have come up through the ranks of squad commanders. They know nothing, can't see beyond the rulebook, and interpret the regulations in their own, crude ways.'

Will it be any wonder if I quietly, or perhaps violently, go out of my mind before I get released? They've brought firefighters into security and told Deputy Platoon Commander Khomenko to get them up to speed. The top brass didn't say a word about it to me. They've disbanded the operational group, transferred the men to me, and taken away the hired volunteer guards, referring to some supposed order from the Third Section. Torpan let slip that they want to put Marzlyak and the others in the punishment cells. Quite an action plan.

21 July 1936

An operational meeting, another working through of the order, with a reminder that this is the last time. The usual indoctrination.

Typically, they don't address anything to me, the platoon commander. Everything is directed at Political Instructor Sergeyev. Adjutant Kamushkin says, 'Yes, Comrade Sergeyev, absolutely correct, Comrade Sergeyev!' and so on.

Actually, the very first question was addressed to me by the head of the Third Section.

'Why are you late? Do you expect to be issued a special invitation, Comrade Chistyakov?'

I replied that I came as soon as I was phoned. I was at Lavrov's. This sort of farce should have gone out of fashion with the tsarist army.

When Brench spoke, he said, 'As soon as we leave this meeting, we'll forget everything said here.'

Khodzko chimed in, 'Good for you, Brench – it is absolutely true that as soon as you leave the meeting you will forget everything.'

The words could be straight out of *Capital Overhaul*.* Tsarist officers questioning an accused sailor ask, 'It is true, then, that you said the officers, the "bastards", deserve a beating?' Reply: 'Correct, Your Excellency, that is what we said. You bastards deserve a beating!'

Another comic turn. The political adviser accuses me of sketching and taking photographs and so on. That I am going on tour round the phalanxes, leaving in the morning and coming back in the evening, and that during that time I am sketching and taking photographs, and therefore not working.

Everyone is calling for well-rounded commanders, and here I am. They are mired in their own stupidity and narrow-mindedness and think everyone else should be too. It's true that Political Adviser Khrenkov has found his place in life, and good luck to him, but BAM is no place for me, no job in security is, no matter where. A narrow-minded commander is a boil that needs to be lanced.

Lavrov rides over: 'If they made you an offer to be a good commander until the end of the project, after which they would let you resign, would you agree?'

I said, 'No.'

* A play by Leonid Sobolev, written in 1932, about the deterioration of the tsarist navy.

At night the cramp in my legs was so bad I thought I would die. It rains every day, mud and sludge.

22 July 1936

I ride to Phalanx 11 on the railcar with Medintsev, the Third Section commissioner. He tells me, 'At Phalanx 28 I put a prisoner into the punishment cells one winter. Kept him three months without charge on 300 grams of bread a day, and sometimes without water. I ordered the guard to restrict his exercise, and made sure he didn't get too much sleep or firewood. He wasn't supposed to be at a holiday resort! I got in a bit of hot water over that, because I nearly finished him off, he was just skin and bones, could barely say "Mum!" through his mouth or nose.'

23 July 1936

Torpan in Phalanx 6 is little better.

'I was with Phalanx Leader Sivukha at one point. Sometimes I dished out punishment my way. Smash one of 'em in the face in front of everyone, blood everywhere. The convicts didn't mind, didn't snitch. They opened an investigation and called one of them in: "Did the duty officer ever hit you?" "What? Hit me? No! He'd never lay a finger on us!" They all said the same. When I had to get them out to work, I'd go straight up to the top bunks: "Right, are you parasites going out to work?" They would all chorus, "On our way!" They would just attack Sivukha with a plank.'

At Phalanx 6 I come across Commissioner Morozov from the Third Section. He has no time for political morale-boosting. I am trying to encourage the guards by telling them that the end of the project is in sight and we just need to keep to our orders, but he butts in:

'I don't care what Grishakova says, she won't be going any-where. She'll be working exactly as she is now.'

He swears his head off, trying to show that the guards count for nothing.

'You can write as much as you like, nothing's going to happen to Grishakova. It's none of your business and none of ours.'

Nothing is being said about me, they avoid mentioning my name, consciously or not, but say things that hint at me.

Adjutant Kamushkin: 'The situation is unsatisfactory with Krivoruchko and perhaps someone else,' and that sort of stuff. They manage things without leaving their office, offer no practical support.

An example. In front of Kamushkin, a guard fires at a prisoner running away through the compound and a *zek* shouts, 'Missed! Try again!' Kamushkin's reaction? Nothing. When someone rather urgently raises the question of the use of firearms in this situation, he smoothly avoids the question.

Khodzko says bluntly, 'We need to withdraw these sawn-off firearms before the devil knows how many people get killed!'

I would very much like to hear, even just once, our superior officers do something other than issue orders for disciplinary action or threaten us with the Revtribunal, to see them doing something practical and helpful. How about some political rhetoric, some morale-boosting: 'Each one of you, when this project is completed, will be remembered.'

I think what will actually happen is that some will be kicked out, some transferred to other camps and, as the icing on the cake, we'll be told, 'Certain of your number have had a negative, criminal attitude to this project!'

I have come to the conclusion that no matter what I do, it will all end badly and the sooner I get it over with the better. Our section's Plan has not been fulfilled for four months in a row. Is that evidence of outstanding leadership? Divisional Political

Adviser Rodionov is half asleep and under reprimand from the Third Section.

At least Khodzko in the Third Section is now acknowledging that Moskvin and Golubev have been playing games, carried away by their pursuit of lozenges for their collar tabs, and that they released and redeployed career criminals to guard-free phalanxes to 'incentivize' them.

Once again, I'm being blamed for the escapes from Phalanx 11. They are saying outright it is all Chistyakov's fault and he should be put on trial. Then they add, slamming a fist down on the table, 'You should condemn him yourselves! It's a matter of your attitude to your work. These figures will reach the Third Section and they will draw their own conclusions. He is not willing to work. That is all there is to it. What is going on? You, Comrade Kamushkin, will have to explain yourself over the fiasco at Phalanx 11. You have not taken this matter seriously, you have failed to create, whether deliberately or not, I don't know . . . but heads will roll!'

It's enough to tell the likes of Krivoruchko and Sergeyev in the political section, 'You are showing vigilance,' for them to purr with pleasure.

One minute they're all in favour of a certain measure, the next they're against it, until you haven't a clue what is right and what is wrong.

Brench, afraid he may be expelled from the Party, tries to save his own skin by blaming everything on me in the hope of advancing his career and showing how ideologically sound he is:

'The platoon commander does not live at Phalanx 11 and shows little enthusiasm for his job.'

At Phalanx 19 new people are received by a common criminal while the commander and deputy platoon commander go off in search of fun, wearing white tunics.

Khodzko: 'A right pair.'

Krivoruchko: 'In 1 Platoon the guards are walking around in plimsolls. They have no suitable footwear and will soon be refusing to work.'

The reason for Divisional Political Adviser Rodionov's surprise visit to our apartment has also become apparent. Khrenkov let the cat out of the bag:

'Chistyakov paints, he takes a palette with him to the phalanxes and spends half his time on that. He's a photographer.'

Plug: 'I have to admit the camp is a disgrace. I have travelled from Urulga to Tamarchukan and nowhere have I seen anything comparable to what we see here.'

Khodzko responds that Plug is a walking embodiment of opportunism.

24, 25 and 26 July 1936
I was woken at 2.30 a.m. At Phalanx 11 a hut has collapsed, crushing people. I get on the railcar and head out. It's a lot of fuss over nothing. One person has scratches, but only minor. I don't remember anything else, it's all confused.

27 July 1936
Amazingly, there have been no new escapes from Phalanx 11 for three days. I conducted classes on how to prepare a rifle for firing, and the new agricultural tax law.

I walked the track from Tyukan to Deya. Everything in order. There's great news waiting for me in Zavitaya: eleven escapes from Phalanx 11, eight while under guard by Zhusman, who fell asleep on the track. If the whole lot had wanted to escape they could have, and taken his rifle with them into the bargain.

Is there a connection here? They gave him 100 rubles and he let them escape?

I'm summoned by the head of the Third Section and, of

course, he immediately starts barking. I'm so nervous, my stomach is upset. I ask permission to sit down. Granted.

'Let's deal with the escape and then come back. We need to talk.'

What about? Is he not sufficiently informed about my mood and desires? Or perhaps someone else wants to hear about me from him, in which case it's better to keep my mouth shut.

I spend all day hunting escapees, barely able to move my legs. No lunch or dinner. Walking through the forest from Tyukan to Rodionovka takes it out of you. I'm disguised as a convict, not even our agents would recognize me. I travel back on a goods train with a hired worker who is leaving Phalanx 11. Not recognizing me, he says:

'The bastards have driven us into the ground and never let us out of the phalanx. But we earn good money. The criminal convicts make extra on the side. They ask the commander to let them out to Zavitaya, and then come back with stacks of cash.'

I ask, 'What's in it for the commander?'

Evasive reply that civilian workers are paid 204 rubles a month, but the *zek* foot soldiers are on the breadline and only get 14 rubles, barely enough for tobacco.

'Still, we can buy good cigarettes on 300 rubles and get something to eat. You give something to the guards sometimes, they're human too.'

I just have to get out, through a conviction if need be. If you're sentenced you at least know how long you've got to serve.

4 August 1936

No time to write anything. Persecuted, scared, escapes from 11, review such a shambles you wouldn't believe it.

On 28 July the local NKVD was organizing a sports competition, first in Zavitaya and then at district level. No preparation, no athletes, no stadium. They urged me to compete in the 100 m and 1,000 m. I was going to be brilliant in the 100 m without a single training session.

Golubev drove by the District Department in a cab and drunk out of his mind. Real athletes, these! There's no physical education or sport in Zavitaya, nowhere to practise, no stadium, not even a sports ground.

The sports competition didn't happen, someone somewhere cancelled it the night before. They play volleyball in Phalanx 8 and I practise starts on the stone-hard clay track in the yard. I tried it outside, dire! Potholes, bricks, sticks, no turns, sharp corners.

Tsvetkov, when asked why he is giving Golubev a hard time, replies, 'He's messing about: Khodzko puts someone in the cells then Golubev lets him out; he doesn't come to meetings, just sits in his office like a lone wolf and complains, "I've been deprived of my vote."'

The company is a complete shambles and the entire Audit and Distribution Unit should be in the cells. They've forged documents: one from the group leader releasing prisoners using the signatures of Khodzko and Tsvetkov, and documents for another three.

Lavrov tells me, 'Adjutant Kamushkin invited Political Adviser Khrenkov to attend a meeting of the Organization and Staffing Section. He replied, "No way! To hell with them and the other five!"' He only turned up to the second half of the meeting.

Divisional Commander Inyushkin again orders me to come out to Phalanx 11. We have another heart-to-heart. Sergeyev has denounced me to him, saying that I'm still disobeying orders.

Why can't these people just understand that I am the wrong person for this job, so the sensible thing would be to replace me, send me to a different platoon, or think of something, anything else?

What measures have the top brass taken to stop the escapes? None. Their only solution is to tell me to go and live there, and everything will sort itself out.

I arrive at Phalanx 11 with the divisional commander and have a talk with the guards. Inyushkin listens but doesn't have anything to say.

On 1 August, I conduct a review meeting. Khodzko from the Third Section is present, and comments, 'You're good at that!'

I couldn't tell if he meant it or was just trying to be encouraging.

Back to the District Youth Section. The girls get on their marks and the instructor tells them, 'You need to take off at speed, leaving both your arms behind.'

These would-be sportsmen!

Every day there is some disaster in the canteen. Some days we wait hours for the cook, some days he's ill, or the server hasn't arrived, or someone's holding a meeting there and we have to wait. I am sliding further and further downhill, getting increasingly jumpy, and losing weight. I don't know how it will end. Everyone is counting the days till the project is over. They just want to get away, but won't say it where it can be heard.

Political Instructor Golodnyak arrived and made his report. He appeared at the review sporting a new lozenge on his collar tabs from the Armed Guards Unit HQ, and gave such a dreadful speech I shot him down and showed him up for the fool he is.

Settled weather, four days with no rain. I put Political Instructor Sergeyev in his place in front of Golodnyak and Ogurtsov:

'You're an informer, are you?'

He answered that he was only replying to Inyushkin, who had asked why I had not gone out as ordered.

Who makes the laws that specify you get three days off in

the month, ought to work eighteen hours a day, and get paid pocket money like a little child? What sort of republic is this?

5 August 1936

Back, inevitably, to Phalanx 11. A contingent of fifty prisoners is being sent to Phalanx 12. It should be quieter now, but we'll see. There's no escort. I take two armed guards and a dog-handler guard as a guide, and arm myself to the teeth: truncheon, revolver, a pistol in my pocket. The wretches get as far as Tyukan and want to stop. Very well, if you really want to spend the night without a campfire and with the mosquitoes. It's a cold night, but fortunately a moon lights it. Three guards rotate on sentry duty. I don't sleep as there's no one to relieve me. The guards and guide each get two hours' rest.

Not a single train stops. It's risky to take them by train to Zavitaya at night anyway, they'll jump out on the uphill stretches. I have plenty to think over. *Zeks* sing their prison camp songs, which aren't devoid of poetry and realism. They're typically anti-Soviet.

A Chinaman is asked, 'What's it like in a Russian prison camp?' He replies, 'Beds good for some, floors bad for some.'*

'I'll tell you about my red letter days,' one sings, listing all the miseries of life in the camp: a bullet from the guards, the cold, the bad gruel, and the hard labour from sunrise to sunset.

I brought the contingent to Zavitaya. They want to buy bread, they want to buy rolls, they want to buy this and that. I treat them humanely, let them make their purchases. They buy two half-litres of vodka. Well, it's too late to stop them. They'll make a fuss if I try to confiscate it, I'll get it off them on the next stretch. The train takes us back beyond Tyukan to a place we can stop. One half-litre bottle goes flying out on to the

---

* In Russian, 'Komu nary khorosho, komu niza plokho', which can also be understood as 'Communards good, Communism bad'.

embankment. I keep an eye open for the other, and when they start drinking from it I take it off them, and, after a struggle, empty it out and smash the bottle.

Bureya. It's hot. They sit down near the station wailing, 'We're thirsty! Water!' Kingpin Borisov is the group leader. When we reach Malinovka he stops and the rest of the group stop too.

'Hey, boss man, let us buy some booze, then I'll keep moving!'

I relent, with the intention of moving the group on and then smashing Borisov's vodka bottle. I put Grishitsky in charge, a gunsmith temporarily promoted to NKVD agent. They insist on walking by the river. All right, I think, wait till I've got you outside the village, then I'll show you what hot is.

Greybeard Kostyuchenko throws his things down on the riverbank and insists: 'Stop! Let us have a swim!'

I put a cartridge in the chamber and they move on. How quickly [illegible] load their pistols. Just wait! We reach the phalanx safely. When we get there they insist on bathing. I agree. The heat takes it out of you, especially after a night with no sleep. Everybody is drenched in sweat. It's not just our throats that are dry but our stomachs too, and the dust rasps.

6 August 1936

That crook Dovbysh is up to something. The *zeks* bring him potatoes dug up from the plots of the hired workers and he accepts them. Aizenberg says Dovbysh may have taken a bribe to let the prisoners out. The food is consistently unspeakable. The meat is rotten, the macaroni musty. The top brass think only about themselves. Gridin got two extra rations from HQ, had some boots made for him, sold them when they didn't fit and had a new pair made. Pakhomov and Burov helped. Pakhomov was caught with the boots at the market. Why does nobody care

Zek with pickaxe. *BAM – the Second Track*

Zeks eating in the open. *BAM – the Second Track*

about the guards walking around in plimsolls, bootless, sleeping in attics, ragged?

7 August 1936
Three escapes from the territory. Dovbysh bought a stolen watch, confiscated the money he'd paid and put the receipt in his pocket. Minkov passes on what Guard Zhusman said: 'Some time I'm going to let them all go to the bathhouse, get boisterous, steal each other's clothes and beat each other up.'

Platoon Commander Ogurtsov warns me, 'Watch your back, stay alert! They want to put you on trial. Khrenkov is insisting, but Khodzko is wavering for and against you.'

What's that about? Is Ogurtsov trying to encourage me to act conscientiously, or does he feel his position in the Party is insecure and wants to use me? People like Slenin never want to leave BAM: 'What could I do? Thieve? Where would I go? No, I'm better off in the camps. Perhaps they'll send me for accordion lessons.'

I received a circular from the Central Red Army Club, and once again it brought back, with devastating force, the reality of my life at BAM. Slenin wants to be nowhere else. His one aim in life is to learn the accordion. Since coming to the camp his singing has certainly improved.

They will be in raptures over people like Slenin: 'The camps have given this man a new life, enabled him to find his vocation,' and so on.

What vocation has BAM offered me? A career in crime? Despair has become a habit. My whole life in the camps is a tale of despair, and I've stopped believing that anything else is possible.

8 August 1936
Phalanx 11 has been moved back to its old location. It should be to the good to have them closer, but I will get more 'talking

to' and threats. Lighting is to be installed somewhere at some point. The nights are dark and invite escapes. What are the top brass thinking, and what do they think with? Everything can always be blamed on the platoon commander.

The division is asking for character references on Devyatkin. I reply that we can't help, we have no right to provide that sort of information.

'Just let us have it!'

That proves the division does not know its own commanders.

I'm at Phalanx 11 till late evening; go to bed without supper, my entire body aching. Rain again. We saw no sign of summer, neither in terms of good weather nor of fruit and vegetables. What a life!

I want to play sport, to learn about radio, I want to work at my real profession, study, keep up with metals technology and try it out in practice. Live among educated people, go to the theatre and cinema, to lectures and museums and exhibitions. I want to sketch. Ride a motorbike, and then perhaps sell it and buy one of those catapult-launched gliders and fly.

Khrenkov and the maniacs like him are welcome to the Armed Guards Unit. There's no end to the things I'd like to do. Is any of it possible here? No. Freedom will have to be won with blood, at the cost of my health, a chunk out of my life, and what I value most. By serving time, by committing crimes, those are the ways out of this unit. So far there doesn't seem to be an alternative.

9, 10 and 11 August 1936

First at Phalanx 11, then at 6. At 11 there is no kitchen and no accommodation for the guards. Crockery is shared, and some of the prisoners are syphilitic. Another blessing from BAM. I travel to Phalanx 6 with the dog-handling instructor. He tells me about Political Adviser Zhila, who is marked by the same grotesque illiteracy. He mentions the 'Chinese' version of the ditty 'Building Bricks'.* Recalls the 'Chinese' answer to 'What's it like in a Russian prison camp?'

Talking about early release moves us on to more serious matters. There is a telegram inviting applications from *zeks* who have served half their sentence. But what about us? I am classed as an employee and get 300 rubles, enjoy all the delights of life in the camps, am totally demoralized and deprived of everything that makes life worthwhile. Why am I treated differently from a *zek*?

12, 13, 14 and 15 August 1936
Back to the old routine, ours, of course. The early release scheme has had its effect on the *zeks*. We've had no escapes, but I feel no better. The sense of depression remains.

A few scenes from recent days: our local top brass wrote to the Armed Guards HQ about me. Item: failed to report and remove Zhusman in a timely manner, resulting in escape of eight persons. Reluctant to work, guilty of sabotage, blah-blah-blah.

They were very confident they would get me put on trial, but the response surprised them: 'Issue a reprimand and deal with the matter yourselves.'

Now they're sulking. Even Khodzko is no longer talking to me. Gridin's tsarist landowner-style pretensions and his would-be aristocratic bumptiousness emphasize his ignorance and uncouthness. He phones our HQ at 11 p.m.

'Call Pakhomov to the phone! Get me some cigarettes!'

The pathetic bootlicker, trying to curry favour with his superiors, dashes about trying to satisfy this whim. Platoon Commander Zhusov is less than complimentary about Adjutant

* A sentimental 1920s ballad with a happy ending.

Kamushkin: 'He's a gossipy old woman, tut-tutting with Political Adviser Khrenkov and always about you, Comrade Commander. But they don't seem very bright. There's their answer and they've got their fingers burned.'

One row behind us in the theatre is Gridin, with his ears flapping. Today, 15 August, Khrenkov's wife, bumping into us on her way to the canteen, spills the beans:

'You should be flogged for that stuff you keep writing.'

Evidently I am a topic of conversation with her husband.

I'm doing geometry with Political Instructor Khomenko, and Inyushkin and the dog trainer are nearby. They go out to talk about the kind of commander I am. What's his education like? Where is he from? What's he doing at BAM?

When they come back in, the trainer says, 'It's good to have someone like that as a platoon commander.'

Khomenko adds, 'BAM is no place for him.'

I wrote a letter to Krylov at GHQ. Let's see how he responds.

16 August 1936

Rain, bringing with it even greater gloom in my soul. I go out to Phalanx 11 in the evening. Have dinner and sleep with the bedbugs. I'm waiting for something, but my thoughts invariably turn either to being allowed to resign, which would be ideal, or facing trial. By accepting imprisonment I can win freedom.

17 August 1936

I'm sitting with Divisional Commander Inyushkin. We get to talking about Gridin. Both Inyushkin and Political Instructor Sergeyev now have a low opinion of him, and of Political Adviser Khrenkov. They're wondering when Khrenkov will be shipped off to you know where.

Inyushkin comments, 'Gridin has been a bad influence on Khrenkov.'

Chekists in charge of the BAM camp and construction project. *BAM – the Second Track*

They said nothing before, fearing for their own skins. Party members! Khrenkov appears at the platoon at 10 or 11 in the morning and goes off at 2 for lunch. In the evening he sometimes puts in two or three hours. Nobody accuses him of sabotage or anything like that.

He's a right idiot. Worked as a guard, resigned. Lived two months in Novo-Sibirsk, then came here and got taken on in the company as a commander. In the outside world he was evidently completely unemployable. People like that infuriate me and I feel nothing but disgust for them. I'm sad about my own life, but what can I do? A stretch in the camps seems the only way out. If they won't let me resign, I'll go off on leave and just not come back.

My pay only covers food.

18 August 1936

A miracle! We are moving to a six-day week and today is our first normal day off. I feel quite strange. I go on a trip 'to the country' with the head of combat training and lie down on the bank of a puddle locally referred to as a lake. Along the way we talk about resigning. We come to the conclusion that we can choose to serve here for the rest of time, or get ourselves convicted of something as a way out and get discharged. Logic suggests that, if you carry on waiting to be discharged, there's no guarantee you ever will be. If you get a two to three year sentence and you're then released, the problem is solved.

The sole ambition in life of the commanders here is to be a lieutenant at BAM. They have no aspirations or wish to leave. So they vegetate here. It's life of a sort.

19 August 1936

Everything leads us back to talking about how much longer we will be here. They've started maintenance on the living quarters, so we're here for the winter; they've sent an order for new uniforms, so we may be able to resign.

Paskevich reasons, 'I'm a trade union member, so I expect an eight-hour working day. I'll hang around till 4, but then it's bye-bye.'

They're not issuing any new boots as the project winds down. They'll have to lay off 30 per cent of the workforce to avoid unnecessary expenditure. Presumably the same goes for the new uniforms. Not only do I not want one, I don't even want to lay eyes on one. Just dismiss me.

I walk the 24 km from Phalanx 11 by night. In the darkness you trip over the sleepers, cursing everything and everyone. Nothing to eat from one morning to the next. Nothing to cook at the phalanx; they've gone out for food, will they bring anything back? Temporary, partial calm is interrupted by the intercom. There's been a group escape from the isolation cells in Phalanx 11. We should shoot the occasional bastard as a warning, but instead we're soft with them. Many of the phalanx leaders do damn all and leave all the work to the Armed Guards Unit. Gusarov, the deputy commander of 11, doesn't even go out there. He just lies about, sleeping a lot.

20 August 1936

It's a nice autumn day, but after the night's rain the mud's up to your ears. There's some chitchat about the new uniforms. They'll be black with blue collar tabs. Instead of army-style badges we've got round buttons and a cockade on the cap.

Will they try to keep us here and not let us resign? We're to have boots with gaiters or leg wrappings. Real warriors. Look out, Moscow, here we come!!!

21 and 22 August 1936

Political Officer Borisov, a Muscovite, has just arrived at the Organization and Staffing Section and does not mince his words.

'The project is to be completed by the 7 November holiday, and that's when I submit my letter of resignation. We've not been mobilized into the Workers' and Peasants' Red Army but assigned to a project, so kindly let us go when it's finished.'

There's a meeting in the canteen about the Trotskyite-Zinovievite bloc. Golubev burbles some sort of nonsense. People who've gathered for lunch are just thinking, 'Get it over with, will you?'

Orlov, reading from a note, blurts out, 'May they be punished by the arm of the law!'

Everybody laughs, evidently thinking, 'And may you be punished by the arm of the Lord God!'

Sergeyev also blathers a lot of nonsense, trying hard to look intelligent by opening his eyes wide and using a special tone of voice. Brench was making a note of something but, apparently not knowing where to start, stood up and sat down again.

Not one rousing speech! None of them can carry the masses with them, inspire them, know how to guide the listener's mind. Anyway, is it really possible to direct the masses?

23–30 August 1936

Strange goings-on in the division. There are no lights, so the top brass are nowhere to be seen in the evenings. That's regarded as an acceptable state of affairs. They imprison *zeks* in Wagon 98. One goes for the guards with a knife. They bundle him out and Butayev gets heavy with him, and not quietly. They twist his arms behind his back and he howls like a wild animal and rants at them. You just have to put up with it, you may be fuming but your job is to re-educate them, after all, and the law doesn't say you can swear at them. Besides, there is no law protecting us. Even if they punch you, you are supposed to show understanding.

At HQ the clerks arrange a booze-up. The top brass do nothing, just deprive them of some nominal credits.

Orders from the Armed Guards GHQ are becoming highly original. All items classified in the army regulations as state property are to be taken back from commanders. We have to return our mattresses, so what are we supposed to sleep on when there is nothing to make a new one out of and you can't buy them?

Everybody is waiting for the end. The top brass are being less officious and trying exhortation. The head of section, when he meets me on the station platform, asks suspiciously what my profession is. Interesting. I have to bear in mind I may do a bunk from the Unit. In the office Moskvin reprimands me and wants to know if I was ever in the Party. Why was I expelled?

'You think you are unfairly treated here, but you cause short-comings in the work quotas and staff training. You are politically more educated than many of our commanders,' and so on.

Brench, hanging around in the division one evening, does nothing but boast to the guards about his watch:

'How much do you think it cost?'

'150 rubles!'

'No, you try and buy one! It'll set you back 300.'

You contemplate this representative of the political commanders and think it's a waste of effort trying to make anything of him. They don't want to live in the countryside where they would have to work hard, they're happy in the army. They are, after all, taught something and get paid for doing nothing. They have no ambition. Anyway, what more does he need, and what more could he do?

Sapozhnikov, chief of staff at GHQ, comes to explain that the Organization and Staffing Section is not an official body and community activity is entirely voluntary. Our best and brightest agree but keep quiet about the new approach. Where their superiors go, they follow. They were incapable of showing initiative and finding that out for themselves. They are feckless and treacherous.

31 August 1936

Commanders had half a day shooting practice. After lunch I go hunting with Zaborsky. We are going through open country covered with undergrowth and not a single mature tree. I hear the quail crying, and decide to spend a few rounds on them. They are the only game. I kill the first to take off. It's getting dark and we need somewhere to spend the night. We find a haystack. The nights are already cold. There's nothing to make a fire from, no branches, no kindling. Only Korean birch. It reminds me of paintings of hunting scenes in Russia.

My heart is all over the place and my chest seems about to burst. Morning brought another quail but that was all we bagged. What a bounteous land! No firewood, no animals, no birds, no berries. Not a drop of water.

1 September 1936
Day off. Today is International Youth Day. There's no difference here between working days and holidays.

Khodzko in the Third Section is phoning everywhere, looking for me so that he can order me to Phalanx 11, evidently to conduct a review meeting. No peace even on your day off.

2 September 1936
One day is so much like another it could drive you nuts. There's no way to vary them. Even Divisional Commander Inyushkin wouldn't mind getting away. Goes to Potseluika for his rheumatism.

The day is as empty as the Torricelli vacuum. Everybody just loafs about but I can't. What's the point? There is none. It's nice that the weather is good, makes things seem less awful.

Sapozhnikov from GHQ is secretly living in the company to observe what goes on. Let's see what he has to say after lunching in one of his own subsections.

We're preparing for winter and there is not enough work to go round. Phalanxes moved from one place to another, finishing off what's left. If they don't let me leave in November I'll have to go all the way, take off on holiday and not come back. What a life!!! Khrenkov isn't bothering to ask for leave, evidently thinking he'll be off when it all ends. Or so I would like to think.

6 September 1936
This is supposed to be a day off, but they've organized a commanders' training day. What does that involve? Adjutant

175

Kamushkin reads out the first exercise from the marksmanship textbook and that's it. I could have read it for myself, better than him too.

Borisov, in vowing that we will work even better, says, 'We will complete the Second Track, there's just two months left, and then we'll all see.'

It transpires that Borisov has no qualifications either. Kamushkin is another autodidact. Here, in his own words, he tells us all how much he knows and just how keen he is to work:

'This training day caught me out, I hadn't prepared for it. I'm self-taught, so I can't teach courses properly.'

You just wonder how people at that level can lead anyone, and how they have the cheek to pretend to teach a course. They review the deployment of the company's 5 Platoon, and appoint me to 1 Platoon.

Political Instructor Sergeyev quips, 'Chistyakov to the west, closer to Moscow!'

I answer, 'Don't worry, I'll get back to Moscow. How about you?'

Kamushkin interjects, 'I've been working five years in the camps and would like to go back to Leningrad, but there's no way I would leave.'

He evidently does the bare minimum, without enthusiasm, not thinking, just slogging away. His time is passing by pointlessly, and so be it. He has no aspirations and it seems that, in addition, he has a court conviction, which he has to work off, holding him back.

Kamushkin now has little time for Gridin: 'He did nothing at all to train the commanders, and Khrenkov hasn't been seen at company HQ for the past three months.'

The two-day gathering was supposed to have us burning with enthusiasm, but somehow we never caught fire. They needed to give us a quick shot of indoctrination before they wrapped up, to stop us thinking about nothing but how soon we could leave, so they decided on a training session. I went out with Lavrov in the evening in search of quail, but didn't see a single one. Kozhedub, one of the guards who's a *zek*, got drunk in Bureya with Chechulin, an operations sergeant, and lost his rifle.

7 September 1936

I am gradually handing the platoon over to Nikolenko. We go to Phalanx 11. Nikolenko tells me about Lilin. He had a *zek* guard, Borisov, who was a thief. Lilin knew and covered up for him. One time Borisov brought him a whole bucketful of eggs, 200–300 of them, and puts them under Lilin's table. 'Lilin was drinking and everything. He gave some to me. I asked where they came from. He answered, "Just eat them. 'Where', indeed!" I asked Borisov and he said he had nicked them. Lilin issued an order that Borisov was not to be given fatigue duties other than special assignments outside the camp. Lilin himself swapped his old boots for new ones from the storeroom. Plug and I knew what he was up to but didn't denounce him.'

8 September 1936

I'm far away in Kaganovichi now, out of the way of the top brass. Brench is accompanying me as political instructor and is not at all happy. It's a bit rich, they've promoted the political instructor of 1 Platoon and Divisional Commander Inyushkin to 'inspector' (whatever that means), and demoted him. He's probably offended about it. He's conceited enough for that.

They've given me a strip of land, like a disgraced vassal. It's 80 km from Pozdeyevka to Zavitaya. There's no point in despairing, I need to think of something. Well, I could at least get them to take out the area to the bridge between Tur and Troyebratka. Acting Platoon Commander Kravets is displeased.

He has been in command of this platoon for two years, under the title 'acting' for the whole time. He wants to write a letter resigning as of 1 January 1937. They've dumped me in a new place with no accommodation, no fuel, nothing, and nobody gives a damn. Sort it out yourself! I have chest pains, an expectation of bad news. I'm sick at heart, bitter. I've been lumbered with Phalanx 11 again. Khodzko of the Third Section has withdrawn the guards from ten prisoners sentenced under Article 59 to ten years. They are effectively released. Run for it, villains!

The way I understand it is, the workers here don't need to be under guard, so with less responsibility for me it should be easier, but as long as you don't mess up, Petrovich! I want the days to pass quickly, the sooner we reach October the better. And then the matter will come to a head, one way or the other.

I sometimes picture Moscow so vividly it gives me a headache.

12 September 1936

It's my day off, but what use is that if there's nothing to do with it!

Zaborsky came, we played billiards, sang, that was it.

13 and 14 September 1936

I spend the night at Phalanx 11. It's a foul situation but the guards are resigned to it. Thus are people's wishes stifled, their aspirations reduced to nothing.

Platoon Commander Vasiliev, a Muscovite, wanted to get out, hit the bottle, and was fired after serving ten days in the cells. He must be so disappointed!

Uncertain situation. One day everything seems to suggest we'll be finished in November, the next it looks like we're going to be here all winter. I am comforting myself with the hope that I am just about to be discharged. I got the top brass to reduce the platoon's area of responsibility by 15 km down to Phalanx 28.

15 September 1936

I got a good rest after a sleepless night. Thoughts invade my head. Here's one: the volunteers employed as armed guards choose to come and live here and are not depressed by the absence of anything human, cultural, artistic, literary, sporting, technical, and so on. They are not at all burdened by their complete mediocrity. They are not interested in society, and have a petty bourgeois outlook on life. 'A samovar and a canary in a cage' is happiness.

It's awful, but can it really be true that my only salvation is self-annihilation? Can I live with that?

I don't feel good about admitting that I have lived with that thought for over a year.

And the future? What does Political Adviser Khrenkov mean when he says, 'Soon I will be sitting on a bench doing nothing'?

16–19 September 1936

It is just impossible to get things sorted out here at BAM.

I go round the phalanxes. I walked 50 km to Phalanx 9, from 9 to 11, and to the platoon in Kaganovichi. It's wet: rain, sludge. I have cramp in my leg and an ache in my right arm. No chance of getting dry or warm. I expect shortly to go mad.

A group escape from Phalanx 11. Girenko either let them out to gather nuts, or, in his words, lost his head, and six people have done a runner. In Phalanx 35, four *zeks* have disappeared. It beggars belief. I still cannot imagine why anyone would assign me to the Armed Guards Unit.

Gave courses at Phalanx 3 as well as at 11. Told them off.

As I'm walking down the track, a sandpiper takes off from the quarry: bang! Dead.

I go to pick it up – a teal flies out: bang! Dead. Right, I'll be having game soup.

I sleep with the guards for five nights, without taking my

clothes off. Adjutant Kamushkin and Kalashnikov arrive. I go to meet them at the station. I report to Kamushkin; he shakes hands first, to my surprise, and doesn't lecture me about the escapees. Some big chiefs are due and we need to go out along the track. We talk about hunting and boots. There are hunting boots in the retail store. I ask Kamushkin to get me a pair. He replies that he'd only do that sort of thing for me. All a bit baffling. Anyway, who cares, I want those boots.

Another 25 km on foot. My feet haven't dried out yet. There's nowhere to rest, either. That's my life, may it burn in hell. Now Political Instructor Novikov has returned from Moscow.

Oddly enough, the man says he doesn't want to live there. Why on earth not? He says everything is too expensive. But people do manage to live in Moscow, and everyone else, or at least most of us, would like to. He says a non-Party member can just resign quite easily.

We'll bear that in mind. I must get through October somehow. Freedom freedom!!!! Autumn is all around. 'Already autumn gilds the maples, birch leaves come cascading down and, like a carpet, deck the pathway.'* A pleasant, warm autumn day with a pungent aroma of rotting leaves. There's a sense of well-being and serenity, but … This is only a moment, an instant. I could find peace if I resigned. Could it be? Will I really not be allowed to resign? I wander over the hills with a rifle and remember hunting in autumn in the countryside. Joy, only fleeting, but so welcome. My tormented soul floundering.

Perhaps I'll feel calmer after I settle into my new quarters. I'll be able to forget everything when I'm on my own, do some painting, do some writing. It's my day off, but there's no way

* Quotation from Apollon Maikov, 'A Landscape' ('Peyzazh', 1853): *Уже румянит осень клены,/* […] *Осыпался с березы лист/ И, как ковер, устлал дорогу.*

to enjoy it. What sort of a day off can you have when there's nowhere to go apart from your guards unit accommodation and a railway track. The food's bloody awful too. Come on, project, end!

20 September 1936

Something isn't right. In a month's time it's the anniversary of the October Revolution, in a month's time we're supposed to hand over the project, but no one is making any preparations. There's just a dozy, unbroken silence. It's like a stagnant pond covered in slime with nothing good visible underneath. Makarova is the *zek* leader of Phalanx 35. In every phalanx she has been in charge of there has been nothing but trouble. I wonder what effect all this 're-education through labour' has had on her.

The rulebook is just a fence separating us from the real world. We need to tear one or two boards out to get through to reality.

21 September 1936

I would so like to be writing that this is the end. The end of this record of my stint at BAM. But the days still go by, cluttering my mind up with escapes, robberies, knifings. I walk the 18 km to Phalanx 11. The weariness from all this trekking every day is getting to me. My body feels drained. At Phalanx 11: more joy, an escape. I join the search, having completed my course on the rules of shooting. On the way I hop on a train carrying ballast and ride it as far as Kaganovichi.

Adjutant Kamushkin is at the platoon. The atmosphere thaws gradually. He is the first to mention the boots, informing me that, 'The retail shop wouldn't let us have them, but I've ordered fourteen pairs and will keep a pair especially for you.'

The 97 baggage train has been ransacked. When I arrive there is nowhere to relax – I'm in with the guards.

22 September 1936

A new day greets me with rain and cold.

Yesterday I told the guards about the seasons, and night and day. They don't know these things. In the evening I went with Soldatov to the puddle people here call a lake. I gave one duck a fright but that was all. With every day that passes I recall life in Moscow in greater and more torturous detail. The wet weather turns my thoughts to boots, but there's no way of getting new ones.

Come on, November! Come on, discharge! I give a talk about the international situation. The guards' and commanders' wives are present. I'm received with the usual illiteracy and indifference to politics. Philistines, philistines! I just want to stay at home without anyone summoning or bothering me. The trains are going to the west. The 1 rumbles by, the passengers counting the kilometres and hours to Moscow. I steel myself against the pain.

23 and 24 September 1936

After lunch, went to spend my day off in Zavitaya. There's a canteen there where you can get a decent meal. Rain and sludge. I'm wearing boots that don't function as boots, with more holes than leather. The water leaks in and my health leaks out.

I'm called in to the Third Section by Khodzko and we have a heart-to-heart. It kicks off with the observation that the weather is abominable and everyone is feeling the same way.

We begin with the escape of Gershevich [illegible] from Phalanx 35, move on to how I'm feeling, then we talk about hunting.

'So, how are you feeling?'

'Not good, Comrade Chief!'

I tell him about my profession and how I view the local commanders:

'They are not concerned about being so poor at everything. Neither the political instructors nor the commanders are up to the job, and if a unit is holding together, it is only out of fear. How can a political instructor be expected to give a literary reading or a talk on a general subject when Brench, Sergeyev, Mikhailov and many others are barely literate themselves?

'I've had a couple of days of rest, though that's only relative, of course. I've been able to relax a bit.'

Khodzko consoles me, 'We'll all be leaving soon, Comrade Chistyakov!'

We've been hearing that for a while now. What I am surprised to hear is that, with the need to finish the Second Track in the near future, there is more slipshod making-do than proper work going on.

25 and 26 September 1936

The days are as empty as a blank sheet of paper. I seem to be descending into a state of idiocy.

I have no thoughts, as if all that is human about me is atrophying. I am content to be fed whenever and whatever, to sleep, get yelled at, and expect nothing more. I am almost an animal, not a human being.

Brench, my political instructor, continues to live somewhere else and do something else. He's working on some task he's been given by the Party Committee. What about the work he's supposed to be doing here?

I ask him, 'Are you going to move here to the platoon?'

He replies, 'No, what's the point if we're only here for a month?'

By Order No. 423 of Company Commander Gridin, various bonuses are to be paid to those working in the phalanxes. Will that include prisoners working as guards? No, because guards don't have any quotas to exceed, and so on. They have not been paid for two months and have nothing to smoke. They are reduced to begging tobacco off the 'soldiers of the track'.

I walked 32 km to high-security Phalanx 35 and back, gave a talk about the end of the project and tested their knowledge.

I can barely walk. What's it all for, I ask myself. Is the pay good? Is the work interesting? Is it hell! Brench turned up for a day, no activities, no political talks. Great job he's doing.

27–29 September 1936

I give a talk to the guards and their wives about the speeches of Hitler and Voroshilov.

There's a hullabaloo at Phalanx 9. A sheep has been slaughtered, two rifles and a greatcoat and some other stuff stolen. Galkin orders the culprits to be sent to Zavitaya but they refuse to go. There's three days of turmoil over that. I'm at Phalanx 11 because of escapes. Nochayev, a hired guard, doesn't want to work any more, releases *zeks*, refuses to go on sentry duty or escort a contingent. The rest of them just want to get away from 11.

Kardanets announces, 'I'm going out searching for escapees and won't be back for fifteen days. I'll live in one of the villages.'

Vasilchenko and Gribenko say, 'It's time they sent someone to relieve us and we went to an open phalanx for a rest.'

I'm trudging 40–50 km every day. I came upon some game, took a shot at them and got four jackdaws straight off.

30 September 1936

It's our day off, but we are not idle. I thought yesterday I might go hunting but Golubev appeared.

Phalanx HQ, ten-day Stakhanov shock-work campaign declared, etc. Lavrov and the head of combat training came by. What hospitality could I offer? How do you spend a day off when it's your first day in rented rooms and nothing has been tidied up or organized? We went for a walk in the hills. It was russet-brown all around. It's a shambles at the top, in the section. Golubev is being dismissed. Yershov already dismissed.

Golubev travelled the track and reported everything was fine everywhere, but the section Plan was only 80 per cent fulfilled. Yershov had failed to organize a Stakhanov movement. Romanov, the foreman at Phalanx 35, was also working indifferently, delaying planned output, failing to assign brigades to specific objectives.

Makarova, the phalanx leader, comes in and reports, 'I sent for the foreman, but he said, "I'm already in bed."'

Golubev didn't say a word about completing the project by the October holiday, commenting only that it was important to have a gift for the anniversary. There's almost no work being done but no evidence that the end is in sight. Tinkering.

1 and 2 October 1936

Some bastard is spreading false rumours. We received a report that a group of 14 *zeks* had escaped, supposedly while being escorted from Phalanx 11 to 47. It turns out to be completely groundless, total nonsense. We're surrounded by people trying to wreck, disrupt, goad. We spend all night on our feet searching for escapees. I wrote to Adjutant Kamushkin to say that, following his example, I had conducted a first commanders' day. I don't know how he'll take that. I wrote another letter of resignation. I also wrote upstairs to Krylov. Something to GHQ [illegible].

Political Instructor Brench still going off somewhere, doing something. I wrote to complain about him too. These are Party members, the enthusiasts, the instructors, conduits of culture, the people who're supposed to be organizing everybody else.

I'm glad the weather is good. No mud or we'd be done for. My boots are wearing thin and my legs are aching. I went off to do some sketching, freeing my head of too many thoughts. At times, though, Moscow flares up again, explodes in my memory.

They say my junior commanders are unsatisfactory, as am I. But if Gridin was a satisfactory company commander, why would he have an unsatisfactory platoon commander under him? Nobody asks that. Gave fifteen talks on different topics: the Moscow Metro, the situation in the East and West, Voroshilov's and Hitler's speeches, the creation of the Earth, the creation of Man, the formation of hills and mountains. The guards and their wives enjoyed it.

Only the wife of Kravets replied to my invitation by saying, 'I'm stupid, so there's no point my trying to learn, I'll leave that to them as is smart.'

Suffering from a general weariness, mental exhaustion, increasing forgetfulness. My memory is losing its edge.

Old age a witch as black as pitch
now step by step will come,
and clutch at you and leave you blue
and starved without a crumb.

Winter is coming. There's frost in the mornings. We have no firewood, and no legal right to compel the phalanx to bring us any. The *zeks* go out of their way to make the guards' life a misery.

3 October 1936

I went to Phalanx 11 in the evening. The admin head from HQ materializes in all his glory. In the guards' quarters he bellows at Squad Commander Bezrodny for not wanting to transfer *zeks* to Territory 8000 without an armed escort:

'I'll send you off under armed escort! You're disrupting the Stakhanov ten-day shock-work campaign, you saboteur!'

Aizenberg is spinning like a top. After reading the order for Bezrodny's arrest, he says he's already eaten one empty-headed idiot for breakfast and is quite prepared to eat another. He read out the order to the 'soldiers of the track', undermining the guards' authority. He never reads out any of the orders about him.

Bezrodny is accused of 'regularly disrupting the unloading of ballast'. I'm surprised that's only being mentioned now . . .

At a territory I ask a man in uniform, 'Who are you?'

'The platoon commander!'

'Of BAM?'

'Well, I'm the head of admin [illegible] unit, but what are you shouting at me for?'

'I'm not shouting, I'm talking to you!'

'In that tone?'

'You don't like my tone?'

The tents people live in are full of holes and it's pouring with rain. Well, to hell with them. But nothing has been done for the guards either. They just ignore the guards, everybody's enemies.

Aizenberg is breathing down my neck: 'We've got a train with ninety wagons and can't get it unloaded!'

I sense he's lying, so I lie in return and say not all the wagons are for us. What a farce.

I tell Mozgovoy, 'I would not have done that. I would not have told Bezrodny I was sending him off under armed escort. In the first place, we answer to the company commander, and in the second only a commander can escort another commander under convoy.'

'Why are you telling me what to do? I work for the Third Section.'

Night, cold, rain. The water is freezing. The guards' premises are leaky and draughty. Mozgovoy has even thoughtfully removed the canvas from the roof over the kitchen. Rain leaks straight into the soup.

Uneasy sleep, cold. I have cramp in my arms and legs. We

187

need to put an end to all this. Health can be undermined in a single day. I go home in the morning, my hands numb with cold. I come across some ducks at the quarry. One teal falls, six fly up but settle again 300–400 m away. I sneak closer. There's one swimming. Bang! Dead. Soup.

See! That's our right as the top of the food chain, the strong, the powerful!

There is no firewood or paraffin and the phalanx doesn't bring us any. I don't have authority to order them to. Sergeyev wants to get out of the Organization and Staffing Section and has written to Krylov. Brench also wrote a report which he is sending by mail, so that is going to the Armed Guards GHQ. I've completely given up all ideas of continuing to serve here and I'm concentrating on resigning.

4 October 1936

I spend the whole day at company HQ in Zavitaya. When you're with people who see things the way you do you can talk and get things off your chest. You can eat like a human being. There's a very respectable frost, the water is freezing in the washbasins. It's last year's nonsense all over again; you splash water in one eye and the other opens by reflex. In unheated accommodation you forfeit your health. There's nothing heroic about it, you just make your rheumatism worse.

I went to see Adjutant Kamushkin to raise the matter of resigning. He replied, 'Sapozhnikov from GHQ has already told you, you can resign when the project is completed.'

We have a chat. He touches on our relationship, wants to know why I raised the question of resigning.

One fisherman spots another from afar. As do birds of a feather.

I got talking to Shishov, a senior surveyor; turns out he is a hunter. We agreed to go goat hunting on our day off.

Is something about to happen?

Company Commander Gridin, when I suggested the end of the project would be 8 May and that I was not intending to wait that long, said, 'The project ends on 8 November. We're ditching some finishing touches.'

Everyone has stopped talking about the project ending. You don't even hear the things that were previously being said. Perhaps they're deliberately keeping quiet to avoid an outbreak of demob fever. I sit on the platform at Zavitaya and chat to Parkhomenko about this and that.

I learn that the bridge at Arkhara was built 2 m higher than specified so they had to raise the subgrade at the last minute. They overspent and had to alter the cross-section, and so on. Oh, dear!

5 October 1936

It's my day off tomorrow. I plan to go hunting but it rains and rains. It makes you weep. There are shadows, darkness and uncertainty in my heart. It is extraordinary that in every area of life you retain hope and never give up, but here you don't even trust hope.

I sat at home all day. Come the dark of the evening, there was no paraffin. Now I'm not even able to read.

The works supervisor of Phalanx 35 asks, 'What are you, a well-educated man, doing serving as a platoon commander in the armed guards?'

Search me. Someone has a nasty sense of humour?

At Phalanx 35 they're digging a vegetable clamp for the winter, and the devil only knows what's going on with the project's end date. More escapes from Phalanx 11. Company Commander Gridin, instead of giving the guards an order to get over there, simply asked them to and three days later they still haven't arrived. At high-security Phalanx 35, Rodak and

189

Sager got drunk and ran amok, maybe because it's so dire there. The guards have no tobacco but the railway workers get a ration so the guards beg from them. The top brass don't give a damn. I've written to them, spoken to them, nothing helps. You can't tell what's going on up there. I'm writing in the dark so that I can save the last drops of paraffin in the lamp. There's no lamp at all in my room.

6 October 1936

It's my day off and I've received more joyful tidings of an escape from irrepressible Phalanx 11. Do I need to go? I stomp out there. Political Instructor Sergeyev is to sort out the living conditions of the 'soldiers of the track'. What the hell is going on? The *zeks* have care lavished on them, get discussions, representatives, leaders and the like, but the Armed Guards Unit never gets a look in. To this day the guards' accommodation has no heating, no firewood, and Aizenberg makes no attempt to conceal his outright hostility towards them.

My political instructor, Brench, arriving back at the platoon, asks, 'Did you write to GHQ to say that I never show up in the platoon and all that?'

I reply, 'Goodness me, no! I'd be better off without you. At least then there would be no one informing on me to Political Adviser Khrenkov.'

He laughs at my application to resign. Acting Platoon Commander Kravets has applied, and so has Political Instructor Brench. That's a clean sweep.

We sit with no light and no firewood and get no response to requests to company HQ. Half rain, half snow. Foul. Nobody notices when you do your job well. There's supposed to be a ten-day Stakhanov work campaign, but there's little sign of it. I seem to smell asphalt being poured on a street in Moscow, and my whole body quivers. I need to act, and decisively.

Every day brings us closer to winter and excessive work. I just want to hide somewhere for the entire day, but there is nowhere. If I had half-decent boots I would go hunting. But I haven't. The day will pass anyway.

17 October 1936

Over the last few days, events have swept chaotically forward. I saw Krylov at GHQ in Svobodny. We went through my letters.

In the evening at GHQ with Loshchinin we reminisced about Sergeyev's courses at our local HQ. The political instructor mentions that a new fuel called apatite – an aggregate! – has been discovered in the Khibiny Mountains of the Kola Peninsula.

They don't really believe I'm only going on vacation, they suspect something more.

Political Adviser Khrenkov and Adjutant Kamushkin treat me with respect and affection, and humour. A few raised eyebrows when I mentioned I was going back to Moscow in a few days' time, when I had also said I only promised to serve at BAM for one year. Too much of a coincidence?

Outside it is already winter. My room is cold. We have no wood or coal.

Lavrov appeals to Kamushkin: 'Comrade Chief! I need to be able to light a stove in my office!'

He replies jocularly, 'But maybe I am deliberately preventing that, so you don't get too comfortable!'

Translator's Note

We have little information about what happened to Ivan Chistyakov after he wrote that last entry in his diary on 17 October 1936. We know he was under arrest in 1937 when Stalin's purges were at their height. He was evidently released in 1938, only to die at the front in Tula Province in 1941 during the first months of the war with Germany.

From his diary, it seems possible that he did what he said he would on 18 January 1936: 'The guards are going away on leave and I'm actually pleased for them. I'll do the same sometime, and not come back.'

On 9 June 1936 he writes about possibly choosing to commit some minor offence to get himself a conviction: 'I'm here till October and then either they let me leave or I'll choose to stand trial.' In fact, he very nearly does land in court through the efforts of his exasperated local superiors. On 7 August he is warned, 'Khrenkov is insisting, but Khodzko [the head of the Third Section] is wavering for and against you.' In the event, when they do denounce him to General Headquarters in Svobodny ('reluctant to work, guilty of sabotage, blah-blah-blah'), it is his superiors who are told brusquely to 'issue a reprimand and deal with the matter yourselves'.

In early August and again in October, Ivan writes to the

very top of the BAMLag administration. In his last entry, on
17 October, he tells us he has had a meeting with Krylov in
Svobodny and that 'we went through my letters'. He evidently
spends a pleasant evening with the staff at GHQ, laughing at
the ineptitude of the people he has to work with in Zavitaya
(although even there, not all his superiors are hostile to him),
and mentions that it has been agreed he should return to
Moscow on vacation. The fact that he was arrested in 1937
may or may not be related to his not returning to the Far East
Region. There may simply have been tacit agreement that he
is a square peg in a round hole, has served his year, that the
project is close to completion and he should quietly be allowed
to leave.

After the last entry in the diary, the notebook contains
some more extended writing, which appears in the appendix that follows. 'Rebels' seems to be a fantasy – or perhaps
a parodied, journalistic report – prompted by the speech
Chistyakov wishes he had given to Budnikova's brigade, but
didn't, on 6 November 1935. 'Shock Workers' seems to be a
fantasy about how much more effective an imaginative and
humane approach to those constructing the railway line, rather
than threats, violence and coercion, could be. Chistyakov
envisages a ten-day Stakhanov campaign to complete the
Uletui–Zhuravli section of BAM in which, despite various
administrative setbacks, as an intelligent engineer, he successfully appeals to the better nature of the workers and achieves
results of historic significance.

Two other short pieces, one a graphic evocation of the
callous awfulness of the regime in the camps, and brief notes
about a fight among the prisoners, have been given as foot-
notes to 4–5 November and 8 November 1935 respectively
[on pp.10 and 12], just a month after Chistyakov's arrival at
BAM.

In addition to the diary and pieces found in the first note-book, we have an earlier (although undated) second notebook, mentioned by Irina Shcherbakova in her introduction, which is also included in the following appendix. 'The Hunt' is an illustrated manuscript which describes an expedition to a swampy area south-east of Moscow. In it, we get a glimpse of a happier Ivan Chistyakov.

Arch Tait
Cambridge

Appendix

Rebels

Ivan Chistyakov

In nature, the day began as normal, but in Phalanx 7 it did not get off to the usual start. A ten-day Stakhanov shock-work campaign was declared, effective as of today, but it was only announced last night. So, we've had no time to prepare. Whether this was done intentionally or not, and by whom, we were unable to discover.

The blackboard with the statistics about brigades' percentage fulfilment of their quotas under the Plan, which hung next to the guardroom, had been wiped clean, and next to it stood the phalanx's red banner, the pride of Samokhvalova's brigade. This banner knew all about shock workers, knew all about Stakhanov campaigns, and knew what women are capable of.

These were the early days of construction of the railway bridge. It was March 1934 and the stream of the River Uletui was still icebound. The temperature was in the region of minus 25 degrees, but the Second Track and the bridge could not wait for it to rise. Before the river thawed, foundation pits had to be dug and piers laid, because otherwise the deck between the spans would not be in place before the frosts of autumn, and that would disrupt the Plan.

While the preliminary works were under way, backfilling the dam, the women were talking among themselves about who would go down into the pits. Sceptics warned of dangers:

they would flood; you would never get out; you would con-
tract malaria, rheumatism. Some claimed the cold would give
them all scurvy. Sit in a wet pit and you'll soon know about
it! Climb in if you've given up on living, because you can
drown as well. You'll drink your fill of water then! What do
they care?

This last referred to the NKVD officers. They travel around
in their special trains and watch us slaving here as they go by.
We should feed them on gruel. The top brass won't issue us
rubber boots or gloves, and they suck up the last drop of our
juices.

'I'm coughing up blood.' A juicy gobbet of spit landed in the
snow. 'Sodding screws! Don't do it, girls! We're not going down
there! We're just not!!'

Samokhvalova, brigade leader of these career criminals,
shouted loudest of all.

'What's up with you? Are you out of your minds? You think
we're going into a pit! That's not work for us, that's not wom-
en's work!! I'll croak before I'll do it. Find men to do this job.
Whose bright idea was it to get a women's phalanx to build a
concrete bridge? They want us buried alive, the bastards. Right,
girls, they say it's got to start tomorrow, if they order us, I—'

'We'll none of us go!' the brigade chorused. 'What kind of
fools do they take us for?!'

It was, however, essential to get this bridge built. To redeploy
Phalanx 7 and take one of the men's brigades off their work to
replace them is just not feasible.

The women had to be talked round, and that means
Samokhvalova's girls, because they are the best brigade, exceeding their quota for ditches and trenches by 200 per cent. They're
a robust, cohesive team, a force to be reckoned with in terms
of productivity.

Evening. A time when the meal you have eaten, together

with rest, begins to renew your powers, and all manner of thoughts come to mind. Some are counting the days to freedom, remembering the life they left behind. Some, perhaps, are thinking of a family and so on. And some, no doubt, are thinking of escape. That will all be going on. They mend their belongings, reread letters for the hundredth time.

The hut was quiet, each person immersed in her own affairs and thoughts. Each one thinking only of herself.

The door creaked, describing a semicircle on the floor. The commander of the Armed Guards Unit entered. Some looked up, some didn't. They are so accustomed to visits from the guards they would think it strange if the evening saw no one call. The newcomer sat down without a word, looking round at the women. For half an hour.

Samokhvalova broke the silence.

'Well, why are you sitting there like you're deaf and dumb?! I expect you've come to get us all down into that pit of yours.'

'No! Why should I try to do that?'

All eyes were on the protagonists.

'Give me a break!'

'We're not going into your pit,' a voice proclaimed from somewhere in the upper bunks.

Samokhvalova lifted her head and silenced the speaker.

'What are you doing answering for everyone? Who elected you? Haven't you already got a brigade leader?

'And you,' she turns to their visitor, 'push off. Go try your luck with Finogenova. They're horses, not human beings.'

'What do you mean, they're horses?'

'They're the kind that work like mad. There's no stopping them!'

'But you work more, your percentages are higher, so you—'

'So we are horses, are we?'

'No. That's not what I was saying. I want to say that you are the people we value most in the Soviet Union. That's why I didn't go to Finogenova first but came to you.'

'Go on, give us more!'

'I'm not going to butter you up, but I'll tell you this. I came to talk to you because you are the best brigade. You'll lose nothing by hearing me out, and then you can make your own minds up. It's for you to decide. You're not little children and I'm not going to tell you any fairy stories.'

'You know what? Just pack it in! We'll decide for ourselves on the bridge.'

'Well, Samokhvalova, it often occurs to me that we are all rational human beings, and what we have in our heads is not junk but a brain. We think, we reason. You, for example, like everybody else, are calculating how soon the project will end, whether you'll get remission and be released soon, but you don't seem to have considered that how soon the project ends depends on all of you, and on you personally. Work out just how many cubic metres of spoil you have shifted this month. Pile that spoil up, stand back and take a look and you will see a veritable mountain. Then think how much your whole brigade has moved!

'So, decide for yourself whether we have anything to talk about. You're spitting fire now. The Armed Guards Unit are a bunch of so-and-sos, but when you need anything, a disagreement over measurement of quantities or work credits, it's us you turn to. Tell me, have we ever refused to help? Not once! You think we are your enemies, a bunch of screws, but what harm have the guards done? None! Only good.'

'You shoot people!'

'That's true, we do sometimes kill, but not people, not even something resembling a human being. Fascist degenerates. You have a few wet jobs on your own record, and a lot of people say you should be shot! Have we shot you?

'If you work, benefit the state by honest toil, I promise you

202

no one will lay a finger on you, not even here in the camps. But if you start stepping out of line, well, excuse me, in that case . . .

'If I bring you, your team, free women who've volunteered to work here and say, "This Samokhvalova is in for eight years for violent crime and the rest of the brigade are just as bad," what would they say? They'd be horrified! Why don't you have them under guard? They'll rob honest people, etc. But I have not come to you with any such words, or even thoughts at the back of my mind. I have approached you as an outstanding brigade, as people honestly working for Soviet power. You really ought to understand that.'

'Oh, you all sing so prettily when you need to get us to work, but if we do get into hot water because you turn up late, or if we're late back from work, it's, "Oh, I can't imagine how that could've happened!" Nobody wants to know.'

'We do want to know. We'll investigate and punish where it's called for. But you are your own worst enemies. Why doesn't the phalanx leader treat you with respect? Why doesn't he appreciate his best brigade? You need to make him respect you. You need to make people respect you, not only in the phalanx but throughout BAM. Here people can make all the difference, by honest labour. We are offering you that right. It is a major privilege. That bridge is a crucial section of the project. Force people to respect you! Let the whole of BAM know all about you. I will negotiate with Finogenova's brigade, and others. If not all, then some individuals will want to work on the bridge. We shall set up a new brigade which, just possibly, will not let you near the bridge.

'I am giving you the right to choose and make up your minds. The company HQ has agreed to award a banner to those setting records on it.'

'Don't you be in such a hurry to go talking to Finogenova!'

'I can't delay. They will be offended and ask why I didn't

make them the offer. I simply do not have the right not to talk to them. If you agree to take on the bridge and let us set you to work on the east pier while others take the west, you can win the banner and the right to the centre pier.'

'All right! Just make sure we aren't drowned!'

'Now, then. I was not expecting that from you! Did you drown digging the trenches? I'll leave you to decide for yourselves.'

The silence that had persisted during the conversation was broken by a shifting of benches, a shuffling of feet, and sighing. Late into the night the brigade was talking it over, late into the night nobody slept.

What would the others say if Samokhvalova took on the bridge?

In the morning, the brigade stood by the guardhouse and was not the first to go out to work, which meant they had agreed.

They went to the bridge. They checked the dam was not leaking. They looked at the spall. They touched the wooden frame of the future foundation pit, looked at each other and, without speaking, started driving the crowbars into the frozen ground.

'Scabs!' the other brigades shouted as they passed.

'Samokhvalova! You've sold out!'

Many thoughts passed through the brigade's minds while Finogenova and the other [illegible] went by. Some paused in their work, held the crowbar uncertainly, no longer consistently hit the ground at the exact same spot.

This went on for a couple of hours while they picked out the [illegible] for explosives.

They primed the explosives, moved away and: *A-aarhh!*

Chunks of frozen earth flew in every direction, mixed with snow and smoke. And along with the explosion came the discharging of a tension that had been weighing on them. The shovels were quickly put to work clearing the site, and the crowbars began to bite deeper and more readily. The foundation pit took shape.

'Congratulations on a good beginning, on shifting the first spoil,' the commander of the Armed Guards Unit exclaimed. 'The congratulations when you finish will come from the leader of this great project, and from your friends and relatives.'

'All right, all right. Get out the way!'

On the first day, victory was Samokhvalova's and the banner was firmly placed on the bridge. Sometimes, however, it passed to Finogenova's brigade, which had gone to work on the west pier. The rules of the contest were simple. The depth of the pit was measured at the edges with a batten and the banner transferred to the east or west.

The middle pier was awarded to Samokhvalova, and with it

Zek women's brigade loading wagons with subsoil for track subgrade. *BAM – the Second Track*

the banner was permanently fixed in one place until construction of the bridge was completed.

Today, however, the banner has been taken back, absurdly, over a trifle. Confiscated. Like it or lump it.

The brigade is tense, on edge. The tension could boil over at any moment, and then who knows what might happen. Everything will depend on the situation at the time. It could burst as a storm of indignation, anger and hatred for everything in the world. It could come as an outburst of enthusiasm, pride and delight. Today will be decisive. We felt the tension, sensed that the storm would break in the evening, knew that Samokhvalova's brigade was supposed to hand over the banner to Finogenova, perhaps even to Budnikova, leader of the brigade of down-and-dirty 35-ers. There was nothing we could do to help.

Shedvid, the women's brigade organizer for the whole of BAM, had blundered.* She had decided the banner should revert to being transferable. They knew that today would be Samokhvalova's first day on ballast and that she would not be able to notch up 250 per cent of the quota. They decided to wait and see what happened.

A delegate came from Budnikova to Samokhvalova to see how things stood. Another came from Finogenova. The delegates didn't speak a word, the brigade was silent. Everybody looked glumly at the ground. That evening everything would be decided at the club. The armed guards turned out for the test measurements. The picture was clear to us, but how was it to be announced? Trying to fudge the issue would only make matters worse. Shedvid had created this mess, it was up to her to sort it out.

The banner was awarded to Budnikova.

After that it was sheer pandemonium.

* Oskar Shedvid was overall head of the Third Section at BAM. See footnote on p.151 to 13 July 1936. The use of his name in this context is evidently intentional. [Tr.]

There was noise, chaos, shouting, cursing, and laughter, but what laughter. Cracked, hysterical laughter giving way to hoarseness and hissing, that was how Samokhvalova's women reacted.

'Right, girls, everybody out! Every last one of us.' Samokhvalova's voice boomed through the general uproar.

A silence descended and the brigade walked out of the club without another word.

There was an awkward pause, nobody had a response. Even Budnikova seemed uncertain about whether or not to accept the banner. After half an hour everything began to cool down as people went outside and began talking to each other. Soon the club was empty and the banner languished up on the platform. What would happen now?

The following day we expected refusals to go out to work, from Samokhvalova, from Budnikova, and many in other brigades.

This prediction was spot on. There was no sign of Samokhvalova's brigade in the morning. The rest came out to work, but there would be no records broken today, just enough done to qualify for a basic ration.

If you turned up during this time in Samokhvalova's hut, you would be on the receiving end of logs, bowls, boards, boots, anything that came to hand, anything that could cause injury, and all of it seasoned with a cascade of expletives of such inventiveness you could never hope to match them.

From the direction of the hut we heard a great commotion, shrieking and screaming as Shedvid was seen off the premises. Their strike could go on for three to five days, but the project cannot wait, the building work cannot be postponed, there are deadlines to be met. We decided to try an approach at noon. I was very agitated, no less so than the brigade. Hell! I was met by bedlam.

'Come in, come in, you screw. If you dare!'

Dong! A bowl hurled from an upper bunk clangs against an opposite upright.

'Who are you throwing that at?' My yell cut short a rising chorus of catcalls. 'Is that your way of saying, "Good afternoon"?'

The question extended their moment of uncertainty, which I needed to exploit if all was not to be lost and I was to leave with anything to show.

'Is your storekeeper here?'

'That's me!' a woman washing her hair in a bowl says.

'No wonder I couldn't recognize you, that hair makes you look like a mermaid.'

'More like a witch,' a voice corrected me.

'Ha ha ha,' someone guffawed. 'The witch from Bald Mountain!'

'Not from Bald Mountain, only from Uletui. Give her a broom. She needs a good demon. Saddle the boss! We shouldn't just have them riding us, we ought to have a go on them.'

'I've not ridden you and have no plans to do so in the future.'

'But would you?'

'No, I can't do it with people watching.'

'Would you ride on Shedvid? If she shows herself here again, the whore, we'll tear her apart.'

'The parasite!'

A hail of choice curses filled the air.

'Well, why are you blaming me?'

'Why are we blaming you? Why, are you going to stand up to her? All you security guards grow fat on our blood.'

'And have you had a lot of your blood spilt?'

'More than you!'

'Where?'

'Right here, in your camp!'

'Has somebody knifed you? How and where?'

'Your guards, your secret policemen.'

'That's not true!'

'But we get plenty of bad blood from you.'

'We get more from you. There's thirty of you in this brigade, three hundred in the phalanx, and only four of us. Who gets more grief? You stuff it up our noses and down our throats, enough for lunch and dinner and some to spare. You women are hot-tempered, you sometimes get worked up over nothing, pointlessly. If we look at this calmly, you are absolutely in the right, but when there's all this shouting and screaming there's no telling what you want exactly, and you may end up with the opposite.'

'We know where this is leading. Go on, persuade us!'

Two of them started singing, 'We are not afraid of work, we just ain't gonna do it.'

'None of you? Is that it! Can we put it to a vote?'

'Go right ahead!'

'Enough yelling! Cut it out, big boss! You're just getting on our nerves!!!'

'You're getting on your own nerves. Why don't we leave it to your brigade leader to decide this? I see she's sitting there and pondering. There's no point in thinking up something bad, so she's probably thinking up something sensible.'

'I'm not going out to work!'

'Not today! How about tomorrow?'

'Are you trying to find something out?'

'I'm not trying to find anything out, but I'm interested, because I feel bad for your brigade.'

'Great! Look who's our supporter!'

'First you trample our brigade into the mud and now you come here to sort things out!'

'I didn't trample on you!'

'What, are you against Shedvid?'

'Too right, I am! That's why I'm here. Let's talk business instead of shouting at each other. You think Shedvid is wrong, is that it? Does that mean you're right?'

'Yes!!!'

'And your strike? Your strike only gives Shedvid more ammunition and takes it from you. That's just what she needs, a trump card, something to use against you. Well, let's suppose Shedvid is in the wrong, she's done something stupid; does that mean you should do something wrong?'

'What, are you defending her?'

'What are you trying to get from us?'

'You've never understood us and never will.'

'I paid for this photograph and article in *Builders of BAM* with my own health. I might just have been starting to believe in the impossible. I might just have been starting on the path of honest labour, of breaking with the past. That banner in the corner of our hut always reminded me that while I was working I was the equal of any other citizen. When I'm working, I'm not a criminal, because criminals don't march under the red banner. It could only mean I was a Soviet citizen. The whole of BAM wanted to be like me, the head of the entire project set me as an example.'

There are not many people like Samokhvalova. And then along comes some stuck-up idiot and the banner is transferred to Budnikova. For what? For a single day's work.

'We held that banner for five months. That's not red dye but our sweat and blood. She could have brought another one, and we might have won that one too. The snake! If she so much as shows her face, we'll kill her.'

'What difference does it make? Our lives are scarred.'

'You need to get these thoughts out of your head. The more days you work, the more credits you will earn and the sooner you will be back home. Without today your release has been set back, and if you are not careful it may be put off even longer. Whose fault is that? I have come to join you in resolving your problem and an issue of importance to our state. You live in the USSR and have no plans to live anywhere else. Do you want to live in China?'

'No!'

'In Japan maybe, or Germany?'

'Hell, no!'

'Well, to live in the USSR you have to live by Soviet rules. Labour is a matter of honour, glory, valour, and heroism. He who does not toil, neither shall he eat. This is not something I have to persuade you of.

'Tomorrow, go out to work to get that banner back, and I shall get another from our sectional HQ. You will earn that one too. Agreed?'

Shock Workers

Ivan Chistyakov

The Uletui–Zhuravli section of BAM was the responsibility of Track-Laying Phalanx 30. They decided to lay the track in record time, and complete it as a gift to mark the 18th anniversary of the October Revolution. There were just three days left before the holiday. It is 12 kilometres from Uletui to Zhuravli, which meant they had to lay 4 km of track every day.

For BAM such rates were unprecedented. Nothing had been said or written of any such achievement, which meant it had never been done. Here, just as at Phalanx 7, nobody had been told about the Ten-Day Campaign. Those in charge at section level had evidently ordered it, so there was no advance preparation in the phalanxes. Their only consultation came when it was already time to start work. There were also no guidelines from the section, apart from enquiries: 'How is your Ten-Day Campaign doing?' This called for inventiveness. It seemed entirely possible that our work during the campaign might be at odds with the overall Plan. Nobody knew.

'Lads! They've started delivering the ballast for this stretch. Fifty wagons of sleepers are being delivered. We've got the rails, spikes, bolts and all the rest, so now it's all up to you. We have no track-laying and work tempos we could give as examples. Lads, I invite you to pioneer new quotas. We need to make

212

sure the next three days between now and the anniversary of the Revolution go down in history as one of the achievements of 1935. You are making construction history, so let's start a movement that cannot be stopped. Let's test ourselves and find out what human beings are capable of, what each one of you can do! Our Soviet heroes, our medal bearers are of our stock. You are the same people with the same blood, so each of you has it in him to be a hero.

'We'll go and unload the sleepers now, and start laying the track this very day. We will present this section as a gift to the October Revolution. I know there will be some who won't like this speed, but the shock-work campaign will sweep them aside and cast them from our path. So I say to you now, if you're not with us, step aside. And now, lads, to the unloading. You each know what you need to take, an axe, a hook. Your work will show who is for and who is against.

'Forward, workers of the BAM,

And sun, shine bright on each man's back!

The Far East Region is our home

As we create the Second Track.'

The answer was a heavy, deathly silence. Whether it indicated consent or not was difficult to judge. The whistle of a steam locomotive left no time for reflection.

'Four men per covered wagon and eight on the platform, unloading to both sides. We have twenty-five minutes. What do you say, lads, can we do it?'

'Why ask? Don't you trust us?'

'Right, we'll have breakfast an hour from now and then we'll start laying the track.'

'You're on!' someone shouted from the crowd.

Quick as a flash they were up on the wagons, and immediately beyond the exit points of the passing loop, brand-new sleepers gleamed in the air as the train moved slowly along, a triple line lain along the sides of the track. Ivanishin, the senior guard, stayed back at the phalanx to make sure the breakfast was at its best.

The hands on my watch moved quickly, and seemed to speed up as time began to run out. We won't get the sleepers unloaded in time! Yes, we will. No, we won't. What am I saying? Of course we will!

The covered wagons prevented me from moving the length of the train so I walked along the platforms.

'Well, lads, looks like I won't be able to give anyone a flea in their ear today!'

Less and less frequently do I see the white bulk of the sleepers up in the air, and many of the men were already lighting up, having finished the job. Uletui. I checked them. Empty empty, empty. But what's this? Four locked wagons.

I winced at the thought, which hit me like a sleeper. Can they be full of . . . sleepers?!

I opened one: sleepers, more sleepers, a third wagon of sleepers. In the fourth, a lone worker.

'Why are you on your own?'

'Citizen Commander, it was impossible to get in while the train was moving, so I got in from the top through the hatch. I threw out what I could, but nobody else came in with me.'

'Okay, lads, there's a bit more unloading here. Don't want these sleepers travelling back and forth.'

'Will do!'

I went to the intercom and called up the wagon of the head of security.

'Comrade Chief, your instructions have been carried out. We are doing our bit for the Ten-Day Stakhanov Campaign.'

I got on the ballast shuttle from Zhuravli to Uletui. At Kilometre 758 there was subsidence where the embankment had collapsed. No matter how we tried to reinforce it, it kept sliding away. We decided to dig out the embankment and remake it with ballast. A women's phalanx had been doing the digging and working on the ballast. There was bewilderment and surprise when a shuttle appeared bearing workers from Phalanx 30, who were enjoying a smoke.

'Look, girls! Who are these?'

'Helpers for us!'

'Why haven't they got any shovels, then?'

'Must be a bunch of idlers. Hey, you lot! What are you doing, riding up and down the line? You'll wreck that shuttle! Sprawling in there!'

'Been working hard, have you? Lots and lots?! Stakhanovites! While we're here waiting for ballast.'

'Actually we're just off to breakfast.'

'What?'

'That's right. Did you see the sleepers along the way? How do you think they got there?'

'Come on, damn it. Give us a shovel. We'll give you a hand.'

And ballast, shimmering and gleaming like gold, streams steadily into the gap.

'If you don't fill in that hole for us by 5 November and you hold up the track-laying, you'll have only yourselves to blame.'

'Are you really going to get here that soon?'

'Ask us that when we get here.'

While they were tidying up the slope there was an impromptu political meeting. X stood on the platform and treated the women to a speech.

'Don't you go imagining we are a bunch of lazy bluffers. Don't be in such a hurry to glorify your Samokhvalova. You only have one Samokhvalova and a team of thirty. Well, there are a hundred and thirty of us. We'll do better than Samokhvalova. Admittedly her bridge is pretty good, but we are going to be over that bridge in record time, both by the standards of the Soviet Union and of BAM. Our record will be on top of hers!'

'You certainly talk big, but I bet you've only got a pig in your poke!'

They began laying the track after breakfast, albeit without any spectacular innovations. They just made sure they chose good tools, and left the broken ones behind to be repaired. The foreman took the phalanx banner to plant in the ground at the point they had to reach by the end of the day. He carried it off round the bend. From Uletui to the bridge Samokhvalova had built was a kilometre and a half and they needed to lay that section in two hours. For each rail, with twenty sleepers and a hundred spikes, they had just twelve and a half minutes.

Mathematics likes precision in calculations and that is the only way to arrive at the correct answer. You need the same kind of mathematical accuracy in work, but work needs something beyond dry mathematics, and that is a sense of competition, lively commitment, enthusiasm. The phalanx was divided into two teams, one for the left and one for the right rail. Both sides got drawn into the contest. As soon as the spiker on the left rail got two or three sleepers ahead, you heard a commotion and trampling on the right rail, and vice versa.

They got over the bridge in one hour and fifty minutes.

On the grey concrete of a pier they scrawled in charcoal, 'Pull your socks up, Samokhvalova.'

The banner didn't stay in place either, they moved it ahead one rail at a time. The left team went one rail ahead and, to keep things even, laid one rail on the right side. Competition flared, and in the evening, returning from their work to the phalanx, Samokhvalova's brigade were taken aback.

'Not bad rails, eh, girls?'

'Good rails, boys!'

216

They reached the subsidence on schedule but it had not been filled in. The rise at the quarry and also the Amur road sometimes slowed down regular movement of the ballast shuttles. They erected trestles at the dip and laid the rails on those, rejoining the main track at the points. Now the shuttle could deliver ballast along the second track without causing hold-ups.

The Hunt

Ivan Chistyakov
[taken from the second notebook]

1934
First day of the six-day week
1 August
The day begins, and with it the lying
Shoot an animal low down and a bird in flight
Aim ahead and aim high.

There's a certain amount of the truth in every lie. It can be impossible to determine the boundary, so let everyone decide for themselves what is true or false.

August 1934

Day 1

The marsh begins 180 kilometres east-south-east of Moscow. It extends another 100 kilometres to the south-east of Ivanovskaya and the River Kobylskaya.

My companion, Alexander, known as Doc, overbalances on the first step he takes and sinks knee-deep into clinging peatbog. 'Oh, feet and fiddlesticks!' he exclaims. 'Pardon?' I ask in mock surprise, on which note our conversation ends.

Low-growing birch scrub surrounds us. Our gundog disappears into the undergrowth. I whistle periodically to call him back, and occasionally have to shout 'Halloo!' when Doc gets lost. We walk for an hour, with no luck – no berries, no game – and head for Lake Malovskoye. The dog stops and points his muzzle. A brood of partridges rises up. Two right-and-left shots go wide. Another point from the dog, another brood, another two double shots, another miss. The day is getting hot.

'Let's make for Lake Dolgoye,' Doc suggests. 'We can rest, and a bite to eat wouldn't come amiss.' We set off. Covering two kilometres of marsh takes the same effort as eight kilometres on dry land. From time to time, Doc, trailing behind, asks, 'Are we nearly there yet?'

'Yes, it's just round the bend!' I say encouragingly, but the bend is never-ending. A sliver of lake, glinting like a knife blade, raises our spirits and I surreptitiously increase the pace. Lake Dolgoye lives up to its name as a long lake; it's four kilometres long, and one and a half wide. Now there are pine bushes among the birch, the grass is waist-high and the moss is a quarter of a metre deep. There are dead trees and tree stumps here and there. A pungent smell of resin. Water gently lapping. Stillness. An old man fishing by the shore looks at us sleepily and says in a dull voice, as if to no one in particular,

'You shouldn't have been there. That's a game reserve, that is.' We sit down on the shore, eat, and drink the lake water, which is warm, with a savour of peat. After our rest stop we move on to Lake Karasovo, taking a shortcut part of the way. Nothing from the gundog, not a shot fired. There is seemingly no game, even though there has been a reserve here for a year. Doc, completely whacked, now thinks nothing of sitting down in a puddle. It's no wonder: you pull your left leg out, your right sinks in; you pull your right leg out, your left sinks in. Evening is falling. We reach Lake Karasovo and move stealthily towards the shore.

Ducks maybe? A couple of teal rise. I shoot. Miss. We settle down by a haystack. 'Our lodging for the night,' I announce. 'We'll burrow in and sleep under the hay. It'll be warm.'

'How about making some porridge?'

'Good thinking, Alexander. A man sleeps more soundly on a full stomach.' I go for firewood and the dog comes too. Thirty metres from the haystack, I'm breaking up a dead birch but freeze in a way that has Doc shouting, 'What's wrong?' I indicate the dog, which he can't see in the grass. 'What?' he asks, as if wanting an answer repeated.

I beckon. He jumps up and comes running with only socks on his feet. I shout in great agitation, 'Bring the gun! He's pointing!' The dog takes a couple of steps forward, lies down and stretches its muzzle forwards. Doc runs up, gets ready, a grouse rises. 'Missed! Ouch!'

I look at Doc. Doc looks at me. 'Some Voroshilov sharpshooter you are!'

'Yep, we missed!' (from five paces, point-blank)

The birch tree has been reduced to firewood, the millet rinsed, the porridge is cooking, darkness is falling. Dusk. A campfire, a lake splashing gently fifteen paces away. Somewhere cranes are calling. The shadow of a bat flickers by and gets us talking about Fenimore Cooper, Mayne Reid and their like. 'You're a real pioneer on the prairies of America,' Doc declares.

'And you seem to be the last of the Mohicans, only instead of moccasins you're wearing Moscow socks, darned by the USSR State Stocking Repair Workshops.'

'I admit it.'

'If we were real Indians we would be looking away from the fire.'

'Well, yes, but we can sit like this while we're waiting for the porridge to cook.'

'Come on, it's nothing to do with Red Indians or watching the porridge – you're not that intellectual – you just need to dry your socks before you go to bed.'

'All right, all right! Now tell me about the porridge you made last year!'

So I do. The first time we took the cooking pot, but forgot the millet; the second time we remembered the millet but forgot the cooking pot; and the third time we remembered both but couldn't find drinkable water.

'And did you burn it that time too?'

'No! We had to finish cooking it when we got back to Moscow.'

'Well, let's make tea with it now and then sleep.'

'Good idea.'

The burnt porridge serves as tea leaves, and the peat-infused waters of Lake Karasovo produce a brew that could pass for Ceylon tea, or perhaps mocha coffee.

'I've never seen game in such abundance, and today has been no exception.'

'And if we carry on missing like this, we'll never have bagged such a round number before either!'

The day's exertions have taken their toll. Doc, twisting and grunting, works his way under the haystack and, securely installed, is soon snoring. I fall asleep too and don't know how many hours have passed or what the time is when I wake, but it's as dark as ever. Doc's boots, kicking me repeatedly in the head, have woken me.

'Why do you keep tossing and turning? If you can't sleep, at least let me try!'

'I'm not comfortable in this haystack! Perhaps we should get the campfire going again.'

'That's not such a bad idea. My legs are sweaty and shivery.'

We resuscitate the fire and it's much warmer beside it than under the haystack. We can just make out the first glimmer of dawn, or perhaps we're still half asleep and imagining it. 'Thanks for thinking of the haystack to keep us warm,' Doc says drily. 'Sleep tight!'

The water boils in the pot, we eat tinned food, and it's time to be on our way. 'What'll the kill be today?' Doc wonders.

'Even if we don't kill anything, our feet will kill us.'

It's a good forty-five minutes' walk from Lake Karasovo to Lake Glubokoye, but after hiking for an hour and a half there's still no sign of the lake. Or, come to think of it, any game. We spot the lake and make a beeline for it. There are said to be ducks there, but so far that seems no more than a hunter's tale. There probably were sometime in the past. How touching that their memory lives on.

'What times those were in America!'

'Yes, real hunting they had there! You'd see a herd of stampeding buffalo, no need to aim. Blam! You fire your Colt, get all the meat you can eat and a buffalo skin to boot!'

'Ah, so that's why you keep missing. You're a Red Indian in disguise and your shotgun is only for shooting big game, so how can it be expected to hit something as small as a grouse or a partridge? If an elephant turned up now, I bet you'd really show us!'

'You don't shoot elephants. In Africa they hunt them without a gun.'

'How's that?'

'They track the elephants to where they sleep. As I'm sure you know, elephants sleep leaning against a tree. They quietly saw the tree down and the elephant falls over. Once it's fallen over it can't get up again, so the hunter comes in the morning, and . . . '

'I see. They find a whole herd of elephants with their legs in the air trumpeting piteously.'

'Yes, then the Africans arrive, tie them up, put them in carts and get a donkey to pull them to an elephant pen.'

'I've a feeling you should stuff your donkey up a priest's beard.'

'I'm telling you, explorers have seen it with their own eyes and written about it. What's so odd about using donkeys?'

'I suppose they also feed them semolina to make them as manageable as babies.'

We have come at the end of the pine scrub to some higher ground, a kind of triangulation point. It's dry, with lots of berry-laden bushes growing between clumps of birch scrub. 'A good place for game, this,' Doc reflects and, before I can answer, the dog is pointing. A grouse rises up. We both shoot, two barrels. Two hunters firing twice at one bird proves effective and the grouse falls to earth. Hunting tradition dictates that when it's debatable who brought a bird down it goes to whoever shot first. 'Alexander, I congratulate you. It's not an elephant but you hit it.'

A finger extended in front of his nose silences me. The finger is redirected towards the dog, which is pointing again. We advance, barely able to see each other through the bushes. It's the kind of situation which could result in one of us shooting the other, but partridges cut out the risk of that, some flying my way, others towards Doc. Two shots ring out, two souls are dispatched to avian heaven or hell, and their mortal remains consigned to our soup pot. 'Hurray!' Doc exclaims proudly. 'Another kill.' Further conversation is again interrupted by the dog pointing. This time we both miss, unforgivably. We should have shot at the partridges rather than open sky.

'Think we've done enough for one day?' I ask Doc.

'Speak for yourself,' he retorts. Fifty paces on and the dog is pointing again. The partridges are becoming downright insolent, almost sitting on our gun barrels. Doc finds this so insulting that when a very young one lands on his gun and cheeps at him, he murders it. His trophy is a mishmash of flesh and feathers.

'We'll have to sew a chicken's head on it,' I say, 'or no one will believe that's edible.'

'Other people may think it's inedible, but I don't, and intend to eat it.'

Our feet and the dog are beginning to weary.

'Do you think it's time we called it a day, after all . . . '

He doesn't need to go on. ' . . . you can't shoot every game bird in the world!' I finish his sentence. 'As simple souls say.'

'Simple souls? Are you calling me an idiot?'

'No, at times you really seem quite intelligent, but don't let it worry you. I expect it will soon pass.'

'And while you were busy being witty, did you see what's just flown by?' Engrossed in our tit-for-tat, we failed to notice the dog pointing again. 'A grouse! And a black one at that!'

'You're a grouse yourself, a big one!'

'What about you?'

'I am too.'

'Okay, nil–nil.'

We head back. The trail snakes this way and that so that at times you think you are back where you started, at others that you are going in completely the wrong direction. 'Carry that gun like a hunter, will you?' Doc protests. 'I'm not a grouse planning to land on its barrel!'

'All right! All right!'

'What's "all right"? You hold it like it's a stick, and you're even squinting at me with half an eye. Don't kill me or you'll come off worse!'

'What if I don't kill you but just wing you and you die all by yourself? Who'll come off worse then?'

We're back at the birch scrub, so in another hundred metres we'll be on firm ground again. 'When we get out, shall we sit down for bit?'

'Good idea!'

The trail from the marsh leads us to a hill called Trushkin Wood. After all that wading through the marsh, walking on dry land feels like relaxation, but we sit down anyway.

It's so good to stretch out on soft moss after the marsh. My legs are tingling pleasantly. I look up through the treetops, and when they sway the sky looks like water rippling in a great lake. I decide to make a suggestion: 'What do you think, Alexander, about walking on now to Karasovo?'

I shiver. It will be six *versts*, kilometres near enough, from the marsh to the village. We take the shortest route, through the woods. 'It's true what they say! Hunting is worse than captivity!' Doc says after a long silence. 'It feels as if we've struggled a hundred kilometres through the marsh, worn ourselves out, worn the dog out, given the game a nasty fright, and now here we are stumbling along like the undead, and all in pursuit of our pastime!'

'Non-hunters would never understand,' I reflect. Another silence. I just want to walk without talking or thinking about anything. It is very, very quiet in the woods. A stick snapping underfoot jolts us out of our torpor.

'Hunting was better before the revolution,' I propose. 'You

226

would be packing and getting ready for two or three months before you set off. You would go to Yar or some other restaurant out in the countryside. Shoot game, drink Condor brandy . . . '

'Pick rowan berries [illegible],' Doc interjects.

' . . . and drink Smirnoff vodka, and then either drive to Hunter's Row or send a footman to buy partridges. You would come home with a hangover. There would be enquiries, perplexed sighs and, of course, hunters' tales. A hangover, memories of drunken revelry, your second-hand knowledge of the marshes and how to hunt game courtesy of Turgenev, all combining to create stories your audience would be too embarrassed to question. "Senya! Your grouse are beginning to go off!" a faithful wife observes. "What grouse? Mine were partridges!" "No, they're grouse!" "Hell, it's probably that wretch Ignashka mixed them up. We agreed I would have partridges and he would take grouse." "What Ignashka? You don't have any friends of that name." "Oh, just someone I met while I was hunting."'

'Well,' Doc observes, 'I couldn't fool my wife like that! If I brought back a dozen grouse . . . '

'She wouldn't say they were partridges?'

'She just wouldn't believe I had bagged them.'

'Why not?'

'Because she knows I'm a terrible shot. She would know I must have bought them.'

We are welcomed at a collective farm by a vigorous, slightly tipsy old lady in her mid-seventies. 'What have we killed? Our feet!'

'Look, Granny, here's what we've killed.'

'You'll be tired, I dare say.'

'We are, Granny, we are,' I agree.

'He's the only one who's tired!' Doc butts in, pointing at me rather petulantly.

'You poor dears. Well, take off your boots and your coats. I'll have some dinner for you in the twinkling of an eye.'

We clean the guns, eat our dinner and quickly head for bed. We climb up to the loft and lie down on the hay, under a quilt. 'The hay seems a bit warmer here, don't you think? Not like under your haystack,' Doc remarks. I hardly hear the end of the sentence as I fall asleep.

Day 2

The chill of morning makes me shiver. Through a crack in the roof I see a luminous pink sky. In the village nearby a shepherd is playing a horn with only three notes. Then we hear the thud of a heavy whip and the cow lying under the hayloft snorts noisily. The sheep bleat. 'Wakey, wakey, Doc!' We get up at once. How wonderful it would be to wrap myself in that warm blanket and turn back over on to my side. The dog at my feet whines, and when he hears us say 'hunting' loses patience. He starts jumping up and trying to lick my face. Fifteen minutes later we are ready to go. 'Have we got everything?' Yes.

The gate in the fence round the village rasps, and we are back in the wild. We walk across a meadow and leave two trails behind us in the dewy, trampled grass. 'We need to turn right through the fields, and in half an hour we'll be at the marsh,' I tell Doc. The sun [illegible] the tops of the fir trees.

The shaded lower half of the forest is still asleep, but up above life is chattering away. A squirrel circles the trunk of a pine tree, making that clattering sound with its claws.

'See those tall fir trees?'

'Yes.'

'That's where the marsh begins. We'll walk about a hundred and fifty paces along the shoreline and . . . '

' . . . start missing the game again,' Doc finishes.

'The birds haven't taken fright here, yet. We'll show them!'

'If you're in too much of a hurry to show them, they'll show you their tails.'

'You're probably right there. How many birds did we shoot yesterday? And how many tails did we see? I'm older and wiser today. I won't just loose off like I did yesterday.'

'How are you going to shoot instead?'

'I'll fire at one bird and move the barrel sideways so the shot sprays them and I get six or seven in one go.'

'Don't give me all the sense in your head or you'll only have the nonsense left.'

The marsh is divided from dry land by a forty-metre strip of meadow, which is always flooded, including today. Doc leaps from tuft to tuft, trying not to fall in. 'How are you doing, Alexander? Not wet yet?'

'No, I've only got my galoshes wet!' Some galoshes they are too, when his shoes are held together with string and the only soles they have are those of his feet.

We keep to the edge of the marsh. At times the pine scrub gives way to birch scrub, then to thickets of willow. We battle through it as if it were a jungle. Somewhere the dog may be pointing, but we can't see him. When we do, he's not pointing so there is no game anyway. We come out of the marsh to rest on a horn of dry land. 'Doc, I have a test cartridge I fancy firing.'

'Right, let's look for a place to hang up a sheet of newspaper.'

We search for a spot. 'Why are you lugging that gun around with you? Do yourself a favour, hang it up on a tree,' I say challengingly. Doc falls into the trap, hangs it on a pine tree and walks away without a care in the world.

We fix the newspaper to a tree and walk back seventy metres. I aim. Bang! We go to take a look. Fifty-one out of seventy-two pellets have hit half a sheet of *Izvestiya*.

'Brilliant!' Doc exclaims.

'Yes, really brilliant!' I say with a grin.

'Why are you laughing?'

'Really, really brilliant!'

'What are you on about?' he asks, puzzled.

'Hunter, where is thy gun? Oh, dear. The last of the Mohicans!' Silence.

We start looking again, only this time not for somewhere to fix a sheet of newspaper but for a shotgun. 'All we need now is for the dog to start pointing! Is that a grouse I see rising?' I muse aloud, just to exasperate Doc.

'That's enough gloating,' he interrupts.

'We could have been sitting here having a rest,' I muse, 'instead of being on our feet all the time.'

'Just treat it as good training for your next trip to Peski,' Doc remarks with heavy irony, leaning against the pine tree where we have found his gun.

'Well, now let's hang it on another tree, have a rest, and then we can go looking for it again,' I suggest.

'The bit about taking a rest is good,' he responds. 'I'll have a smoke while you tell me all about how you got lost at Peski.'

'Oh, you're the expert at getting lost in a three-pine forest, and that was in the marshes. In 1930 I was camping at Lake Karasovo with someone I know called Gulidov. We stayed there for a while and then set off back to Moscow. We had a cooking pot the size of half a bucket and had cooked a potful of porridge to take with us. I put the pot with the porridge in my knapsack. Nikolai thought I was daft. "We're not going on a hundred-kilometre expedition. Dump it, feed it to the fishes. It's heavy. What do you want to cart that around for?"

'We got to the bay and met a fisherman. "Tell us, friend, what's the quickest way out of the marsh?" "Ah, you'll be needing to go to the boundary marker, and then it's straight up the firebreak." We followed his instructions. There was only one boundary marker, so that wasn't a problem, but there were five firebreaks leading away from it, all of them straight as a die. Without hesitation, we headed up the first one. It was noon. I went first, Gulidov followed, still going on about the porridge.

'"Your back's hot. Mind it doesn't burn the porridge. I'd better give it a stir." We walked for an hour and a half and should have been able to see Lake Glubokoye. It had started drizzling. "Gulidov, old chap, I'm beginning to wonder if we might have chosen the wrong road." "What do you mean, it's as straight as can be." "It is indeed, but where is it taking us?" "Let's just keep going. We'll come out somewhere in the end." "Indubitably."

'We went on for another two hours and ought to have made it out of the marsh, but instead we found ourselves in such dense undergrowth it was getting frightening. We were also wet through. Gulidov was still harping on about the porridge. "I'm worried it's going to be watery. Perhaps you should put it under that leather coat of yours to thicken." The undergrowth gave way to a quagmire, as I was the first to discover, sinking in shoulder deep. I might have gone in deeper if the knapsack with the porridge hadn't stopped me. I climbed out and Nikolai asked, "What were you sitting down for?" "I didn't sit down, I sank into the swamp." "Oh, I thought perhaps you'd spotted a bear and crouched down." Twilight was falling. We were tired, soaked to the skin, and starving. For the time being, though, we didn't touch the porridge. Gulidov said it was not quite ready. We ate some tinned food, looked at each other, and didn't have to put it into words. "We're lost," I said, nevertheless. "Yup," Gulidov concurred. We couldn't spend the night there: there was nowhere to sit, let alone lie down. We needed to find somewhere tolerably dry. I climbed up a dead birch tree and could see a large fir forest in the distance, which meant dry land. "See anything?" Nikolai asked. "Yes, there's a spruce forest over there, which means a dry shoreline." "Well come down and let's go. My shoes are getting soggy." I spiralled down the trunk and, by the time I was at the bottom, had forgotten which direction we had to go in. "You'll have to climb back up and tell me which way to face. I'll walk in that direction and you can shout 'A bit to the left' or 'A bit to the right' from up there." "And how do I get out of the marsh?" "You don't need to. It's dry up there and you're hardly going to fall off."

'I climbed up, pointed my arm in the right direction, and waved it for greater emphasis. This was too much for the rotten birch tree, which broke but fell pointing in just the right direction. "Ho ho ho!" Gulidov guffawed. "We certainly won't get lost now! Why didn't you think of doing that in the first place? You could have pole-vaulted straight over into the forest, like a glider off a mountain! Might have had to leave the porridge behind though. Well, bring it with you now. Let's go!"

'It was pitch-black. We took our bearings from the silhouette of the tallest spruce and could hear the rustling of a big forest. We squelched out on to the water meadow and tiptoed along a path of tree trunks. "How about that? Just like a pavement in Moscow." The clang of a cooking pot rang out as I fell off. "The porridge! Look after that porridge will you?" Nikolai yelled. "Damn!" I rejoined. "I was so busy gawping at shop signs I tripped over the kerb!" In another half hour we were by the fire of a watchman guarding his horses.

'"Can you tell us how far it is to Tugoles?" "Where's that? Don't believe I've heard of it." We exchanged glances. "Well, what's the nearest village?" "Oh, Peski will be a bare four *versts* from here." "And do you know Krivandino, the railway station?" "That I do! Sixty *versts* that is and more." We glanced at each other again. "Well, Nikolai, it's lucky we chose the right firebreak. That really was the shortest route."

'And you were laughing at me going round in circles in the forest looking for my gun,' Doc notes. 'The two of you didn't do much better going in a straight line. Shall we move on?'

'Let's!'

We have barely gone fifty paces when the dog stops and points. 'What the hell?' Doc exclaims. 'Have the grouse been sitting there listening to us?'

'Difficult to be sure,' I say. 'Maybe they were, and were reassured about the kind of hunter you must be.'

'But you're just fine?' A grouse flies up. Doc shoots, and misses.

'There, I told you they've worked out the kind of shot you are.'

A second grouse rises up. I shoot. And miss.

'And what did I say?'

Silence. The dog stares at us in disbelief. We trek on. Something rises with a squawk. Perhaps a hawk, perhaps not. I fire at it. It banks to one side and falls abruptly behind a bush. I go over. It is an owl.

Doc stands next to me. 'Take your wood grouse, only don't lose it on the way home.'

'All right, all right.'

'We can get it stuffed.'

Things go right when you least expect it. Right at the edge of the marsh, almost on the meadow, the dog halts again. Doc says mockingly, 'What game are we going to find here. A crow or an owl?' In fact, two grouse rise up. I shoot. One falls at the dog's feet, the other is hit by the shot high above the forest. Somersaulting extravagantly, it falls heavily to the ground. That's more like it! That's real shooting! That's ... ha! Bang! I've already reloaded and death comes to one more young grouse that flew my way.

'How are you doing, Doc?'

'Oh, well ...'

'One of mine surrendered instantly and the other is looking for a place to die.'

'Finish it off.'

'You—'

Bang!

'You scared the living daylights out of me there! My hands are shaking. What's up with you?'

'I was leaning down to get the owl and it suddenly flies up and practically knocks the gun out of my hand.'

'Have you killed it now?'

'Yes!'

It seems too early to head home, but we don't feel like going on. We settle ourselves in a place with lots of berries. Doc crawls about on all fours, gorging himself on ripe cowberries. 'Delicious! These are great berries!' My teeth are hurting and I can't join in. I sit down on a tree stump, but jump up as if I've been stung.

'Have you sat on a drawing pin, or what?'

'Come over here!'

'What for?'

'Just come over.'

'What? You want me to sit there too? No thanks. Sit there yourself.'

'Stop fussing and come here.'

'No!'

I pull off the string bag with the owl and the other game in it. Either it decided to remind me of its presence before dying or else it is just bad luck that its claws are now embedded in my body. 'Ah!' Doc murmurs. 'A taste of your own medicine! Poor owl. Next time you'll know to shoot game and not just anything that flies.' Somehow he disengages the claws. 'Is it itching? I'll fix a dressing with nettles. That's supposed to help.'

From somewhere far away, barely audible, comes a peal of thunder, then another. A breeze ruffles the treetops. A flock of crows flies up out of the forest, cawing, and disappears.

'There's rain coming.'

'Let's get home, Doc.'

Another gust of wind, stronger this time. The sky darkens. A thundercloud moves towards us from the west. Its ragged violet-blue edge, tinged with reddish lilac, appears in the gap of the firebreak.

Day 3

It's morning. One raindrop, another, a trickle. The closer they are to the edge of the roof, the more substantial the rivulets and, as they pour into a crack in the roof beneath which Doc is sleeping, they form a stream. But Alexander feels nothing. There is a blissful smile on his face. Perhaps he is dreaming about how happy he was as a child, unaware of how wet he is now. I am reluctant to wake him but the rain shows no sign of stopping. There is a rhythm, even a certain melodiousness, in the tapping of the raindrops on the roof. They seem to be singing:

'Petrovich! Hey, Petrovich, come and drink a cup of tea!'

'Thank you kindly, so I will, come and drink a cup or three.'

I really need to wake Doc. But how? I decide to tie a string to his blanket, lower it from the hayloft and tug. I do so. First, I hear inarticulate moaning. Then, 'Stop it!'

We are in a log hut. The best room is thirty metres long and has three windows looking on to the street. The walls are scrubbed and smoothly planed, as are the floor and ceiling. In the middle is an oilcloth-covered table. Beneath the windows is a wooden bench and there are chairs on the other three sides. The floor is carpeted with home-made runners. On the wall in an oak frame, almost life-size, are Lenin, Kalinin and Voroshilov. There are several family photographs.

Here is the daughter, an agronomist. The grandfather is a hero of the Russo-Turkish war, in gold braid and with a medal on a ribbon; a fine soldier, scornful of his superiors, stony-faced, contemptuous of the world because he is a hero. He has been wounded for his faith, the tsar and his fatherland, but that is as nothing because he has that medal on his chest. No matter that the little land he owns is infertile, the important thing is that the congregation in church point him out as a distinguished ex-serviceman.

Next to Grandfather is his granddaughter's husband. He too is a hero, having been decorated for his courage in battle by People's Commissar Klim Voroshilov. On his jacket he sports the Order of the Red Banner. He is an engineer but people do not point him out. But occasionally there will be a note in the newspaper that 'the generating machinery at the plant is now operational and the power station is delivering electricity to the mains. Engineering work was carried out under the direction of N.' He too has little land. He descends deep underground into mines and ore workings. There is even talk of building an underground railway in Moscow. This commander of the army and industry is sitting here now, squinting with one eye at the grandfather and with the other at Voroshilov. He is reminiscing about the Civil War and how, after the Battle of Volochaevka, he and Blyukher developed the plan for carrying the offensive forward. We settle ourselves down. The samovar, burnished with crushed brick, murmurs hospitably.

Steam rises from potatoes newly fried in sour cream. Next to them are two gamebirds, the partridges we brought down yesterday. There is fresh and boiled milk, lightly salted cucumbers. Maria Sergeyevna, the wife of our host, Ivan Bolshak, is at the samovar. Bolshak resembles Turgenev's hunter: tall, with curly hair and a lean, tanned face. He wears a shirt, once blue but now faded in patches to grey, and a rope belt. The grey striped trousers that don't reach to his ankles emphasize how thin he is. If we add that he is the best hunter in the neighbourhood, that his old 'cannon' has a broken stock held together by two metal clamps and has been fired so many times that the ends of the barrels have widened like the muzzle of a musket and that one of the triggers is operated with the aid of a piece of wire, and that this hunter manages ten to fifteen kills a day as he sways from side to side, limping on a broken leg, then you will have a good overall picture of the man.

A crow settles on another dead birch tree fifty metres from the window. Doc gets up and loads his small-bore. 'That's the stuff, Voroshilov sharpshooter!' The Voroshilov sharpshooter spends ages taking aim, then: click. A misfire. He reloads.

'Get it in the head!' Bolshak recommends.

'Of course.' He fires, but the crow caws and flies off. 'The shot went through its open beak,' Doc asserts. Another crow lands. Another shot. This crow also caws, but falls to the ground. We go over to take a look. The bullet has hit the base of its tail, breaking one leg.

'You're a crafty one, though, Doc! If you'd missed you would have said it waggled its rump at you.'

'Excellent! Right in the head!' Bolshak comments ironically. 'Next time, load salt. If you hit it in the rear with salt the bird will stay put.'

The sun peeps out. 'Shall we go, Doc?'

'Let's be off.' But then the thunderclouds come back and it starts raining again. 'Why don't we go back to sleep in the hayloft?'

'In the army, I served in the Caucasus,' Doc begins. 'That's the place for hunting bears. But I know you're a man with a lot of experience: you're something of an expert on how to hunt elephants in Africa, so I expect you already know how to hunt bears in the Caucasus.'

'Actually, I know how to hunt lions in the Sahara.'

'Really? Tell me more!'

'Well, as you are no doubt aware, lions roam the sands of the desert. Sand and lions, lions and sand. So you take a sieve, sift the sand, and what's left is lions.'

'That's really clever!' Doc admits.

'But,' I enquire, 'how would you hunt bears in the Caucasus?'

'You just take a plywood shield and draw a man on it, with a hole for the mouth. You fix handles at shoulder height, take a hammer with you, and run straight at the bear, holding the shield in front of you. It works best if you also stick your tongue out through the hole. The bear lunges at the shield and its claws go straight into the plywood. You keep your head and hammer its claws down to the plywood from the back. The animal is now stapled to the board, and you can just push it on its back and cart it away.'

'I notice, Doc, it's always the big game you go for down there in the south. We hunt bears in the north too, of course, only polar bears, and we have a different approach.'

'What's that?'

'Well, you choose a day when it's around minus 70 degrees, take all your clothes off and go hunting in your underpants. The bear can't believe you're a man. You take him by the ears and lead him away. He still doesn't believe you're a hunter. You skin him, and he's still not believing it. You start smoking the meat and he realizes you are a human being, but by then it's too late. Once he's been smoked he's no longer a bear but a ham, and a ham is really nothing to be afraid of.

'Actually, we don't go hunting bears all that often. Usually the weather isn't right. We go looking for wolves, hares or ducks. By the way, do you think hares like cabbage?'

'Of course they do!' Doc obliges.

'So that's the way to catch them. What we do is take a brick, sprinkle snuff on it and put a cabbage [word crossed out] on top. The hares eat the cabbage, take a sniff of the snuff and start sneezing. They bang their heads on the brick and die. Then you just go round with a sack and pick them up.'

'Do you catch many that way?'

'It all depends. Mostly it's the older hares you catch. Their parents don't let the young ones indulge in tobacco.'

'What about wolves? How do you hunt wolves?'

'Wolves? I'll tell you. With them you need vodka rather than tobacco. Surgical spirit, ideally.'

'All your animals up there seem a bit neurotic. Some of them are taking snuff, others getting drunk—'

'Don't interrupt. You don't give the vodka to the wolf, you fool, you drink it yourself to give you courage. Right, so you drink a litre or so and off you go. The wolf comes charging towards you and you run straight at it. As soon as it opens its jaws you stick your hand in, but right down to the end of the brute, catch its tail and turn it inside out. Without its fur it ceases to be a proper wolf.'

'That sounds splendid. It's nice that you get to have fun, and the wolf is probably pleased too because it won't be so hot in the summer without its coat.'

'Mind you, I've only done it once myself, and the wolf was quite short. I was feeling around in there and just couldn't find the tail. The wolf was suffocating and I didn't know what to do. Luckily some lads ran up and yelled at it and the wolf ran away.'

'Do you know what?'

'Well, what?'

'What do you mean, "Well, what?" Have you read Baron Munchausen?'

'Of course I have!'

'Well, nowadays we think he was an eccentric, but in his time they called him a [word heavily blacked out] lunatic.'

'Take a look, will you? Has the drizzle stopped?'

'The drizzle has but the rain hasn't.'

'I'm asking you a serious question.'

'Well, don't you think that's a serious answer? Supposing it had stopped, it's only going to start again.'

'When it will start again is another matter altogether. What is important is whether it's raining now.'

'I hope you're not thinking of going hunting.'

'I'm not thinking about it, but I may just up and go. The game will be sitting there getting wet right now, and won't feel like flying very far.'

'In that case, I'll come too.'

'Get ready, then!'

I notice how much everything has changed since the rain. The dust has been washed off the leaves and now we can see they're bright green. The grass has perked up. Just three years ago you would have seen individual strips of land and that hillock which had been sown was barren because the boundaries between the private holdings took up maybe more than half the land, plus there were blank areas, plus some of the seed didn't germinate. Now, though, over an area of three square kilometres there is a lush carpet of buckwheat. The path running diagonally across it is lost to view: you can't see it for a solid wall of potential porridge. How could people in the past not understand how wasteful boundaries and private smallholdings were? And now there are so many haystacks that it's impossible to take them all in. They stand there so proudly, as if they want to shout 'See what a lot of us there are' and that's only the ones still left in the meadow. An equal number have already been taken away. I'm moved to breathlessness.

Beyond the forest we glimpse the marsh. 'Are there ducks here, then?' Doc asks.

'Yes. It's a pity we haven't got any melons.'

'What do we need melons for?' he wonders.

'Catching ducks, of course! Never fails, although sometimes you catch frogs by mistake because they have the same webbed feet.' I begin explaining how to catch them. 'What you have to do is get, say, a wagonload of melons and dump them in the lake where the ducks are swimming. They get used to them being there. Then you take a melon and put it on your head and get into the water yourself. You make eyeholes to look through. A duck swims up to you, you grab it by the feet and put it in your bag. It's an admirable method, and you don't need gunpowder or shot to do it. Simple and convenient! The only snag is, while you're sitting in the water, someone might steal your clothes, but you don't need to be upset because there is a straightforward solution. In order to get back home you can just hang the ducks round your waist. No one is going to check whether you are wearing underpants or not. You can pretend you're getting a tan. In fact, none of the local villagers pay any attention to me, even when I'm not wearing ducks.'

'Even if you're not wearing underpants?'

'No, I was wearing underpants. But they know I'm from Moscow. One time they saw me wearing spiked running shoes. I told them they were special shoes for going up trees after grouse, and the whole village turned out to watch. They asked me to run up a telegraph pole and hang out a flag.

'I remember in 1930 I killed a wood grouse at just this spot.'

'How big?'

'Twelve pounds.'

'Was it old?'

'No, probably about two years.'

'You should have waited. If you shot it now, I bet it would weigh eighty pounds.'

'You want everything to be like those animals of yours down south, the size of buffaloes and elephants, to suit that gun of yours.'

'While you, being a northerner, only want them the size of a polar bear?'

You do need to have an understanding of detail, though. White partridges, for instance, favour birch scrub and the brood stays together, but afterwards, in the autumn, they form flocks close to the edge of the marsh. Grouse, on the other hand, adore resinous pine scrub. In the evenings they move towards the water and lakes. In the autumn they fly off on their own, as they are moulting into black plumage, and start sitting up in the trees.

Wood grouse like pines too, and will flee from right under a dog's nose across grass. They need to find an open space to take off from, because there's not enough room among trees for them to bank if they need to turn. They make a lot of noise when they take off. It can give you quite a fright.

You can shoot a whole brood of partridges. If you don't let them rise up from the ground, one shot can kill two or three at once. Sometimes they hide. You think they've all risen but you notice the dog is not moving and find one cowering behind a hummock, so close you could pick it up. Partridges rise up one after the other and fly off in different directions. There no need to fire in haste, there's plenty of time. At the start of the season everything except a wood grouse will let you come as near as fifteen paces, but even in late autumn, at the beginning of October, you can get close for a shot.

The weather finally clears up completely and it gets hot. The land is steaming. We're still warmly dressed. A pine tree towers skywards like a landmark. Summer heat. A rainbow-coloured swarm of insects shimmers above the top of it, humming and whining. Hmmm ... A bumblebee flies by and disappears.

'Let's have lunch, Doc, and then sleep till evening.'

'Fine.'

We heat up some tinned food, eat the partridges cooked back

at the hut, along with tomatoes and gherkins held by their stalks. We go to the lake for water, and it soon boils on our campfire. We slake our thirst and lie down to rest.

A persistent fly is giving me no peace. I brush it away from my nose but it settles on my forehead. I chase it from there and it lands on my cheek. I try to catch it, flap at it, nothing helps. Groggy, I don't want to open my eyes. Now the fly is trying to get up my nose. Time to swat the brute. That scares it off but I know it'll be back in a moment and open my eyes. Oh, irksome vet! Oh, chicken-hearted Comanche! That was no fly: Doc has been tickling me with a blade of long grass.

'Can't you sleep? You still want to sleep, Paleface Brother? It's seven in the evening. Is sleeping from noon till now not long enough?'

I get up. We've a three-hour hike ahead of us before catching the midnight train back to Moscow. Well, come on, dog, show us what you're made of! This is the last day of our first hunting expedition.

We don't have to wait for long. The dog runs straight to a bush. A grouse? Yes indeed. It rises. Bang! Dead. Beyond the bush another shot. Did I miss? No!

'Let me beat about in that bush a bit,' I say to Doc. 'Only don't kill me if something flies out.'

'Go ahead, see what those grouse have been up to in there.'
Bang!
'Did you find anything?' Doc asks.
Yes, actually.
'Was it a big one?'
'Only the size of a polar bear.'

Memorial International
Human Rights Society, Moscow
and the Preservation of Historical Memory

Memorial is an international historical and educational charity, set up in 1988 on a groundswell of public opinion from different generations. Its supporters had very varied biographies, and sometimes divergent political outlooks. They were not only former political prisoners and their families, but young people and others in favour of establishing a democratic state under the rule of law.

Memorial's first chairman was Academician Andrey Sakharov. Today, Memorial is a network of dozens of organizations in Russia, Belarus, Germany, Italy, Kazakhstan, Latvia and Ukraine who conduct research and educational work and defend human rights. In 1991, on Memorial's initiative and with the society's participation, a law was passed on rehabilitation of victims of political repression. It declared 30 October a Day of Remembrance of Victims of Political Repression.

From the outset, Memorial has considered one of its principal tasks to be the creation of a tradition of informed remembrance of political repression in the USSR. An essential part of this work has been collecting and preserving the testimony of over

4 million people persecuted during the Stalin era. In the course of twenty years, Memorial has established the only systematic public archive of its kind in Russia, museum holdings, collections of documents, and a specialized library.

Another aspect of the work is restoring and making publicly available the identities and biographies of victims. A Book of Remembrance provides the foundation for an electronic database of more than 2.6 million victims of political repression.

Memorial organizes discussions directly related to remembrance and analysis of current policy towards history.

The charity is constantly studying not only the means of transmitting historical memory from generation to generation, but actively encouraging this by organizing a nationwide history essay competition for older school students on the topic of 'Man in History: Russia in the Twentieth Century'.

Memorial sees scholarly and research work as an integral part of its mission. Among its main projects are:

- creating maps of the Gulag and a definitive work describing the Gulag system;
- creating reference works giving the biographies of the organizers and perpetrators of the Terror;
- studying the role and significance of social-democratic opposition to the Stalin regime;
- researching the administrative structure and statistics of the Terror;
- studying sites associated with the topography of the Terror;
- studying family memories of the Terror;
- monitoring museum collections relevant to the history of the Gulag;
- studying the fate of different groups of victims of political repression, such as Poles, Germans, and Harbin Russians.

Memorial's archival and museum collections

Memorial's archive began acquiring materials from the very inception of the society in 1989, when victims of repression, their relatives and friends began passing documents, photographs and manuscript memoirs from their family archives to the movement's activists. The archive consists of several themed collections.

Archive of the History of Political Repression in the USSR, 1918–56

The backbone of this collection is personal files of people who were persecuted: shot, sentenced to prison camp terms, exiled, or 'dekulakized' in the case of more prosperous peasants. The collection contains in excess of 60,000 personal archives. These consist of such materials directly related to the persecution as originals and copies of official arrest warrants, records of searches; pages from archival, criminal, prison camp or surveillance files; notifications of sentence, death certificates, certificates of release and rehabilitation; and such personal documents as lists of parcels sent to prisons and camps, and appeals by prisoners and relatives for a review of their case. There are also documents from the period of detention: character references, poetry, posters for camp amateur performances, certificates of good behaviour, home-made cards, sheet music, and personal notes.

Correspondence between prisoners and their families is of particular interest. This includes not only officially authorized correspondence, read and often with deletions by the censor, but also letters passed to the outside world illegally: snatches of news from prison trains in transit, notes scrawled on fabric or cigarette paper and hidden in the seams of clothing or in buttons. The personal files also contain documents from before arrest: birth certificates, school-leaving and degree certificates, membership cards of various organizations, service records, diplomas and award certificates, letters, family and work photographs, and the like.

246

Memoir and Literary Works Collection

The Memoir and Literary Works Collection contains some 600 files and represents a unique source of personal testimony about life in the USSR in the twentieth century, about arrests, investigations, camps, and exiles (the latter reflecting the entire history and geography of the Gulag). In addition to memoirs, the archive includes collections of letters, diaries, sketches and articles, and literary and journalistic works. Most of these texts have never been published.

Archive of the 'Victims of Two Dictatorships' Programme

This archive of materials, on the fate of Soviet people deported to perform forced labour in Germany during the Second World War, contains some 400,000 case files. Many of these people were subjected to harassment and persecution when they returned to the USSR. The files contain biographical information, letters and memoirs, documents issued by the German administration; documentation of their passage through 'filtration' when they were repatriated; data from Soviet state and ministry archives, as well as from the International Tracing Service of the Red Cross; personal papers (photographs, letters and postcards from Germany and filtration camps).

A database on individuals has been compiled, drawing on the archive's holdings, which, among other things, gives information on where '*Ostarbeiter*', slave labourers from the East, lived and worked in Nazi Germany.

Archive of the History of Dissidence in the USSR, 1953–87

Memorial's collection of documents on the history of dissidence in the post-Stalin era is the largest in Russia and one of the most extensive in the world. It comprises seventy-four holdings and collections, as well as a photograph archive and collection of rare publications which appeared in very limited editions.

The holding comprises some 300,000 sheets of documentation.

These include a collection of Samizdat works assembled by Memorial International. Personal collections and archives include letters, diaries, memoirs, drafts of articles, and other working materials of prominent dissidents, totalling about thirty personal files. The archive contains photocopies of around 13,000 index cards of prisoners sentenced in the 1950s to 1980s for political and dissident activities. The collection is an important source for research into oppositional social and political activity and the repressive policies of the USSR during this period. Samizdat and other materials connected with dissidence come in a variety of shapes and forms: typescripts, photocopies, home-made albums with illustrations. Some are truly unique: a letter from exile typed on cloth, a tape recording made secretly in the camp, and so on. The collection also contains some 5,000 photographs.

The Centre for Oral History and Biography
The Centre has ongoing projects on Women's Memories of the Gulag and Children of 'Algeria' [the Akmolinsk Camp for Wives of Traitors to the Fatherland, opened in January 1938], which have recordings of some two hundred interviews, as well as thousands of documents, photographs, memoirs, letters and diaries, depicting the fate of wives of 'traitors to the fatherland', who were sent off to the camps, and of their children, who were placed in 'orphanages'. The collected materials and, in particular, the oral evidence, enable us to trace how the history of mothers despatched to the Gulag affected the destiny of their children, and to re-assess the traumatic experience of families under the Soviet system.

In the course of the projects Survivors of Mauthausen, and Forced Labour in National Socialist Germany, about three hundred audio and video interviews were recorded with former prisoners of concentration camps and *Ostarbeiter*, which portray the tragic vicissitudes of these people during the war and their long experience of discrimination in the post-war era.

Memorial Museum Collection

The Memorial Museum Collection began to be formed as early as 1988. Along with documents, relatives of the persecuted brought memorabilia, drawings and photographs for safekeeping by Memorial, and in 1990 a museum was set up. The main source of acquisitions was families of the persecuted, which had kept relics, paintings and drawings; some of the exhibits were acquired on expeditions to the sites of former camps. The museum currently houses some 2,000 items. With 1,500 exhibits, this is the world's largest collection of works created in captivity. The greater part of the collection is paintings and drawings by imprisoned artists: genre drawings, portraits, interiors, landscapes, and sketches for scenery and costumes for productions in the camp theatres. Some of them are by famous artists who ended up in the camps and exile.

Closely related to the museum collection are some 12,000 works in the photograph archive. These are originals or copies of documentary photographs depicting the history of political repression in the USSR from the 1920s to the 1980s, the life and labour of the prisoners of the Gulag, the everyday life of the USSR, and Soviet propaganda.

Address:
Memorial International
5/10 Karetny Ryad
Moscow 127006
Russia
tel. (+7 495) 650 7883

e-mail: nipc@memo.ru
websites: www.memo.ru; www.urokiistorii.ru

Pages from Ivan Chistyakov's diary.